A Crime of Vengeance

An Armenian Struggle for Justice

EDWARD ALEXANDER

THE FREE PRESS
A Division of Macmillan, Inc.
NEW YORK

Collier Macmillan Canada
TORONTO

Maxwell Macmillan International
NEW YORK   OXFORD   SINGAPORE   SYDNEY

The Free Press
A Division of Macmillan, Inc.
866 Third Avenue, New York, N.Y. 10022

Collier Macmillan Canada, Inc.
1200 Eglinton Avenue East
Suite 200
Don Mills, Ontario M3C 3N1

Printed in the United States of America

printing number
1   2   3   4   5   6   7   8   9   10

Library of Congress Cataloging-in-Publication Data

Alexander, Edward
    A crime of vengeance : an Armenian struggle for justice / Edward
Alexander.
        p.   cm.
    Includes bibliographical references and index.
    ISBN 0-02-900475-6
    1. Armenian massacres, 1915–1923.   2. T'ēhlirean, Soghomon,
1896–1960—Trials, litigation, etc.   3. Talât Paşa, 1874–1921
—Assassination.   I. Title.
DS195.5.A42   1991
956.6'202—dc20   90-27258
                                                                CIP

*To my
mother and father
In memoriam*

Contents

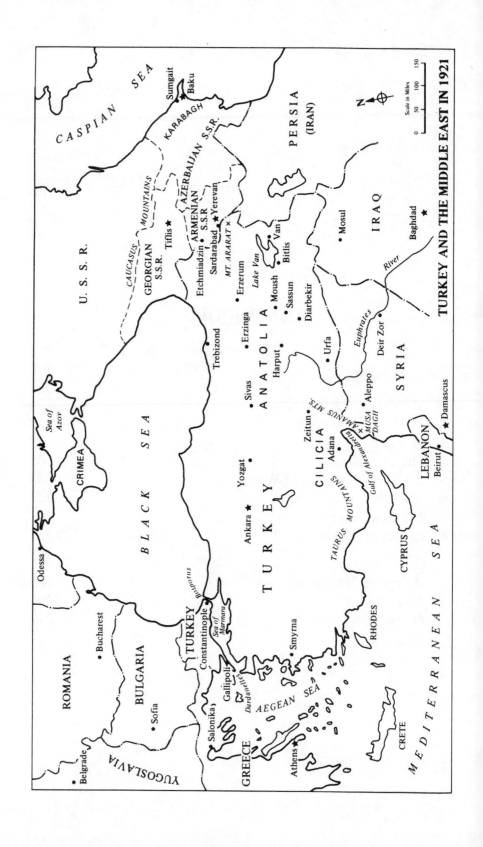

TURKEY AND THE MIDDLE EAST IN 1921

Introduction

*F*rom the closing years of the last century into World War I, a deadly wave of Turkish fanaticism—so shocking in nature that it was an assault on the credulity of the civilized world—swept over Armenian towns and villages. Unable to cope with such horrors, the world dismissed them from memory.

The universal indifference to these horrendous events made such a lasting impression on an obscure Austrian corporal in World War I that he later cited it as a justification for his own genocidal policies. In 1931 Adolf Hitler gave an interview to a Leipzig newspaper editor in which he described his new world order and explained that for Germany to have more *Lebensraum* (living space), there would have to be mass reductions of populations: "Think of the biblical deportations and the massacres of the Middle Ages and remember the extermination of the Armenians."[1] Eight years later, in an exhortation to his general staff assembled at the *Adlerhorst* (Eagle's Nest) in Bavaria on the eve of the Nazi invasion of Poland, Hitler called for ruthlessness in dealing with the Polish people and sought to allay any fears of future condemnation by noting, "Who, after all, speaks today of the extermination of the Armenians?"[2]

There is a terrible irony in the fact that while the rest of the world seemed to have forgotten the Armenian tragedy, its memory was fresh and useful to this tyrant as a model of world apathy toward organized cruelty.

Viewed from a historical perspective, the Armenian massacres represented a spasm in the final convulsions of the Ottoman Empire. In human terms they translated into the ruthless destruction of 1.5 million people. This decimation of a nation—without historical parallel either in magnitude or efficiency—had its preamble in the last decade of the nineteenth century. The Ottoman sultan Abdul Hamid II, defying European governments that protested his despotic rule, proceeded to vent his anger on his Armenian subjects in a murderous rampage carried out by cavalry troops in Anatolia, the central part of Turkey. There, in the six provinces inhabited by Armenians, the sultan's troops slaughtered and ravaged the unarmed population and pillaged its property. News of these terrible events was slow to reach Western countries, but largely through the efforts of American and German missionaries it was eventually established that close to two hundred thousand Armenians had been killed.

A decade later the sultan was deposed by a political party that came to be known as the Young Turks—reformers who wished to erase the dreadful image of Turkey that existed in the Western world. Although they introduced a constitution that granted freedom and equal rights to all minorities, including the Armenians, the Young Turks soon betrayed their principles by scuttling the reforms on which they had based their revolution.

Under cover of World War I, in which they (like the sultan before them) were allied with Germany, the Young Turks began a systematic campaign of carnage, more cruel and far greater in scale than Abdul Hamid's. Beginning in April 1915, Talaat Pasha, the leading figure of the Young Turk government, issued a series of decrees ordering the deportation of every Armenian man, woman, and child from Anatolia to the desert areas of Syria and Mesopotamia three hundred miles away.

Talaat's decrees used the term *deportation,* but it quickly became evident that *deportation* was synonymous with *death.* Most of the Armenian men were taken outside their villages and shot or killed with sabers and axes. The women, children, and the elderly, sick, and infirm were herded into columns of caravans extending for many miles, in month-long marches to the southern deserts. There was no protection from the blistering sun during the day and the piercing cold at night. The Turkish "gendarmes"—really criminals released from Anatolian prisons—took their pick of the most attractive women and raped in full view of their husbands and parents. Others were soaked with gasoline and burned alive in caves. Mothers hurled their babies to their deaths to spare them further suffering; pregnant women were bayoneted and the fetuses flung around for sport. Half-naked, barefoot, hungry, and exhausted, the straggling procession arrived at their destinations with 90 percent of the caravans strewn along the way, their passengers dead of typhus, dysentery, and cholera, the corpses rotting on the roads or choking the rivers. Many of those who survived drew their last breath on arrival.

These incidents were witnessed by schoolteachers, orphanage directors, nurses, doctors, and missionaries of many nations—but mostly from Germany, Turkey's wartime ally. Other witnesses were German soldiers assigned to the interior and German engineers engaged in building the Berlin-to-Baghdad Railway in Anatolia. These Westerners were incredulous at the barbarity with which the deportations were enforced. No less aghast were the many consuls, primarily German and American, stationed at diplomatic posts throughout Turkey. They provided countless eyewitness reports to their embassies in Constantinople, which relayed them to Berlin and Washington.

The sheer magnitude of these cataclysmic events so shook the United States ambassador in Turkey, Henry Morgenthau, that he wrote: "I am confident that the whole history of the human race contains no such horrible episode as this. The great massacres and persecutions of the past seem almost insignificant when compared with the sufferings of the Armenian race in 1915."[3] Fleeing Turkey, they settled in Western countries, in Arab lands, some even in Soviet Armenia, and almost one million in the United States. Three-quarters of a century later, the trauma of those tragic days continues to haunt the few thousand who had actually lived through them. But the heritage they hand on is that same trauma, which has come to haunt the new generations of Armenians.

It is a heritage governed by two imperatives: the retention of memory and the search for justice. Armenians are both saddened and embittered that a catastrophe of such immense proportions goes unacknowledged by the United States, and is altogether denied by Turkey. They cannot believe that despite the factual reports of its own diplomats on the spot at the time, the United States Department of State views "the historical record of the 1915 events in Asia Minor as ambiguous," and "does not endorse allegations that the Turkish Government committed a genocide against the Armenian people"— comments made in State's *Bulletin* of August 1982.[4] Armenians equate the systematic killing of their compatriots in 1915 with genocide and look to the United States to officially recognize the loss of one million Armenian lives as nothing less than a deliberate genocidal policy of the Ottoman Turkish government. They can appreciate that the United States does not wish to injure or alienate an ally, but they also deplore the sacrifice of morality to political expediency.

Armenians are incredulous that the present Turkish government, despite having had no part in what transpired in Anatolia seventy-five years ago, denies that the massacres took place. If justice cannot be satisfied even by the simple fact of acknowledgment, then memory must remain to keep the search for justice alive.

As time moves on and new generations emerge, however, memory will dim. It sometimes seems as though there exists a conspiracy to traumatize the Armenian psyche for a second time in the same century. But the ghosts of the national disaster of 1915 will not evaporate so easily. Mainstays of the Armenian character are its tenacity in the face of adversity and a capacity for survival over the centuries despite invasions and domination by Persians, Greeks, Romans, Arabs, Mongols, and Turks, militant neighbors, hostile ideologies—and calamitous earthquakes. As long as they exist, Armenians will neither forget 1915 nor will they allow the world to forget.

They take heart that they are not alone. In Strasbourg, the European Parliament refuses Turkey membership in the European Economic Community until it acknowledges its crimes against the Armenians. In Paris, a Permanent People's Tribunal—comprising European intellectuals and Nobel laureates—has determined that the Turkish government must assume responsibility for the crime of genocide committed by the Young Turks in 1915.

Armenians have found the greatest sympathy and support from members of the U.S. Congress in Washington. Every year since 1984 Congress has considered a resolution marking April 24, when the massacres began in 1915, as a National Day of Remembrance of Man's Inhumanity to Man. Each year the resolution has failed to pass, owing to concerted opposition from the White House, the departments of State and Defense, and Turkish diplomats and American ambassadors recalled from Turkey to lobby Congress.

In 1990 the Senate sought to commence debate on a resolution introduced by Robert Dole designating April 24 as a National Day of Remembrance of the 75th Anniversary of the Armenian Genocide. Senator Dole made it abundantly clear that it was the earlier government of Young Turks and not that of Turkey today that was at issue, but he was opposed by Sen. Robert Byrd, who engaged in a filibuster. Those arguing against the resolution feared that Turkey would retaliate by abrogating its NATO obligations and closing American bases. The final vote was the closest in the resolution's six-year history—51 to 48—prompting Senator Dole to say: "I still think 'David' won the debate, but it is pretty clear that 'Goliath' won the vote."[5] Weeks later, even though he had encouraged opposition to the resolution, President Bush felt compelled to issue a statement saying he wished to join Armenians in "a day of remembrance for the more than one million Armenian people who were victims."[6]

In Soviet Armenia the memory of 1915 has remained alive, just as the ever-visible sight of Mount Ararat just across the border in eastern Turkey is a constant reminder to citizens of the small Soviet republic of the tragic Armenian past. Although prevented earlier from engaging in any public demonstrations commemorating the events of 1915, in Soviet Armenia citizens assembled on the fiftieth anniversary of the massacres in 1965 for a modest parade and speeches in the capital city of Yerevan. For the first time since becoming a Soviet republic, Armenia was making a political statement that was not in accord with the policy of the central government in Moscow. Although there was no love lost between Turkey and the Soviet Union, both countries maintained a correct relationship, due in large part to considerations of trade.

But there was yet another aspect to this demonstration, an aspect that has gradually grown in twenty-five years—namely, the emergence of a nationalistic spirit born of the craving for freedom. This, after all, had been the ultimate aim of Armenians for centuries, from the earliest times under Roman rule through the Ottoman Empire, whose excesses motivated Armenian political leaders to organize, resist, and struggle for national identity. Under Soviet domination, this had been a virtual impossibility. But the struggle could not be suppressed, as the small nation increasingly sought recognition. Nationalist motifs crept into the work of Soviet Armenian writers, poets, and artists, and despite criticism and often condemnation by Communist party officials, the movement grew, not only gaining widespread support but spawning underground political parties.

In 1985 it received its greatest impetus when Mikhail Gorbachev introduced his policy of *glasnost,* or openness. Now freedom, democracy, and independence could at least be discussed, if not yet practiced. But Armenians had only to be patient. In August 1990 the

Soviet Socialist Republic of Armenia issued a declaration announcing itself independent of Moscow's control and changing its name simply to Republic of Armenia, claiming the right to control its own army, natural resources, banks, economic system, and foreign policy. After centuries of servitude, in the last decade of the twentieth century Armenia appeared to have taken a major step in its struggle for independence, which has often been inseparable from its struggle for justice.

This courageous action carried with it a major implication for the future of Armenian-Turkish relations. Even though the memory of 1915 is fresh, the Armenian declaration, while calling for Turkey to acknowledge the massacres, appeared to recognize that Turkey would not repeat them. Unlike the lands of the Ottomans, Turkey today is not isolated. As a member of NATO, a signatory to the Helsinki Final Act, and a recipient of much American aid, Turkey cannot emulate the violent policies of previous regimes without profound damage to its international standing and possibly to its very survival. Its greatest ally, the United States, has never through any of its representatives pointed the finger of guilt at the present Turkish government. But by denying the guilt of a previous regime, present-day Turkey is transferring to itself and to its people the burden of that same guilt. A Turkey owning up to its past, however, will be respected for its courage and welcomed into the community of civilized nations. It will be an ally with which the United States will no longer feel discomfort, while Armenians will cease to dwell on the past.

In the United States, England, France, Germany, and Armenia, historians, scholars, biographers, academics, and filmmakers are digging deeper into archives to extract new information about "lost episodes" in the Armenian struggle for justice. The story of Soghomon Tehlirian is one such episode. But, viewed from a historical perspective, it has a significance far exceeding the mere commission of a crime.

The event with the greatest impact on Armenia's destiny may well have been the adoption of Christianity at the very beginning of the fourth century. Church and state became as one, and in time of war the supreme patriarchs marched into battle side by side with the rulers of Armenia. When Christianity became its state religion, Armenia earned the hostility of all the neighboring peoples, unwittingly inviting a series of invasions over the next ten centuries by barbaric armies incited by religious hatred. The invaders ravaged the

country and decimated the population, dimming all hopes for freedom. Those hopes vanished completely by the sixteenth century,
when Armenia was conquered and absorbed into the Ottoman Empire, whose Moslem rulers then and thereafter looked upon the
Armenians as "Christian infidels."

The Armenian yearning for freedom and the nation's intransigent
adherence to its religious faith fused in the Armenian psyche and
became a projection of the collective national will. As the treatment
of Armenians in Ottoman Turkey in the late nineteenth century
shifted from the deprivation of human rights to persecution and
massacre, the first steps toward conscious and organized resistance
were born.

Soghomon Tehlirian, too, was born at this time, the most harrowing time for his people. His early years saw the turmoil of Abdul
Hamid's reign and the horrors inflicted by the Young Turks, the
consequence of which would transform him from a tragic and tor-
mented youth into an avenging angel. In acting out that vengeance,
Tehlirian followed the only law he knew, not man-made but biblical
law—the simple dictum that if a man kills another, he should himself
be killed. But in committing the crime, which he viewed as an act of
revenge, Tehlirian may not have been aware that his deed represented
yet another salient moment in a historic continuum dating back to a
time when the Armenian Christian state first lost its freedom. His
deed spoke for all the generations of Armenians who had been
deprived of their human dignity, their right to worship, and their very
right to live, and was perpetrated in response to events in Turkish
Armenia. But even as his blow against tyranny was anchored in the
past, it seemed an augury of events yet to come in the continuing
struggle of the Armenian nation for political independence.

In the eastern part of Armenia, which since the mid-19th century
had been under Russian administration, a Soviet republic was created in 1920, under Red Army coercion. During the seventy years of
dictatorship that followed, Armenians were once again bereft of
freedom and denied the open practice of their religion. When their
ancient churches were converted into museums, they nourished their
hunger for freedom by retaining religion in their hearts, even secretly
baptizing their newborn. But once the bonds of servitude were
loosened and the declaration of independence from Moscow made,
the newly elected president of Armenia did a highly significant thing.
After seven decades of atheistic propaganda, his first official act was
to travel to Etchmiadzin, the Holy See of the Armenian Church, and

ask for the blessing of the supreme patriarch. By this symbolic gesture the president was confirming once again what Armenians had always known and believed—that for them faith and freedom are inseparable. The great curve of Armenian history, in which Soghomon Tehlirian had played such a palpable role, thus came full circle.

1

Murder in Berlin

A slender young man parted the heavy curtains of his furnished room and peered at the doorway of the villa opposite. It was a March day in 1921 and the weather was damp and cold—*nasskalt,* as Berliners noted on that day. But the midmorning sun was already illuminating the sumptuous residence across Hardenbergstrasse. It was a few minutes before ten o'clock—time for the familiar figure to begin his morning walk. Seeing no one, however, the young man returned to his daily study of German.

There was a knock on the door, and a maid brought in his morning tea. He sipped it slowly, his eyes on his book but his mind elsewhere. Out of the corner of his eye he detected some movement, and he went to the window again. The bright sun was now full on the windows opposite. Through the reflected glare he beheld the object of his interest.

A heavyset man had come out into the front yard and cautiously onto the sidewalk. He looked up and down the wide street as though fearful of something. Then he lowered his head and slowly rubbed his brow. After a few moments, he went back into the house. The youth held his breath.*

Shortly thereafter, the door opened again to reveal the middle-aged man clad in a long gray coat. He walked to the sidewalk, turned

---

*This and all other similar phrases are drawn from Soghomon Tehlirian's *Memoirs*; my sources are discussed in "A Personal Postscript."

right, and began a leisurely promenade toward the Zoological Garden in the center of the Charlottenburg district.

The young man sprang to a closet and from a suitcase filled with laundry seized a revolver. He shoved it into his breast pocket, hurried out of his first-floor room, and, spotting his target, crossed the street. The portly gentleman was walking casually, swinging his cane.

The youth walked behind him until they were parallel. He approached from the rear, passed him—they were now two blocks from the villa—and turned so they were almost face-to-face. For a moment they looked into each other's eyes, and the man broke his stride to avoid a collision. The youth passed him, turned again, drew his gun, aimed it at the back of the man's head, and pulled the trigger.

The loud explosion stunned a number of pedestrians, who turned in time to see the victim stiffen and fall to the ground. A woman's scream pierced the quiet of Charlottenburg, and one of the witnesses fainted. The youth bent over his victim, intending at first to empty his gun into the prone figure. But seeing that he was dead, he threw his weapon to the ground and stared at the dark blood that poured from the wound.

Recovering from their momentary shock, the pedestrians now began to shout and run toward him. "He killed a man," someone yelled. "Seize him!" The youth turned and ran toward the nearest side street, Fasanenstrasse, upset at having failed to plan things better. He almost managed to escape the mob but was grabbed by someone running toward him. On the corner of Hardenbergstrasse and Fasanenstrasse an angry crowd quickly gathered and began to beat him with fists and any objects they had in hand. One struck his head repeatedly with a key. He felt a hot flame in his head, and his vision began to fade. His face now covered with blood, he fell to his knees as the crowd kicked him.

In panic the youth shouted in broken German, "I foreigner, he foreigner, this not hurt Germany."[1] But before they could injure him further, he was rescued by the same eyewitness who had stopped his flight. His head bleeding profusely, the youth was rushed to the guardhouse at the entrance to the Bahnhof Zoo (Zoological Garden Railroad Station). Once inside, he asked for a cigarette, as an even greater crowd now surrounded the small guardhouse and threatened to inflict further harm.

The frantic guard telephoned the Charlottenburg Police Station, where Criminal Inspector von Manteuffel promptly dispatched Sgt. Paul Scholz, who took the youth into protective custody.

More police arrived and cordoned off the area where the body lay in a pool of blood. Sergeant Scholz emptied the dead man's pockets, then escorted the injured youth from Bahnhof Zoo to the Charlottenburg Police Station on the nearby Kaiserdamm. Some two hours later, around 1:30 P.M., after the body had been examined and photographed by the criminal police, it was transported to the morgue for an inquest.

The crowd milled about, still agitated, people talking among themselves about the shocking scene some of them had witnessed. Ignorant of its meaning, they were in fact compelled to wait until the entire German press erupted that afternoon with the spare but significant facts. But although they were able to identify the victim and his killer, not even the newspapers understood the full consequences of that single pistol shot. For the murder committed that day on a street in Berlin would produce a trial attracting international attention, affect the foreign relations of several Western nations, inspire a form of terrorism that continues today, and expose deeds of mass violence by a wartime German ally of such barbaric cruelty as to shock not only Germans but the entire civilized world.

═══

The initial front-page stories Berliners read that day and the next contained variations and contradictions. The young man was identified as a twenty-four-year-old student named Soghomon Tehlirian—that much was agreed upon, and it was accurate. But he was variously said to be a Turk, then a Persian, and finally (correctly) an Armenian. (He had been born in Turkey but bore a Persian passport, hence the confusion.) The fact that he was ethnically an Armenian, coupled with the identity of the victim, completed the equation for those with knowledge of recent history.

Visiting cards found in the victim's clothing indicated that he was Ali Salih Bey, a Turk, described in the press as well-dressed and a person of apparent distinction. But the police learned within hours that he was really Talaat Pasha, former Turkish minister of the interior and grand vizier. Further digging by the police and newspaper reporters established that following the end of World War I and the collapse of the Ottoman government, Talaat had escaped from Turkey with his wife and had been living in seclusion in Berlin for the last two years—without the knowledge, said the press, of the German government.[2]

Fanciful journalists wrote that Tehlirian had approached Talaat, tapped him on the shoulder, and exchanged friendly words prior to killing him. Others wrote that a second shot was fired, which had severely wounded Talaat's wife. Neither of these reports was true. Tehlirian had not had any contact with Talaat, who was walking alone without his wife; only one shot had been fired; and the woman who had screamed and fainted was a stranger who had not been injured.

It was widely reported that Tehlirian's German was poor and that a preliminary hearing could not be expedited until an interpreter was found. A second reason for delay, according to the *Tägliche Rundschau,* a mildly liberal organ of the German People's party, was that Tehlirian was weak from loss of blood because of the head wound inflicted by the mob—a wound described as being twenty-one centimeters long and running from the crown of his head to the nape of his neck.[3]

Once the interpreter arrived—a local Armenian merchant whom Tehlirian had befriended, named Kevork Kalustian—the criminal police were able to ascertain the following facts: that Tehlirian freely confessed to killing Talaat with premeditation, as revenge for the violent death of Tehlirian's family, for which he held Talaat personally responsible; that Tehlirian had come to Berlin in January 1921 and had lived for several months in different apartments; that on discovering that Talaat was in Berlin and living in Hardenbergstrasse, Tehlirian moved on March 5 to a room across the street to observe Talaat; and that he had been unable to carry out his plan until he had the means to flee. When arrested, he had on his person twelve thousand marks, which he said he had obtained only the day before.[4]

A postmortem on March 15 by Drs. Schmulinsky and Thiele established that the victim had a large circular hole, which contained countless bone splinters, at the rear of his head; that his brains were blackened and swimming in blood; and that the skull was so shattered and the brains so destroyed that death had been instantaneous. Both coroners also agreed that the victim had probably suffered a heart attack as well.[5]

Finally, a firearms expert identified the weapon as a self-loading pistol in use by the German Army, able to fire eight bullets. The pistol bore the date 1915 and the stamp "German Weapons and Munitions Factory."[6] Tehlirian freely admitted that he had bought the gun two years earlier in Tiflis (now Tbilisi), fearful for his life in the event of a Turkish invasion of Russian Georgia.[7]

Most papers labeled his deed a political crime, but the right-wing *Deutsche Tageszeitung* confidently claimed that it had been committed out of jealousy, adding: "Such personal disputes are not unusual among our foreign guests."[8]

The criminal police were still grappling with the question of whether Tehlirian had accomplices "in knowledge or deed" or whether he had acted alone. Inquisitive reporters were told by some people at the scene that following the murder, several persons "of Oriental appearance" had driven away from Bahnhof Zoo toward Friedrichstrasse. This information was eventually declared invalid, but the thorough Inspector von Manteuffel ordered Tehlirian's room at the Dittman Boardinghouse locked and sealed and all his papers confiscated.[9]

According to the Treaty of Versailles, as leader of the Young Turk party Talaat would have had to be delivered up by the authorities if it were known that he was anywhere in Germany. Hence, he had selected the cover name of Ali Salih. The leftist-liberal *Vossische Zeitung* maintained that Talaat did not occupy himself with political matters, and had no ties with the German government.

None of this was true. Far from living in seclusion, Talaat traveled freely, attempting to persuade Europeans that there had never been an Armenian problem and that the persecutions had never taken place. In the hope of returning to power one day, he and his fellow exiles endeavored to lay the foundations for positive attitudes toward Turkey in postwar Europe. As for relations with the postwar German government, not only had Talaat and Enver Pasha, the two most prominent Young Turk leaders, been the most loyal allies of the wartime German government, as attested by the huge German military presence in Turkey during World War I, but Talaat's refuge in Berlin was arranged primarily by pro-Turkish sympathizers in the German Foreign Ministry. By declining to extradite him to Turkey, they provided him with the protection necessary to carry on his political activities. Fully aware that he was sought by the Allies, Talaat was extremely cautious, adopted a false name, and kept a low profile.

But one enterprising journalist from the *Tägliche Rundschau* reported:

From a friend of Talaat Pasha, we have heard today that he felt pursued and even had premonitions of his fate. Talaat had very specifically told his friends that if Mustafa Kemal [the new head of

the Turkish government, known also as Atatürk] should have suc-
cess at the London Conference [convened from February 21 to
March 14, 1921, in which Kemal sought to alter the sultan's peace
treaty with the Allies], his, Talaat's, final hours would be at hand.
He believed that a secret organization supported by the Entente
[Allies] was out to get him. In those circles which are familiar with
Oriental émigré politics, there is disagreement with Talaat's theory, but it cannot be dismissed that such murder organizations
could exist.[10]

The mass of newspaper readers, however, would have had to look
deeper into the stories and the lengthy editorials that followed to
comprehend that Tehlirian's crime was more than an act of private
vengeance. An editorial in the liberal, pro-Armenian *Berliner Tageblatt,* seeking balance in Talaat's career, stated:

> He was indisputably the strongest and toughest head of the Young
> Turk Party. He was also one of the few who did not seek personal
> enrichment, who did not stretch out his hands towards foreign
> treasures, and therefore, it is regrettable that these same hands are
> not clean of blood.[11]

The latter observation must have been obscure to many, for the
perpetration of the massacres was not widely known to the public.
But some clarification emerged in other editorials, and by the time
the background stories had appeared, readers were able to comprehend the simple historic truth behind the reference to Talaat's bloody
hands, as set forth, for instance, clearly and explicitly in this front-
page editorial in the Catholic organ *Germania*:

> The Armenian massacres comprise a dark page in the late Grand
> Vizier's career. The German side attempted repeatedly, alas in
> vain, to stop this bloody endeavor which cost tens of thousands of
> Christians their lives. The Turks, regarding this as an internal mat-
> ter, did not allow any interference. If anyone thinks that Talaat
> and the others guilty of these massacres acted justly, then it should
> not be forgotten that the Turkey of the 20th century is in no way a
> civilized European state, but that Asian methods are employed to
> rule, and that its rulers, despite their European education, are un-
> able to free themselves of those methods because such methods are
> not incompatible with their innermost views. It is because of the
> Armenian murders that Talaat is wanted by the Entente.[12]

The *New York Times*, on the other hand, in reporting the sensational crime for its American readers, neither explored nor even mentioned a possible motive. Its Berlin correspondent submitted a story describing how the German press mourned "the loss of a friend of Germany's who remained true up to the last few days before Turkey finally collapsed." The paper quoted German authorities as saying that they had been ignorant of Talaat's presence in Berlin but that many of his countrymen knew of it because he went to the Turkish Club on Motzstrasse, "where he was generally regarded as the coming man who would pull his country out of its misery." The *Times* also reported that Talaat's ample supply of money enabled him to "surround himself with European and Turkish comforts," and that the Deutsche Bank was said to be holding Talaat's fortune of ten million marks in safekeeping.[13]

Once the sensational facts had been published, discussed, and digested, Berliners returned to the normal menu of news that preoccupied a defeated Germany only two and a half years after the end of World War I—unemployment, inflation, reparations payments, and the public speeches and activities of foreign leaders such as Warren G. Harding, David Lloyd George, and Vladimir Ilyich Lenin. Berliners also began preparing for Holy Week, to start in five days. The Easter observances included performances throughout the city of sacred music, especially Bach's *St. Matthew Passion,* which was an annual ritual and in these times a solace for people's souls.

Criminal Police Sergeant Scholz, on the other hand, along with the state attorney, was busily working on his unusual murder case. Even more unusual than the case, however, was the culprit himself, who never denied having committed the deed, did not appear to suffer any remorse, and merely sat patiently in his cell smoking one cigarette after another.

Scholz had first taken Tehlirian to the Charlottenburg Police Station, where he was brusquely put in a cell. But within minutes he was taken out again, his head was bandaged, and he was driven to the Secret Police Division, where he was put in yet another cell. But despite his harrowing circumstances, he felt an inner contentment such as he had seldom experienced.

The prisoner was taken out again for his first interrogation, which was to be in French. Unable to respond with any clarity, he was returned to his cell.

Toward evening he was taken from his cell once more. This time, one of two escorting policemen devised a primitive set of handcuffs. He took from his pocket a ball of cord whose ends were tied to a pair of cylindrical wooden blocks. The cord was wrapped around Tehlirian's wrists and joined to the cylinders in his hands. (Tehlirian smiled to himself as he recalled that as a child he used to play "horse" like this.)

With the two policemen, the second now holding a mountain of paper, he walked out of the station and through the streets, until they arrived at Central Police Headquarters on Kantstrasse. They entered a large room where several officials were present, to one of whom the policeman handed a package containing the murder weapon. The room was very still as the officials examined the calm young man. His name was entered in a ledger, and he was taken out into a corridor where he saw prisoners cleaning windows and sweeping the floors.

His new cell was of medium size with a small window, a folding bed attached to the wall, a chair, and a table equipped with a plate, wooden spoon, two earthen vases—one filled with water for washing—but no soap. Twilight was falling, and an electric light bulb, which hung by a wire from the ceiling, was suddenly switched on.

Now, for the first time, Tehlirian's tranquility seemed to leave him, and his emotions became chaotic. For one thing, he was beginning to feel the pain of his injuries. His ribs ached, his head throbbed, his knees were scraped, and his body shivered with fever.

In the evening he was taken to a room on the second floor. A bearded, bespectacled German official was seated opposite the door through which he entered. On a table he saw his own gun. Nearby stood a young man with Asiatic features who glared at him with obvious hatred. Tehlirian sensed him to be a Turk. Another official sat at a desk, while on a table close to Tehlirian was a hat soaked with blood, and a cane.

The official began the interrogation in German, but Tehlirian had difficulty understanding him and asked for an Armenian interpreter. The official appeared to ignore the request and stubbornly repeated his question. Tehlirian grasped that the question pertained to how and why he had killed Talaat Pasha. For a moment he was overwhelmed, wondering how he could possibly describe the crimes of the former Turkish grand vizier. The official picked up the gun and asked Tehlirian to demonstrate how he had used it. When Tehlirian hesitated, the official looked pointedly at the other young man, who blurted out in Turkish: "You criminal! How could you have killed this man?!"

Tehlirian retorted in Turkish: "The same way he killed one million innocent people."

"So you know Turkish!" the German official said, brightening.

"As well as I," responded the Turk.

"Then you can help me conduct this investigation. Ask him why he killed Talaat Pasha."

The young Turk looked at Tehlirian strangely and repeated the question. Tehlirian curtly refused to answer any questions in Turkish. When it became evident that the Turk could not be helpful, the official handed him Talaat's hat and cane and waved him to the door.

Now the official bade Tehlirian be seated. His stern manner melted away, and he spoke in more sympathetic tones. As he talked, Tehlirian gradually realized that the German was speaking about the Armenian massacres and several times mentioned the name of Johannes Lepsius, a German theologian who had written books and articles on the subject. Even so, Tehlirian realized he could make no further progress and asked again for an Armenian interpreter.

He was returned to his cell, where soon thereafter his light was extinguished. In the dark his thoughts and emotions alternated between the tragedies that had befallen his nation and the happier times he had spent in his native Erzinga.

In the morning, after he had awakened and washed, his cell door opened and another prisoner (apparently a trusty) entered, replaced his water, and brought him some hot, bitter coffee and some barley soup. They did not speak.

Two hours later he was taken to a room where he was overjoyed to see his friend Kevork Kalustian, who greeted him with the words: "Have no concern. The entire Armenian community stands ready to defend you. I am here as the official Armenian interpreter." Nearby sat a pleasant-looking man who identified himself as Herr Schultze, the counselor to the Charlottenburg Court, who would conduct the interrogation through the Armenian interpreter as Tehlirian had requested.

Kalustian now sat close to Tehlirian and offered him some chocolate candy and cookies. Seeing this, Schultze exclaimed in astonishment: "You wish to give the murderer sweets?" to which Kalustian immediately responded: "What do you mean—murderer? This is a great man whom we all admire!"

Schultze looked at Kalustian, who was only five years older than the prisoner, and at the prisoner himself, outwardly so calm.

As a court reporter recorded everything in the Criminal Police Protocol (transcript), Schultze asked his first question—Was Tehlirian a Persian subject? Tehlirian replied that he was not.

"Yesterday you said you were."

"Yes, I came to Berlin with a Persian passport but I am a Turkish subject, born in the village of Pakaritch in the district of Erzinga."

"Why did you lie?"

"It wasn't a lie, it was a necessity. [Since] the massacres, no Armenian is able to get a Turkish passport."

"Where were you educated?"

"In the Erzinga National High School."

"Does that school issue a diploma so you can enter the university here in Berlin?"

"No. I merely wanted to audit classes."

"Do you know enough German?"

"As much as one can learn in three months."

"Do you know who Ali Salih Bey was—the man you killed on the sidewalk in front of Hardenbergstrasse 17?"

"Yes, he was Talaat Pasha."

"What compelled you to commit that crime?"

"I am not a criminal. Talaat was. He destroyed our people. I can describe for you the atrocities he committed from Constantinople all the way to Deir Zor" [in Syria].

"Who helped you kill Talaat Pasha?"

"No one." He paused, then added: "But even if there were others, I wouldn't tell you."

Schultze studied him intently for a moment but did not pursue the matter. There was something mercurial about the young man. He was gentle, soft-spoken, but on occasion, the rapid movement of his eyes suggested an inner turmoil. Schultze found himself feeling compassion for the youth, who at times seemed utterly lost. *"Ein echter Fremde* [a real foreigner]," he said to himself. He said he had acted alone, but Schultze didn't believe him. Surely he was merely a soldier in a larger army, and surely he wouldn't admit it. Schultze thought it worth a try anyway.

"On which organization's orders did you act?"

"My own."

Schultze nodded with ironic disbelief, as though he hadn't expected any other reply.

"Personally, what do you have against Talaat Pasha?"

"A great deal. It was on his orders that all the Armenians were killed, including my mother, my brother, and my other relatives. From that day on, I have lived for the hope of revenge against Talaat."

"How long have you had this notion?"

"From 1915 on, but it has taken me three years to find Talaat."

"How did you discover that Talaat was in Berlin?"

"Accidentally, from a newspaper."

"And how did you locate Talaat Pasha in Berlin?"

"Toward the end of February, near the Zoological Garden, I overheard Turkish being spoken. Turning, I saw three young Turks, one of whom addressed a fourth as 'My Pasha,' a rather heavyset man who had apparently been conversing with them. When they parted, all three kissed his hand. He looked to me very much like Talaat Pasha, whose picture I had seen in the newspapers. I followed him to a house on Hardenbergstrasse. A few days later I rented a room opposite. During the last ten days I was able to establish that 'My Pasha' was indeed Talaat. And when on March 15 he came out, I struck."

"In that case, do you admit to having committed the murder with premeditation?"

Tehlirian was confused by the question, and although he replied, "Of course," he was disturbed to see a strange expression on Kalustian's face.

"I can understand that the idea of revenge could have impelled you to commit that act, but doesn't your conscience trouble you after the murder?"

"On the contrary, my heart is filled with gratification that I was finally able to avenge the murder of one million people."

"In other words, you came to Berlin not to study but to kill Talaat?"

"I have dreamed of studying mechanical engineering in Berlin since before the war. But everything turned upside down."

The counselor toyed with a pencil as he looked solemnly at the young Armenian.

"Do you know that by law, you are liable to the death penalty?"

"Yes, but after the successful completion of my task, whatever happens happens."

"When did you decide to undertake the killing?"

"I had sworn an oath on my mother's unknown grave that I would kill Talaat—when I found him, I would most certainly kill him."

Schultze asked for a description of the murder, and Tehlirian patiently reviewed the events, describing exactly what happened. Throughout his recital he felt uncomfortable and perspired heavily. Afterward he was returned to his cell.

The trusty entered and cleaned his head wound, changing the bandage. This time he introduced himself, saying his name was Levine, that he knew why Tehlirian was in prison, and that he also knew a great deal about the Armenian massacres and about Talaat Pasha. Although Tehlirian did not understand everything, it was clear that Levine was sympathetic. At one point he made it clear that if he had been Armenian, he would have done the same. Levine then made a salient point. If Tehlirian had killed Talaat out of a desire for personal revenge, he could get fifteen years of hard labor. But if he said that he killed Talaat for general political reasons and with premeditation, he could be beheaded. (At the time, the death penalty in Germany was carried out by guillotine.)

Tehlirian mulled this over. Certainly, he could not tell all; there were still secrets to be kept. He had noticed the skepticism on the counselor's face during answers to questions about accomplices and organizations. He knew why he had tracked down and killed Talaat, but in taking a life, had he engaged in a kind of one on one? Was there any sense to that, or did it make more sense that his motive was to advance a political cause? Tehlirian shook his head, confused by his own thoughts.

He shared the candy and other sweets that Kalustian had given him with Levine. Later Levine smuggled into the cell a copy of that day's *Morgenpost*, whose headline read: FORMER GRAND VIZIER TALAAT PASHA MURDERED IN BERLIN: POLITICAL REVENGE BY AN ARMENIAN STUDENT.

Tehlirian now began to understand the point Levine had made, as well as the expression on Kalustian's face. Consequently, when Schultze continued the interrogation later that afternoon, laying great stress on the political aspects of the crime, Tehlirian repeatedly played up the argument of personal revenge for the killing of his family.

When the interrogation ended, Tehlirian found an occasion to exchange some words with Kalustian, who told him that the Turkish community was making a great effort to minimize the case, while the Armenian community was doing its utmost to represent it as an international question and to press for an acquittal. Kalustian also said that as the official interpreter, he had not signed the transcript.

Back in his cell, Levine slipped Tehlirian a sliver of mirror, and for the first time since his incarceration, he studied himself. One side of his nose was swollen, there was a cut under his eye, his left cheek was scratched, and his forehead was cut.

The next morning he was confronted by another interrogator, Counselor Mandopfeil from the Court of Assizes, an older man whom Tehlirian found unpleasant. Heeding Levine's advice, Tehlirian sought to stress the personal nature of the crime as opposed to it being a premeditated murder. After the interrogation, Kalustian informed Tehlirian that the community had acquired for his defense attorneys from Berlin's most notable law firm.

Levine seemed to know everything that was going on in the prison. He informed Tehlirian that Mandopfeil was responsible for his own misfortune, which entailed conviction for embezzlement. Levine explained that the sum involved was fifty thousand marks but that it had in fact been an accounting error owing to a sudden sharp devaluation. He therefore shared Tehlirian's distaste for Mandopfeil.

Commenting on what had happened the previous day with Schultze, Levine said that Tehlirian had done well to maintain that it was not he who was the criminal but Talaat. "Save that for the trial," he advised, "for who can prove that this man Talaat, [though he] so recently enjoyed an honorable life here, was not a criminal?"

Five days later, on March 22, Tehlirian was transferred to Berlin's Central Prison. This saddened him since he had not only become accustomed to his former cell, but felt that in Levine he had found a true friend whom he would not see again. Now all his clothes and belongings were registered, and he was given a prison uniform. His new cell was approximately the same size, and he was pleased to find that it was immaculately clean. On the other hand, he learned that in this prison everything was organized from morning to lights out, and he came to dread the strict regimen and iron discipline that were to govern his life until his trial.

The next day was Sunday, and the prison pastor visited him. Tehlirian learned that it was traditional for the pastor to visit murderers. The pastor said that through the writings of Johannes Lepsius, he too was familiar with the agonies of the Armenian people. He delivered a brief sermon and promised to send a copy of the Bible in Armenian.

No sooner had the pastor left than Tehlirian was told he had another visitor. It was an Armenian Catholic priest, who blessed him "for having killed the monster and wreaking revenge for all." The priest was en route to Rome and said: "I shall ask the pope to bless you for the work you have performed as a gift to your nation."

The consoling visit was interrupted by a prison guard, who said it was forbidden to communicate in a foreign language. The Armenian priest gave Tehlirian a cross from Jerusalem and left. Moved by the experience, later that morning Tehlirian attended religious services, after which he received yet another visitor who—despite the guard's earlier admonition—was able to relate to him the details of certain dramatic events he had witnessed.

———

The visitor was a close Armenian friend named Hazor, who had been present at both Talaat Pasha's assassination and his funeral. Six days before, on March 15, Hazor had been in the neighborhood of Uhlandstrasse when he saw two Turks running toward Hardenbergstrasse. One was Dr. Behaeddin Shakir, an old friend and ally of Talaat's with whom he had escaped from Turkey at the end of the war; the other was a Dr. Rusoohi, who, untypically, was bareheaded. Hazor knew immediately that something unusual had happened. A few moments later they reached the spot where the corpse lay, and Hazor recognized Talaat Pasha.

Shakir walked unsteadily toward the body and stared down in disbelief. A policeman held him back. Shakir looked around as though for help and was approached by an elderly official who allowed him to go nearer. With trembling hands Shakir lifted the cloth from the head of the corpse and confirmed that it was Talaat. The bullet, which had entered beneath his ear, had come out the front of his head.

Shakir covered Talaat's head and withdrew slowly. The official came up to him, shook his hand, and said: "This is a most regrettable thing. I am very upset and shaken by this unexpected incident. Please accept my sympathies, Doctor." Hazor later established that this elderly official had spent the war in Turkey and was familiar with the Turkish community of Berlin.

"Extending condolences is not enough," Shakir said sternly to the official. "Talaat Pasha was everything to us. Buried with him will be all our hopes. Of course, the criminal is an Armenian, isn't he?"

"Yes, an Armenian youth, arrested in very bad condition. The people wanted to lynch him."

"But what are you doing here?" Shakir suddenly asked the official, whom he apparently recognized at that moment.

"[My presence] is not accidental. I was sent by order of the foreign ministry to identify the victim and was given a car to get here quickly."

"Very well. But tell me, why is the corpse allowed to lie here in front of this mob? Who will remove it? Do you need a special order from the attorney general?"

The official could not answer. He walked over to one of the police guards and after a long conversation returned and said: "There is no need to get permission from the attorney general. The municipal authorities have already authorized removal of the corpse, but a car has not yet arrived."

Behaeddin Shakir stood there stunned and finally said: "Is this how you honor the . . . premier of a country that remained loyal to Germany until the very last minute, by letting [his corpse] lie here for hours in the street?"

"It's because there are no hearses available right now at the city morgue," was the reply. "If you wish to pay the cost yourself, we can move the body with an ordinary car."

For the next five days, Talaat's body lay in the morgue while the Turkish community sought to have the remains transported to Constantinople for burial. The Turkish government of Kemal Atatürk, however, though not unsympathetic to Talaat and his policies, refused to accept it. The European press had seized on the assassination to recount stories of the massacres, and the Turkish government, now based in Ankara, did not want any association with its predecessors.

In consequence Talaat was given a modest funeral in Berlin, which began with a Muslim religious service at his residence—Hardenbergstrasse 4.

Countless bouquets and floral displays began arriving well before the appointed hour of 10:00 A.M., as several hundred people, largely Turks—most identifiable by their red fezzes but others wearing turbans, fur caps and bandannas—and some Germans, filled the street and sidewalk in front of the villa. A special force of Berlin security police watched from the sidelines as photographers filled the air with the clicking and whirring of their cameras.

Inside, Talaat lay in state in a zinc coffin draped with a red Turkish flag, a red fez at its head. Moslem coreligionists—such as Egyptians,

Indians, Persians, Arabs, and Afghans—were present, but most notable among the mourners were past and present officials of the German government. Paying their respects were a representative of the Weimar Republic, two former foreign ministers—Richard von Kühlmann and Arthur Zimmermann (author of the famous telegram concerning Mexico which ultimately brought the United States into the war)—representatives of various other German ministries, several generals and other military officers who had served in Turkey, and the director of the Deutsche Bank.

Talaat's widow mourned quietly by the side of the closed coffin as wreaths continued to arrive from the Dresden Bank, the Oriental Bank, the Deutsche Bank and the German-Turkish Club. Finally, there was a large wreath from the German Foreign Ministry with the inscription "To a great statesman and loyal friend." Although the new Turkish government had refused to let the burial take place in Constantinople, it did send a representative to Berlin, in the person of Heydar Pasha.

The service began punctually at 10 with Muslim prayers by the imam of the Turkish Embassy, Shukri Bey, whose cry—"Allah Akbar [God is great]!" filled the packed ground-floor rooms of the villa. The imam then proceeded to the various rites for the dead. His sermon concluded with the words: "He who lies here before you, Mehmed Talaat Pasha, was a man of high virtue and a servant of God. Is there anyone present who knows otherwise?"

There was a murmur of denial by all those who understood Turkish as the service ended and the coffin was borne out into the street and placed on a hearse. The funeral procession moved slowly toward the cemetery of Saint Matthew's Church. Behind the hearse and the wreath-bearing cars walked the imam, resplendent in a purple cloak, white turban, and gold headband. At the end of the procession were some twenty Turkish youths dressed in old uniforms with German Army caps.

At the cemetery the imam held another service, and then twelve brief speeches were made, one by the former director of the Anatolian Railway, who said: "We Germans carry a monument to him in our hearts, a monument to the purity of his character." The final speaker, Dr. Behaeddin Shakir, Talaat's confederate, was now senior émigré Turk in Berlin. But few could understand Shakir; he was so shaken with emotion that the words stuck in his throat.

The funeral service drew to a close. But the coffin was not lowered into the ground. Instead it was placed in a special hall where, the corpse embalmed, it would remain until the call came from Ankara to have it transferred to Talaat's native soil for burial.

Between March, when the crime was committed, and June, when the trial began, the public learned nothing about the pretrial examination of the accused Armenian student. In the absence of any news, the press nevertheless succeeded in prodding public memory through the periodic publication of letters and statements from partisan individuals and groups sympathetic to the Armenians or the Turks. While some of the authors were Germans, most were from the Berlin émigré communities of 4,500 Turks and 500 Armenians.

One Berlin newspaper apparently more willing than others to lend its columns to such public debate was *Vorwärts*, the official organ of the Social Democratic party. Two weeks after the crime, it published an article containing what it termed "the views of the local Armenian community." In summary these views held that the German people could not know of the Turkish crimes against the Armenians during the war because of military censorship, which had cloaked the atrocities in a mantle of silence. Tehlirian's deed was an act of revenge for the persecution of his people by Talaat and Enver (minister of war), an act that would be understood by all Germans sensitive to justice. The deportation and annihilation orders, signed by Talaat and Enver, "resulted in acts of unparalleled horror against women, children, and the elderly."

Vorwärts then quoted two charges from the statement. The first claimed that "the one-and-a-half million Armenians had been martyred because of their Christian faith." The second maintained that Germany had poured money into Turkey "to win Turkish favor during the war," and this booty had found its way into the pockets of Talaat and Enver, adding: "At a time of extreme shortage of living space in Berlin, Talaat came here and with German money rented a nine-room house on Hardenbergstrasse." While expressing sympathy for the Armenian cause, this socialist newspaper did not aid Tehlirian's case by placing the murder in a political context when it wrote: "The Armenians see in Tehlirian's deed not a murder but an act of political liberation and hope that the German jurors will interpret it as such."

These charges were soon answered in the columns of the same newspaper when, one week later, a letter—"one of a large number commenting on the character of the deceased"—was published from an unidentified German who claimed that he had lived for many years in Turkey and had known Talaat personally. The author admitted that the Armenians had suffered extensively but not because of their Christian beliefs. Attributing to the Muslim faith a tolerance of other religions "which is without example," he went no further in explaining why the atrocities took place. The author also conceded the existence of corruption in Turkey but said it was a defamation of Talaat "to throw him into the general pot of *baksheesh*-devourers and profiteers."

It was not, however, until in mid-May, shortly before the trial, that a major effort was made to influence German public opinion. Circumventing the press entirely, a pamphlet (written in German), which bore the intriguing title, *The Secret of the Murder of Talaat Pasha*, was circulated throughout the city. Its author, one Mansur Rifat, appeared to depend on his readers' ignorance of history, and especially of recent events. He presented a convoluted view of the situation in Turkey by accusing the Young Turks of chauvinism, exploiting nationality and religion, and circulating poisonous ideas, yet praising their successor Kemal Atatürk for his "new and healthy ideas." Inasmuch as Kemal, himself a former Young Turk, was at that time avidly pursuing the same policies, especially against the Armenians, as later developments would reveal, Rifat's arguments led nowhere.

Similar contradictions nullified some of his other points, such as the charge that Britain had ultimately caused Talaat's death because Britain saw raising the Armenian question as the "surest means of destroying the Ottoman Empire and humiliating Islam." This, too, was in direct contradiction of British foreign policy, for it had long been the objective—from the time of Prime Minister Disraeli in the late nineteenth century—to preserve the stability of the Ottoman Empire, thereby guaranteeing that Russia would not have access to the Mediterranean and the Persian Gulf and protecting British interests in the Middle and Far East.

Rifat's pamphlet discussed a number of other minorities in the Ottoman Empire, which had been for more than a century a mosaic of many nationalities, disparate in their political beliefs and held together only by oppressive Ottoman military power. As the influence of western democratic ideas spread throughout the empire, independence movements sprang up and spurred nationalists into action. Thus, when Rifat accused the Greeks of "inhumanity" and the Bulgarians of "barbarism," he was actually using euphemisms for revolt against Ottoman subjugation. But Rifat's main focus in the pamphlet was on the Armenians, the blame for whose unrest and its consequences he laid on British and American missionaries for instilling revolutionary ideas in young Armenians.

Unmentioned by Rifat were the government abuses inflicted on the Armenians, which led them to rise up and resist Ottoman oppression, leaving the impression that Armenians were anarchists who had to be suppressed.

As with many pamphlets motivated by burning contemporary issues, Rifat's was highly tendentious and proved, in the end, to be a shrill and unconvincing political tract. It even sought to play on German sensitivity to charges of wartime atrocities in Belgium, which, Rifat reminded his German audience, General Pershing himself had found it necessary to deny.

Finally, it sought to sway the public against the Armenian student prior to his trial by labeling Tehlirian's comments about Talaat's responsibility for the death of his parents "a pathetic tale to gain the sympathy of the court." Rifat cited a letter to a Berlin newspaper (again *Vorwärts*) from members of Talaat's family in which they justified his policies but blamed a typhus epidemic for the greatest Armenian losses, accused the European powers of giving prominence to the Armenian question for their own imperialistic purposes, and concluded: "The motive for the murder will be clarified by the trial."

These were to be prophetic words.

For his part, Tehlirian was kept aware of developments outside his prison cell by occasional visitors from Berlin's Armenian community. They gave him news of events in Armenia and provided him with moral and material support. Late in March, he met his defense attorneys. Adolf von Gordon was a tall dignified gentleman, apparently well-known to the prison officials, who greeted him warmly. Von Gordon came to familiarize himself with details of the case and to get Tehlirian's signature authorizing him to proceed with the case. Tehlirian's second defense lawyer, Friedrich Werthauer, was a pleasant man with sad features, who asked many questions about the massacres, about Tehlirian's childhood, and about his dreams.

Meanwhile Tehlirian's sealed room at the Dittman Boardinghouse was opened and carefully sifted by Sergeant Scholz's Criminal Police staff. No evidence linking him with any coconspirators or organizations was discovered.

The weeks passed quietly with a minimum of contact and activity, and in May he was visited by several doctors, including two psychiatrists and two neurologists, who examined him. Thereafter, informed by his lawyers that the trial would take place in June, he spent his time quietly and patiently. Sometimes, he would sing traditional Armenian folk melodies, sad songs filled with longing for the homeland, and on occasions such as these, his mind would be filled first with images of his family and then with the face of Anahid. At such moments his heart would be heavy, for Tiflis was so far away in the Transcaucasus, and Anahid even more distant. Would they ever have a life together? Could they have had one, had he made good his escape? He was almost startled to hear the sound of his own voice as, aloud, he asked the same question Armenian émigrés all over the world ask themselves in time of confusion: *"Oor ayee, oor ehga?"* [Where was I before, where have I come?] He answered himself: You are in a jail in Berlin, far from Erzinga, far from Anahid, because you have murdered the man who murdered the Armenians. You have done what your mother wanted. You have done what your political mentors wanted. You have taken revenge for your entire nation. Somehow, though, he was sad, and as he sat in a corner of his cell, he thought of himself less as a hero than as a mere spoke on the wheel of a very large oxcart, unable to guide his own destiny and rolling in a direction away from happiness.

At other times, to all outward appearances, he was at peace with himself. But there were moments when he would muse that given the hard facts—seen by witnesses committing the murder, discarding the weapon, running from the scene, caught by an irate mob, all in a foreign country whose government had been an ally of the murdered man—how could he expect anyone to understand him or his motives?

He was right on all counts. But while the police might not have understood his motives, he was altogether ignorant of the distinction between personal and political motivation on which the German investigators placed so much importance. These concepts of German law were totally alien to him. As for the facts, all the police had was his version, which was incomplete and untruthful. It was actually only a small part of the story that would later unfold. For, far from acting alone, Tehlirian had been supported and assisted by a considerable network of expatriate allies who had funded and guided him. In fact, Tehlirian was part of an international conspiracy of vengeance that had its roots in the turmoil of Armenian history.

2

The Web of History

*A*rmenia as a civilization dates back to six hundred years before Christ. Armenians inhabited the areas that are today eastern Turkey, the Transcaucasus, and northern Iran. Prior to that time, this area had been known as Urartu,* and Mount Ararat (a variation of Urartu), where the Bible says Noah's ark finally landed, towered at almost 17,000 feet in its center and became the symbol of Armenia. The country was ruled initially by the Medes, followed by the sun-worshiping Persians, and then the Greeks, when Alexander the Great conquered the Persian Empire. As a consequence, Hellenistic culture dominated pre-Christian Armenian life, as Armenia became a crossroads for trade routes between the Far East, Central Asia, and the Mediterranean.

In the first century B.C., Armenia reached the height of its glory under Tigran II in a kingdom that, no longer landlocked, embraced a triangular area surrounded by the Black, Caspian, and Mediterranean seas, and included Mesopotamia (present-day Iraq), Syria, and parts of Georgia and Azerbaijan.† Armenian, a branch of the Indo-European family, became the language of the country, and political and economic life developed rapidly. The Romans could not tolerate

---

*Urartian cuneiform inscriptions can be found in many museums today, especially in Berlin's Pergamon Museum.
†The USSR's Armenian Republic today represents an area only one-tenth of Tigran II's kingdom.

the existence of such a thriving rival, and twenty-five years into Tigran's reign they conquered and divided the country.

As Christianity spread in the years following Christ's crucifixion, two of his disciples traveled to Armenia, which had worshiped pagan gods, preaching the new gospel. Their efforts eventually led to the adoption of Christianity as Armenia's state religion at the beginning of the fourth century A.D.—a conversion that was to have a crucial impact on the nation's future. In the fifth century, an alphabet notable for its unique characters was created whose first literary fruit—a translation of the Bible from Greek and Syriac—heralded a period known to Armenians as the Golden Age of Literature because of many other religious works that followed.

Kingdoms and satrapies (protectorates) interchanged over the centuries as Armenia was invaded repeatedly by Arabs in the seventh century, Seljuk Turks in the eleventh, and Mongols in the thirteenth. These invasions of the small Christian nation by largely Muslim hordes from Asia were carried out ruthlessly—especially by the Mongol Tamerlane—leaving a trail of death and devastation from which Armenia never fully recovered. In fact, they spurred a migration westward and the establishment of a small Armenian monarchy on the Mediterranean coast in an area called Cilicia, also known as Lesser Armenia. During the Crusades, Lesser Armenia played a prominent role in supporting Christian forces from Europe and thrived for three centuries until its monarchy was ended by a succession of invasions, eventually by the Ottoman Turks. Many Armenians remained in Cilicia and are still there, in the area of Lebanon and Syria.*

After Tamerlane's invasion Greater Armenia was absorbed into the Mongol Empire and sought to recover from the destruction that had reduced the country to ashes. Its population survived under considerable difficulty until one final invasion, this time by Turkish tribes from Persia seeking to escape Mongol hordes. These tribes were the nucleus of what would become the Ottoman Turks. Their leader and

---

*The historical existence of two Armenias has led to the current coexistence of two Catholicoses (Supreme Patriarchs), in Lebanon and Soviet Armenia. Initially in Etchmiadzin when the Armenians adopted Christianity, the Catholicate moved to Cilicia, but with the downfall of that kingdom, it was revived in 1441 in Etchmiadzin, where it exists today, headed by Vazgen I. The continuing Cilician Catholicate, located in Antelias, near Beirut, since 1930, is headed by Karekin II, an Oxford scholar. President Bush received both Catholicoses at the White House when they came jointly in 1989 to thank the United States for earthquake relief.

first sultan was Osman I, founder in the early fourteenth century of the Osmanli, or Ottoman, dynasty, which would rule Turkey for six hundred years. In 1453 Constantinople, which had been the seat of the Byzantine Empire under Emperor Constantine, fell to the Ottoman Turks and became their capital.

The vast Ottoman Empire extended from the borders of Germany to the limits of Persia and embraced a variety of nations, cultures, languages, and faiths. It appeared to be a conglomerate of peoples existing peacefully under Ottoman suzerainty, whereas in fact it was a seething cauldron of ethnic rivalries, its subjugated peoples— whether Hungarians, Bulgarians, Serbs, Greeks, or the multifarious Arabs—united only by a common hatred of their Turkish overlords. It was in the sixteenth century, during the reign of Sultan Süleyman I—called Süleyman the Magnificent because of the skill with which he expanded the Ottoman Empire to its greatest power—that Armenia was conquered and absorbed into the Ottoman Empire.

The Ottoman government constantly levied taxes to defend its volatile empire, and in the centuries that followed, when Armenia was often the battleground for wars between the powers that surrounded it, Ottoman Turkey seemed always to be at war with one or more of its enemies—Poland, Austria, Russia, and Persia—in consequence of which the empire was gradually whittled down. As a result of one of these wars—between the Ottoman Turks and Persia— Armenia was divided in 1639 between them, the Persians acquiring (and 200 years later losing) a small section that would eventually become Russian Armenia.

Throughout the turbulence, meanwhile, an indigenous culture had been flourishing and was being nurtured by the Armenian nation. At its root was the language and the alphabet, employed first in the translation of the Bible. The language, retained still in the church liturgy, later bifurcated into the eastern dialect, spoken in Russian Armenia and Iran, and western Armenian, spoken in all other countries. Armenian architecture and music both drew their inspiration from the Christian bases of the nation. Churches hark back to the fifth century and abound throughout Turkey, Soviet Armenia, and Karabagh, and are noted for their impact on Byzantine architecture. Armenian liturgical music is especially admired by musicologists for its beauty and expression. Armenian painting first took the form of frescoes on church walls, then illustrations for pages of the Bible, primarily the life of Christ. These hand-copied replicas of the Bible became printed books in the early sixteenth century, only sixty years after the invention of movable type by Gutenberg. Many of these "illuminated manuscripts" are to be found in American museums. Miniature painting, metalworking, rug weaving, silversmithing, and coins dating back to the third century B.C. were all part of the ancient culture that Armenians passed on to their children born as exiles in various parts of the world.

In the early nineteenth century, the focus of Armenian history shifted north with the Russian entry on the scene. Until then, the territory of Armenia in the Transcaucasus had been under Persian occupation. But in 1828, after the Russo-Turkish War, the defeated Persians ceded Armenia to Russia. Armenia was now divided between Turkish Armenia, primarily Anatolia or east-central Turkey, and Russian Armenia, the former eastern province.

Armenians in Russia's Transcaucasian cities fared well enough. They made up most of the merchants and bankers in Tiflis, and they were predominantly in charge of the oil wells in Baku. Yerevan, on the other hand, which was to become the Armenian capital, was undeveloped and populated largely by peasants in the service of Russian feudal lords. Even so, the Russian Armenians enjoyed conditions comparatively superior to those of their compatriots in Turkey.

The plight of the Turkish Armenians was the true genesis of Armenian political enlightenment. Armenian intellectuals who had studied in Russian and Central and Western European universities gathered in Tiflis, the capital of Georgia, which had become an Armenian intellectual and cultural center.* They focused their attention on the oppression suffered by their compatriots in Ottoman Turkey, primarily in the six *vilayets*,† or provinces, populated by almost two million Armenians.

The first of the resulting political parties was the Armenakans, founded in 1885 in Van by Turkish Armenians, whose objective was self-determination with the aid of European powers. The Armenakans disavowed terror as a means to achieve their ends, employing arms only for self-defense. But Ottoman military power and the absence of effective European support eventually showed the Armenakan approach to be ineffective. Two years later in Geneva, a Marxist revolutionary party was formed. The Hunchaks were Russian Armenians whose objective was the establishment of a socialist

---

*Even today, Tbilisi has an Armenian population of 450,000.
†The six *vilayets* were Van, Sivas, Erzerum, Diarbekir, Bitlis, and Harput.

Armenian state in Central Turkey. Unlike the Armenakans, the Hunchaks favored the use of terror and agitation.

Then in 1890, an umbrella organization combining all previous political elements was formed in Tiflis called the Armenian Revolutionary Federation (ARF).* The primary aim of the ARF was to achieve self-administration and social and economic reforms for the Armenians of Ottoman Turkey through any means, including terror. Because of internal rivalries and differing ends—the Hunchaks were basically socialists and the Dashnaks nationalists, even though members of the Second Socialist Internationale—they split one year later and operated as two separate political movements.†

With the founding of these political parties, Russian Armenian political writers focused increasingly on the problems faced by Armenians in Ottoman Turkey. There Turkish authorities made no pretense that the Armenians were anything but a subjugated people living in Anatolia in their six provinces at the pleasure and on the sufferance of the sultan. Many restrictions were imposed on them: They could not bear arms; they could not testify in court; they could not become officers in the army; and in some parts of Anatolia, they were forbidden to speak their own language. But harshest of all was the system of taxation, with avaricious tax collectors pilfering amounts far exceeding the poll and property taxes that Armenians and other Christians were compelled to pay. Despite these injustices, however, and unlike many other nations in the Ottoman Empire, the Armenians had never revolted, attempting instead to resolve their differences with the Sublime Porte by negotiation.‡ For centuries, Turks and Armenians had lived peacefully, if not harmoniously, in Anatolia. As one astute historian has noted, "tolerance did not mean equality under the empire."[1] There had been many injustices over the centuries; and yet, Armenians played a vital role in the history of the Ottoman Empire, often achieving high stations in the government, which recognized reluctantly that it needed the support and

*The ARF is known in Armenian as the Dashnaktsutiun, which means "Federation," and its members are called Dashnaks.
†A third major Armenian political party, the Ramgavars, was formed in 1908 in Cairo, and together with its Russian-Armenian counterpart, the Populists, adopted a nonviolent approach to achieving equal rights for Armenians in Turkey. In recent years Ramgavar activities have been largely philanthropic, especially for the benefit of victims of the 1987 earthquake in Soviet Armenia.
‡The Sublime Porte, in Turkish *Bab Ali*, was the term used when referring to the Ottoman government.

participation of this intelligent and industrious segment of the population.

Elsewhere there was considerable agitation for separation from the Ottoman Empire. Western ideas had begun to penetrate and spread among the many subject nations, fueling their hunger for freedom.* These ideas of freedom and independence had aroused the Ottoman government to violent repressive measures. When Abdul Hamid II became sultan in 1876, Turkey had fully earned its description (by Czar Nicholas in 1853) as "the sick man of Europe." The empire was in a state of financial collapse. Its bankruptcy was moral as well, and national movements agitating for independence were rife. In the same year, Bulgarians rose in revolt and twenty thousand were slaughtered by Turkish irregular troops, in what became known throughout Europe as the "Bulgarian atrocities." This unprecedented severity alarmed European governments and their publics. Accordingly the European powers condemned Turkish oppression and recommended reforms, namely the promulgation of a constitution and the establishment of a parliament. The sultan apparently accepted both suggestions but did nothing to implement them, instead applying greater pressure, through exorbitant taxation, on the Christians in Turkey, primarily Armenians and Greeks.

At Christmas 1893, the Greek patriarch of Constantinople closed all Orthodox churches in a passive gesture of protest. The Armenians were more belligerent. In the autumn of 1894, persecuted by Turkish troops and Kurdish cavalry units,† and badgered by aggressive Turkish tax collectors, Armenians in the mountainous areas of Sassun took up arms and fought back. After weeks of fighting they were promised pardons if they laid down their arms. When they did, all were killed in what was the first Turkish massacre. A European commission of inquiry condemned the sultan's cruel measures.

In May 1895 Great Britain, France, and Russia submitted a reform plan to the Sublime Porte. But by October, despite a flurry of diplomatic activity, the Porte, resentful of European intervention in

---

*One cannot examine this era of the Ottoman Empire without drawing parallels with similar multinational structures, simply because the pattern is always the same: forcible absorption, years of oppression, clandestine circulation of subversive—that is, democratic—ideas, and finally insurrection against the central authority. The disruption of the Soviet Union is but the latest example.
†During the massacres Sultan Abdul Hamid often used Kurds, who had been organized into units called Hamidye, named after him. This provided the sultan with a pretext that his own Turkish troops were not at fault.

Turkey's internal affairs from without, and of Armenian pressures—
pleas for freedom of speech, press, and assembly and for the right to
bear arms—from within, reacted with a violent brutality that
shocked foreign diplomats, missionaries, schoolteachers, relief
workers, and other eyewitnesses. The second major massacre took
place in Trebizond in October 1895, and within months Armenian
villages and churches throughout Anatolia had been destroyed, set-
tlements looted and burned, segments of the Christian population
forcibly converted to the Muslim faith, and over two hundred thousand Armenians slaughtered.

Europeans were not the only ones repelled by the sultan's violence
and duplicity. Turkish intellectuals had been gathering in Western
European centers and discussing revolution and reforms in their
homeland. In 1908 a group calling itself the Committee for Union
and Progress, better known later as the Young Turks, took power in
Turkey. They forced Abdul Hamid to agree to a constitutional regime
promising civil and religious liberty and parliamentary representa-
tion for all Ottoman subjects. Armenians joined in the universal joy
at this momentous turn of events and welcomed the arrival of the
Young Turks.

But fanatical supporters of the sultan engineered a countercoup in
1909, and in the process another slaughter of Armenians took place
in the Cilician city of Adana. Abdul Hamid, his loyal forces finally
defeated, was succeeded by his brother and exiled to Salonika. The
Young Turks were now in power. They were led by three men, Talaat,
Enver, and Jemal, who, between 1908 and the outbreak of World
War I, executed a political about-face, transforming the liberal party
they headed into a chauvinistic, imperialistic movement. Their objective was a pan-Turkic empire designed to expand Turkey's borders to
Central Asia. In order to do so, they planned to rid Turkey of all non-
Muslim elements—including Greeks, Jews, and Assyrians. Most of
all they wished to expel the largest minority within the borders of
Turkey—the Christian Armenians.*

In the summer of 1915, under cover of war, the Young Turks issued
decrees signed by Talaat and Enver ordering the deportation of the

---

*At this time, the population of the Ottoman Empire—which still included Syria,
Lebanon, Mesopotamia, Palestine, and parts of North Africa—was approximately
31,000,000, of which the unarmed Armenians comprised only 6 percent.

Armenians from Anatolia, where they had lived for centuries, to points more than three hundred miles away in Syria and Mesopotamia. The government justified this forced migration on the grounds of military necessity—that the Armenians were plotting a revolt and that they were guilty of collaboration with the Russian Army. When the decrees were implemented, the Armenians knew that those arguments were merely pretexts to uproot them, for most of the men were taken away and killed, and it was the women, children, elderly, ill, and infirm who were formed into caravans to begin the long trek on foot through the deserts in which some 90 percent would die of starvation, exhaustion, exposure, and disease.

The deportations took place directly after the defeat of the British at Gallipoli, where an invasion of the peninsula had been planned as the beginning of a land campaign against the Turks. Although the Turkish Army was headed by a German general, his deputy, Mustafa Kemal, was the commander who forced the British withdrawal, and to him went the credit for this major defeat. The Gallipoli victory had two consequences: It encouraged the Young Turks to continue their persecution of the Armenians, unhindered now by any expectation of Allied interference, and it elevated Mustafa Kemal—who eight years later would become "Atatürk, the father of modern Turkey"—to national prominence.

Elements of the Russian Imperial Army, supported by Armenian volunteer units, invaded Turkey and got as far as Erzinga, which they occupied until the Bolshevik Revolution broke out. When they withdrew, Enver commanded a Turkish Army that recaptured all of Anatolia and headed toward Russian Armenia with the intention of proceeding into Central Asia and realizing the pan-Turkic dream. But in May 1918, Armenian forces engaged Enver's army and, though outnumbered two to one, defeated it at Sardarabad. One week later, Russian Armenia declared itself an independent republic. The small state was born in agony, its population hungry and exhausted, cholera and typhus killing thousands, its economy virtually nonexistent, its treasury empty. Somehow, however, the republic survived, with the monetary and material support provided by organizations such as the American Near East Relief Committee and the infusion of funds from Armenian philanthropic groups. (It was at this time that the phrase "starving Armenians" originated.)

The government of the republic, from premier to cabinet members to the legislature, was dominated by the ARF. It hoped for international recognition to ensure its security, but that recognition was slow to come. The Allies, including the United States, granted de facto recognition—de jure to follow on the signing of the peace treaty with Turkey, as late as 1920. The various exile communities, still nursing the wounds of the massacres, sought to begin anew, hoping to forget the catastrophe they had left behind. But their concern for the survival of the republic remained foremost in their thoughts.

The struggling nation had the sympathy of Western leaders, most prominently Woodrow Wilson, who met in the White House with a delegation from the republic. His sympathy extended even more to the Armenians in Turkey. As Wilson had proposed at the Versailles Peace Conference, an international commission—from the United States, France, and England—arrived in Turkey and joined Turkish members to investigate conditions in the areas separated from the Ottoman Empire. Armenian hopes were high that word would reach the American president of the suffering of the survivors.

The Allies negotiated the Treaty of Versailles with Germany in 1919, but concluded a separate treaty with Turkey one year later at Sèvres. Counting on Allied support, the Armenians had expected that the area of the six *vilayets* would eventually become their new home, and this stipulation was included in the Treaty of Sèvres and accepted by Sultan Muhammad VI, the Ottoman ruler at the end of the war. According to the treaty, Turkey would recognize an independent Armenian state, and President Wilson would draw up its boundaries. But the terms of the treaty were never implemented.

The reasons were grounded in the person and plans of Mustafa Kemal, who, although having himself been a Young Turk, was now engaged in a campaign for his own ascent to power. These plans, growing out of a deep-seated nationalism, included the eradication of the Armenian Republic. In 1920 Kemal invaded Armenia with a Turkish Army as, with Lenin's approval, a Red Army invaded from the north. Caught in a pincers between the two, and rather than succumb to Turkish rule, which recent events had shown to be synonymous with extinction, the Armenian republic surrendered to the Red Army, eventually to become one of the fifteen Soviet republics.

In 1921 the Turks and the Soviets signed the Treaty of Moscow, ceding certain Armenian territories to Turkey and satisfying Turkish nationalist aims. This was a bitter pill for the Armenians to swallow, a pill heavily laced with irony. For even in delivering themselves to the Red Army, they could not escape their Turkish tormentors. Despite having engineered the massive crime of 1915 against the Armenian people, the three Young Turk leaders had fled the country immediately after the end of the war and the collapse of their government. All three had sought the assistance of Lenin and Trotsky for a return to power in Turkey, but they had been turned down. Enver and Jemal, however, had ingratiated themselves with the new Soviet leadership and become military advisers to the Red Army. Enver oversaw operations in the Transcaucasus—and Armenia.

Talaat, meanwhile, had traveled on to Germany where he was engaged in quite another strategem, which required the cooperation of Mustafa Kemal. As the acknowledged heads of the Turkish émigré community in Europe, Talaat and his fellow exiles sought the help of European political leaders, foes and friends alike, to assist them in a return to power in Turkey. But Talaat also sought Kemal's help in reestablishing the Young Turk Party in Central Turkey.* For his part, Kemal maintained surreptitious contact with Talaat and other émigrés in Germany in seeking support for his own bid for power, although he never fully trusted Talaat.

Kemal also arranged contracts with Bolshevik representatives to solicit their aid in preserving the Ottoman Empire, now under Allied occupation. The objective was to forge a Turkish-Soviet alliance wherein Soviet support in preventing partition and combating Western-sponsored separatist movements in Anatolia, especially by Armenians, would be reciprocated by Turkish support in stirring the Muslim world against the West. The Bolshevik leaders had already perceived that Mustafa Kemal was the key to Turkey's future and that his growing prominence could be exploited to preserve the young Soviet state through his influence with the Muslims Moscow was hoping to incorporate.†

On October 29, 1923, Turkey was proclaimed a secular republic and Mustafa Kemal was named its president, thereby automatically dissolving the sultanate and the Ottoman Empire. Ankara was desig-

---

*In April 1919 The Times of London described continuing unrest in Anatolia, where Young Turk holdover officials and agents were fomenting demonstrations against "Armenian survivors of the massacres, principally women . . . to keep fanaticism at the boiling point." The Times added: "This hostility is due partly to Armenian claims for redress and for the restoration of property and of women and children who were carried off by the Turks during the massacres."
†The durability of that influence was evident seven decades later, in May 1990, when Azerbaijanis demonstrating against Soviet authority paraded through the streets of Baku with Turkish flags and large pictures of Mustafa Kemal.

nated the new capital of Turkey, and in one of his first acts as president, Kemal rejected the Treaty of Sèvres, which authorized the creation of an Armenian state in Anatolia. As for the Young Turk triumvirate of Talaat, Enver, and Jemal, who had hoped for a return to power in Turkey—all three were dead.

3

Manhunt

Soghomon Tehlirian was twenty-two when he began his zealous search for the one Turk he and the Armenian nation held responsible for the annihilation of more than one million men, women, and children. He also had a personal score to settle with the former minister of the interior and grand vizier.

In 1915, when Tehlirian was in Erzinga with his mother, brothers, and sisters—his father having moved to Belgrade and seeking to have the family join him—the government of the Young Turks in Constantinople issued the decrees ordering the deportation of the Armenian people in Anatolia to the deserts of Syria and Mesopotamia.

Rumors had been rife throughout Anatolia of persecutions, deportations, and large-scale pillaging by Turkish irregular troops, or gendarmes; but in this time of slow communications, Armenians could only confirm them when the gendarmes reached the individual towns and villages. In June of that year, this fate was visited on the Armenian population of Erzinga and the violence the Tehlirian family suffered was so shattering that eighteen-year-old Soghomon fought incessantly to banish its memory from his mind.

World War I was raging. Turkey was on the side of Germany and Austria—the Central Powers—and Tehlirian, in despair at the loss of his family, found his way eastward toward the Russian border, eventually ending his travels in Tiflis, the capital of Georgia, which was under Russian administration. There he learned that since the start of the war, in order to assist the Russian Army in its advance into Turkey, Armenian volunteer units had been organized for the sole purpose of engaging in guerrilla activities against the Turks. The Armenian Revolutionary Federation had been the most active of the political parties in organizing the partisan groups, and Tehlirian signed up as a member, joining one hundred thousand other refugees. Initially a medic, he became incensed at the sight of villages filled with Armenian corpses and transferred to more active resistance duty. During his three years as a guerrilla fighter, he raided Turkish units and participated in major battles, bivouacked in the mountains, and slept on the ground in summer and winter, gratified to be in the company of his compatriots and doing his share to protect the Armenian nation. Only once had he returned to his native village, when Russian forces occupied Erzinga in 1916. The experience of visiting his parental home, echoing with memories of a happier time, had overwhelmed him.

On his initial stay in Tiflis, he had met a lovely Armenian girl named Anahid, whom he saw thereafter whenever he returned to resistance headquarters. Now his life took on a new dimension. He saw her frequently in a number of chance encounters until, finally, he managed to convey his romantic attachment to her. She let him know that she reciprocated his feelings, and for the duration of his time in Tiflis his days were brightened by the company of this girl, with whom he envisioned the possibility of a life ahead. Soon, however, he was called away to service at the front, leaving matters unresolved between them.

For the next four years, as his missions took him from one corner of Anatolia to the other, his love for Anahid gave him comfort and helped him to survive. He witnessed barbarous events: scenes of inhuman suffering inflicted on women, the elderly, and children—thousands of whom had been orphaned—straggling starved, parched, and half naked in long caravans over hundreds of miles into the desert. These sights were a continuing reminder of his own personal tragedy and aroused in him a compulsion for revenge that turned into obsession, blurring his dreams of a future with Anahid. That pleasant dream, he grew to think, would have to be postponed until he carried out one final mission.

When he next returned to Tiflis, he was suffering from typhus. It was Anahid who nursed him through the crisis, and the long recovery period brought them even closer. When he explained his plans and asked her to be patient, she agreed to wait for him.

The war ended in 1918, the government of the Young Turks collapsed, and the country reverted to its earlier status as a sultanate.* In mid-December, following the Allied occupation of Constantinople,† Tehlirian decided to go to the Turkish capital on the chance that by some miracle he might discover family survivors. He also went to start his hunt for Talaat.

Once in Constantinople, like thousands of his compatriots, Tehlirian placed ads in the Armenian newspaper seeking relatives who might have been rescued from Deir Zor in the Syrian desert, the final stop of the deportations. He waited patiently for news. But as the days went by, the youth became despondent. He gave up his fruitless search and decided to concentrate on his second objective—the quest for the former grand vizier, now a refugee himself.

Tehlirian was welcomed into a circle of Armenians many of whom had survived ordeals similar to his. In long conversations deep into the night, he found himself attracted to a group that seemed better educated and more intellectual. A member he held in particularly high regard was a woman named Yeranoohi Danielian, a teacher immersed in political and social issues. They became good friends. The older woman was drawn to the quiet youth, in whom she sensed a quality of sadness. His manner was gentle and his conversations bland except when the subject of the massacres came up. Then he grew agitated, and his voice rose. Yeranoohi came to realize that this young man was not like the others she had befriended—middle-aged men who were all miraculous survivors of the tragedies that had taken place in Anatolia. Most of them were resigned to the deaths of their families and preparing to start life anew elsewhere. But not Soghomon Tehlirian. In the company of others, he was reserved and reticent. But to Yeranoohi he opened his heart, and she learned that he was bent on finding and punishing the murderer of the Armenian nation. He told her of his dreams, of his visions of his dead mother, of Anahid, and Yeranoohi realized that this was no run-of-the-mill survivor. It is possible that at this time she also spoke of him to others in connection with Talaat Pasha.

In any case, it was from Yeranoohi that he first heard of Talaat's flight from Turkey. The news stunned him, but it was an even greater blow to learn that other members of Talaat's government—War

*The sultanate remained until 1923, when the nationalist forces of Mustafa Kemal declared Turkey a republic.
†The name of the city was officially changed to Istanbul in 1930.

Minister Enver Pasha, Navy Minister Jemal Pasha, Education Minister Nazim Bey, and others—had also escaped.

Sultan Muhammad VI, who was recognized by the victorious Allies as the new Turkish sovereign, was quoted as having said that he would gratify the vengeance of the Armenians. This was to be accomplished, according to reports, by the formation of a Turkish military tribunal, approved by the Allied occupation authorities, to try the leading Turkish war criminals. But to what purpose, Tehlirian wondered, if they had all escaped?

Yeranoohi also told him something else that would temporarily divert him from the obsession that had brought him to Constantinople. One evening they passed a house she said was the residence of Talaat's Armenian agent. Incredulous that any Armenian could have worked for the destroyer of Armenians, Tehlirian asked his name.

Harootiun Mugerditchian, Yeranoohi told him, and identified him as the man who, at Talaat's request, had drawn up an initial list of Armenian intellectuals who were arrested and killed. It had happened on the night of April 24, 1915, when hundreds of writers, doctors, editors, poets, teachers, composers, and clergymen were rounded up, herded into prison, and on the following day marched outside the city and murdered. The date had already been enshrined in the Armenian consciousness as the first chapter in the massacres that would follow.

Tehlirian asked in amazement whether there was no one to wreak revenge on the traitor, and Yeranoohi said there was not. He soon discovered that she was right. Hardly anyone he encountered paid any heed to Talaat or Mugerditchian. Most Armenians' attention was directed instead to the Caucasus, where in May 1918 victorious Armenian forces had proclaimed an independent Armenian republic in the territory formerly under Russian administration.

Tehlirian did not take much notice of these developments, however. His thoughts were focused on the informer, whose treasonous acts were confirmed by many of his newfound friends. As though preparing a criminal case, he established Mugerditchian's actions relative to the arrests and deportations—all reported directly to Talaat. For two weeks Tehlirian stalked his prey, watching the house for hours at a time.

In April he attended a mass commemorating the fourth anniversary of the arrest and annihilation in 1915 of the Armenian intellectuals. Constantinople's Armenian patriarch, Zaven, spoke of the thousands who had fallen "as so many grains of wheat which would one day revive and come to life." One of the handful of survivors of that initial deportation, a Dr. Melkon Giulistanian, described the Saturday night when the intellectuals were rounded up shortly before midnight—half asleep and ill-clad, hatless, or in slippers—and marched off to Constantinople's Central Prison. As each new group arrived, the realization of what was happening grew. No one could sleep for fear, and when dawn came a few hours later, they could hear the muezzins' calls to morning prayers from minarets throughout the city.

Giulistanian told of the roll call from Talaat's "black list," as the Turkish police bunched the men into groups of twenty and, with Chief of Police Bedri Bey watching from his limousine, herded them onto Saint Sofia Boulevard. They were taken beyond the city limits, never to be heard from again. He ended the solemn observance by reading in Turkish Talaat's order for the destruction of everyone from one month to ninety years of age.

Such occasions worked Tehlirian into a fury and strengthened his resolve to take vengeance on the author of the "blacklist," who was still alive and in safety.

One night Tehlirian gathered that Mugerditchian—whose son had purchased five bottles of cognac from a café opposite—would be entertaining guests. Looking in the windows of the house, Tehlirian saw ten people seated around a table. He felt contempt for the self-satisfied demeanor Mugerditchian displayed before his guests. His pulse pounded in his temples, and a voice within urged him to shoot through the window.

Tehlirian aimed the gun, which he had owned since his days in Tiflis, at Mugerditchian's heart and pulled the trigger. The glass shattered, and the informer crumpled in his chair. As the guests stared in horror at their host, Tehlirian fled.

The next morning the papers reported that Harootiun Mugerditchian had been injured by an unknown assailant. Desolate that he had failed, Tehlirian reprimanded himself for not having aimed for the head. However, Yeranoohi soon came to him, shook his hand, and said with a smile that she had learned from a friend that Mugerditchian's hours were numbered. He died the next day, and the Armenians of Constantinople celebrated with exuberance.

Tehlirian soon learned from fellow members of the ARF that Mugerditchian's assassination had revived the movement's interest in the matter of the escaped war criminals, its bureaus throughout Europe now consulting busily on the whereabouts of Talaat, Enver, and the others. Whenever he discussed the Young Turk leaders with Yeranoohi, he noticed that she would become very intense and dwell on his every word. So penetrating was her gaze that he sometimes had the feeling she was studying him.

The military trial, which had begun in February, was still in progress at the end of May 1919. The press reported that Talaat, Enver, Jemal, and Nazim had ten days in which to present themselves to the tribunal. If they failed to appear, they would be deprived of their civil rights and all their possessions would be confiscated. Meanwhile, the Turkish press was printing shocking exposés of the horrors inflicted on the Armenians during the deportations. It also reported that Talaat Pasha had fled with ten thousand Turkish gold pounds.

One day Tehlirian was summoned by the Patriarch Zaven. Zaven had been exiled in 1915, and the Armenian church had suffered greatly as a result of Mugerditchian's betrayal. The patriarch received and blessed Tehlirian. He said that Harootiun Mugerditchian was three times worse than a traitor, and he officially condoned Tehlirian's act. Tehlirian then asked for his support in the pursuit of Talaat Pasha, but Zaven said he could not participate in such an endeavor on religious grounds.

To continue his quest, Tehlirian needed money. He turned to Yeranoohi, who had little money herself, and was upset to hear that she had been offered a teaching position in the United States. He had come to look upon Yeranoohi as a sisterly comrade in whom he could confide his innermost thoughts. With her departure, he would be completely alone again, troubled by his visions and condemned by his self-inflicted dedication to the search for the criminal. Late in August Yeranoohi left for Paris, pledging that she would inform him if she found any trace of Talaat. The firmness with which she spoke gave him the strong impression that he would be hearing from her soon.

Meanwhile, since he had not been able to trace any other surviving members of his family in Turkey, Tehlirian concluded they were all dead. With time on his hands, he traveled to Greece where he had distant relatives, and to Serbia to visit his father and brothers. Then he returned to Constantinople, dejected and lonely, his mind filled with doubts about himself and his future, and waited.

Toward the end of October Tehlirian received a note from Yeranoohi, including a poem and a warm greeting. It contained no information, but he took comfort from the knowledge that she was still in Paris and had not forgotten him. The note was also a reminder of his mission—something of which he had no need, however, since he was haunted by recurring dreams in which his mother appeared with a message urging him to kill Talaat.

Impatient at the lack of news, Tehlirian decided again to consult Zaven, who had now gone to Paris. Accordingly, he, too, left Constantinople, though the money from his father's cache was dwindling. Zaven remembered him very well, but when Tehlirian repeated his request for help in finding Talaat, the patriarch again declined.

Frustrated and bemoaning his ill fortune, Tehlirian made a fortuitous discovery. The Armenian Republic's national delegation to the peace conference had just arrived in Paris, hoping for recognition of Armenian sovereignty and claims to territories in eastern Turkey— the areas that, prior to the deportations, had been populated primarily by Armenians.* Through the auspices of the delegation, whose senior staff consisted of ARF members, Tehlirian found a job with an Armenian shoemaker. He learned the trade quickly, working with four other émigrés eleven hours a day, and feeling grateful for even the limited free time he had to ponder his next move. He often ate alone, avoiding Armenian restaurants, where the patrons were largely survivors of the massacres and talked of nothing else.

One evening about a year later, he was told that a Miss Danielian was looking for him. Overjoyed at first, Tehlirian was then confused, for he had been certain that Yeranoohi had long since gone to the United States. He went to the appointed restaurant, where a woman resembling Yeranoohi smiled at him from a corner table. It was, in fact, her sister, who gave him a letter from Yeranoohi that instructed him to make immediate arrangements to go to the United States to accomplish a specific task. Though this would take him that much farther from his beloved Anahid, he could pose against that troubling thought the exhilarating possibility that Talaat himself was in the United States. He felt a deep debt of gratitude to Yeranoohi, who had not forgotten him.

Tehlirian told her sister that he lacked the funds for such an expensive trip. The woman replied that he was to visit the Armenian

*The Allies granted neither, despite innumerable statements of support for the Armenian people in England, France, and the United States, especially by Woodrow Wilson.

national delegation, where further instructions awaited him in a letter from Boston.

In October 1920 Tehlirian sailed from France for the United States. He had never seen the Atlantic, and when he lost sight of land, he felt as though he had left the planet itself. Two days out, a storm struck, and the mountainous waves terrified him. It seemed the large passenger ship had become a plaything of the churning sea and would split in two at any moment. But the storm passed, calm seas returned, and on the morning of the seventh day he saw the shoreline of the United States. Though he was ignorant of English, his French got him quickly through customs. He took a cab to the local ARF club, awed by the tall buildings of New York and amazed at the city's frenetic pace.

Once in the club, however, surrounded by compatriots speaking his native language, he lost all sense of strangeness. He was bombarded with questions and satisfied them all, but eventually arose to go, remembering his mission. He explained that the Central Committee of the ARF in Boston had summoned him, which immediately impressed everyone.

Arriving in Boston, he was questioned closely by the editors of the ARF daily organ *Hairenik* about the situation in Turkey. The editors, as he soon discovered, were all members of the ARF Central Committee, whose headquarters were now in Boston. Their inquiries, at first general, soon narrowed down to his own experience and attitudes, and he gathered that they were more interested in him than in political conditions in Turkey. In the course of the questioning, one of the editors informed Tehlirian that his friend Yeranoohi Danielian was responsible for his being there. She, meanwhile, had settled in California. He began to sense the reason for his presence when he learned of the central committee's distress that Talaat and his cohorts had gone unpunished, even though the Allies, in a proclamation issued in May 1915, had pledged to bring all responsible Young Turk officials to justice.

The editors informed him that the Armenians of the United States had decided to take action, and for that purpose a special fund and organization had been established with the code name Nemesis. To his supreme gratification Tehlirian discovered that in America his dream had taken concrete form, for it was the sole function of Nemesis and its international web of agents to hunt down and assassinate the leading Turkish war criminals.

Tehlirian was filled with a new self-esteem and sense of mission as he realized that he had been singled out to avenge the Turkish crimes against his nation. (It was, to be sure, a happy union, for in Nemesis, Tehlirian had found the perfect agency, while in Tehlirian, Nemesis had found the perfect agent.)

Considerable spadework had already been done. Nemesis had confirmed that the former Turkish leaders were actively negotiating with European politicians, seeking to prevent retaliation for Turkish treatment of the Armenians. Just two months earlier, the Turks had organized a conference in Berlin to influence the British. The latest information placed a number of prominent Turks in the Azerbaijani capital of Baku, among them Enver Pasha and Dr. Behaeddin Shakir. The ARF's intelligence placed Talaat Pasha in either Geneva or Berlin.

Tehlirian discovered that in Boston the driving force behind the search for Talaat was Armen Garo, known far and wide for his services to the Armenian cause and now the Armenian Republic's minister plenipotentiary to the United States.* Garo gave him a very cordial reception, after which they focused on the business at hand. Garo said he had last met Talaat Pasha in Constantinople on June 4, 1914, when they had discussed Armenian reforms. During the discussion, Garo observed, Talaat's hatred of the Armenians had been thoroughly evident, and he had erupted when Garo accused him of reckless disregard for the rights of the Armenian minority. Finally, Garo had said that if Talaat's oppressive policies continued, Armenians would prefer to destroy the Ottoman Empire stone by stone rather than allow Talaat to realize his objective, which he had once stated, of an "Armenia without Armenians."

That night, Tehlirian studied photographs of the Young Turk leaders—Talaat, Enver, Jemal, Shakir, Nazim, and Police Chief Bedri—as well as pictures of Talaat's and Enver's wives, both of whom he found beautiful. He wondered how such angelic women could be married to such monsters.

Although he scrutinized them all—noting the vain pose of Enver, known as "the idol of Turkish women"—he concentrated on Talaat, observing his powerful arms, and heavy square shoulders, suggesting energy and power. Above his lips, like a thick smear of tar, bristled a dense black mustache.

---

*Tehlirian apparently did not know at that time that Garo, whose real name was Karekin Pasdermajian, was also a member of the ARF's highest body, the Bureau, and had been considered for premier of the Armenian Republic.

After a month—most of it spent in Boston—in the United States, Tehlirian was informed that a telegram had come from Geneva instructing him to go there immediately. Arriving in Geneva, he went to the ARF newspaper *Droshag*, housed in a modest, gray two-story building. Tehlirian felt a deep pride as he walked through the iron gate and garden of the building, for within these walls oaths had been taken to aid the Armenian cause, first by Hunchaks in 1887 and later by Dashnaks. There could be no more appropriate place to begin the last leg of his mission.

Tehlirian was greeted warmly and was given a letter whose cryptic contents he immediately understood. It informed him that according to news from Constantinople, a "relative" of his had been traced to Berlin, and that Tehlirian had best go there quickly so that he could be in time to enroll in the university. Now he could be certain that his search was over; Talaat was in Berlin. Nevertheless, he had to hold his impatience in check during the five-day wait for a visa authorizing him to go to the German capital "to study mechanical engineering."

=====

The ARF Central Committee had known for almost two years that Talaat and his colleagues had escaped Turkey. The true purpose of the inquiry was to take stock of the young survivor and imbue him with a sense of his own importance in front of the ARF's senior body. He had come highly recommended by Yeranoohi Danielian, in whose intelligence and judgment the committee had complete confidence. Therefore the committee had authorized payment of all expenses for a round trip to Boston to look the candidate over in person. Earlier, when it became known that the major Turkish war criminals had escaped, funding for the Nemesis intelligence network was established and the assembly of a European staff begun.

Yeranoohi Danielian had been scouting for recruits to perform the demanding task of hunting down the war criminals. The major European centers of the ARF were filled with vengeful Armenians, but none seemed to have the obsessive zeal and fanatical devotion necessary for the critical and dangerous mission of assassinating prominent and powerful figures such as Talaat Pasha. When she encountered Tehlirian in Constantinople, heard his tragic story, and observed the intensity of his obsession to settle a personal score with Talaat, she was partially convinced that he might be right for the task. But all doubt vanished when she beheld his total commitment to the planning and carrying out of the killing of the Armenian traitor Harootiun Mugerditchian.

Tehlirian took solace in talking about Anahid and stressing his deferment of a life with her until he had carried out the mission he had set for himself. That he confided his dreams and visions to Yeranoohi did not hurt his case. In fact, she believed that the fantasy world he sometimes inhabited would not interfere with his mission and might even shield him from the reality of failure. For Nemesis, failure meant either wounding and not killing or killing and not getting away.

The final decision had been up to Armen Garo, the seasoned Armenian patriot, revolutionary, and diplomat. A keen judge of men, Garo had digested everything Yeranoohi had told him of this young man—that he had undergone the most horrific experience while still in his adolescence; that he might, in consequence, have suffered a form of mental derangement (which might explain his visions); and that he had no personal life, so powerful was his lust for revenge. Garo was himself dedicated to Armenian nationalism and had himself made many personal sacrifices for the cause. Consequently he did not view exploiting the zeal of a fellow Armenian as a cynical means to achieve a national end. Though voluntary and personal in nature, it simultaneously suited the political aims of the ARF. Tehlirian was a broken man; that much was clear. Having lost his loved ones, his home, and possibly even his sanity, what kind of life was left for him? Of course, he might still have one with his Anahid, but only if he did everything right and escaped. The time and place of the deed would be for him to determine. He would be given money enabling him to flee.

Garo was also driven by another thought. The long history of the Armenian people was permeated by oppression and cruelty inflicted by one foreign tyrant after another. But never throughout that tragic history had any despot suffered retribution at the hands of an Armenian. Here, now, finally, in the person of this confused but determined youth, was a singular opportunity to vent the rage of a nation. If he succeeded, Tehlirian would become a symbol of the nation's historic defiance, even as he realized an immediate political objective.

There was only one way to describe this confluence of events, Garo said to himself, and it was summed up in the word *fate*—a word widely known, ironically, by its Turkish equivalent, *kismet*. The search was finally over; Nemesis had found its man, and Soghomon

Tehlirian, selected from among other agents, would be the assassin of Talaat Pasha.

It was 10 P.M. on December 3, 1920, when Tehlirian arrived at the Tiergarten Hotel in Berlin, where he was to meet his ARF contact. It was bitter cold and wet, the rain mixing with sleet. He went directly to his contact's room and was greeted enthusiastically.

Tehlirian learned that Talaat Pasha was in Berlin, information he had been waiting to hear for several years. Further, Shakir, Nazim, and other criminals were also in Berlin, and Tehlirian's informant named a few more, ending with Jemal Azmi, the former governor of Trebizond, who now owned a tobacco shop. Azmi had been personally responsible for the deaths of fourteen thousand Armenians and the confiscation of their wealth. That such a criminal was living safely in the capital of a civilized country filled Tehlirian with an urgent desire to settle that score as well. But he quickly realized that to do so would ruin his plans for Talaat.

Some of these Turks were already under surveillance by designated Armenians, and Tehlirian, too, would be given such an assignment. The following morning he was met in his hotel by the first of his Nemesis accomplices, a dark-skinned Armenian of twenty-seven named Hazor, a student at the University of Berlin.*

Hazor was very congenial and said he had fresh news. Enver would be coming shortly from Moscow, where he had taken refuge, to revive the Young Turk Party, which he and Talaat had controlled during the war, as a force in Turkish politics. Since the collapse of the Turkish government at war's end, a rivalry had developed between the two party leaders. Talaat's supporters argued that the party should be based in Berlin, with extraterritorial status. Enver, on the other hand, wanted Moscow as the party's headquarters, because he was so often in the Caucasus. Enver also wished to play a role in adjacent Anatolia, where, since the end of the war, a Young Turk party infrastructure was reviving and aiding the rebellious nationalist forces headed by General Mustafa Kemal.

The source of this information was a fellow Armenian student Hazor called Hrap, whose dark skin, language fluency, and Turkish

---

*Tehlirian never identified Hazor more fully, but in Armin T. Wegner's book *Am Kreuzweg der Welten*, published in 1982 in East Berlin, he mentions that while on a trip to Armenia in 1927, he had a reunion with a Dr. *Ha*gop *Zor*ian, a professor at Yerevan University, whom Wegner had known as a student in Berlin. See p. 307.

pseudonym gained him acceptance among expatriate Turkish students. A dedicated Armenian nationalist, Hrap had become a vital source of information on Turkish activities in Berlin.*

After this interview, Tehlirian walked out into the wintry air, determined to familiarize himself with Berlin as quickly as possible. He looked around him, saw the Brandenburg Gate from afar, and mingled with the crowds of Berliners. A few moments later he entered a side street and walked by chance directly past Jemal Azmi's tobacco shop.

He had an almost irrepressible desire to enter the shop and confront the mass murderer. Instead he found a cafe, where he could sit down and watch the shop while sipping coffee. He repeated this the next day and the day after that. For three days he observed that hardly anyone entered or left the store and wondered to himself why anyone would pay thousands of marks in rent for a store that was so poorly patronized. It could only mean one thing: The shop was not meant for business but for an entirely different purpose.

Hazor's message came to mind, and Tehlirian speculated that if Enver were to win the party struggle, Talaat would go to Moscow or the Caucasus. On the other hand, Turkish national interest would be better served if Talaat remained in Berlin, or at any rate in Europe, where he was already conducting diplomatic business. There was little doubt that it was the Young Turks who were stirring up nationalist feelings in Anatolia, as well as negotiating for military supplies for Turkish armies in the East. Thus, Turkey's future was once again in the hands of the chauvinists who had swept it to defeat.

Tehlirian was drinking yet another cup of coffee, submerged in these thoughts, when he suddenly noticed a woman enter Jemal Azmi's shop. No sooner had he rushed out for a closer look than the woman emerged and hurried away. At the same time another Armenian emerged from the shop, whom Tehlirian, when paying his bill, had not seen enter. The two men conferred quickly, and he told Tehlirian that he had overheard the end of the brief conversation between Azmi and the woman. Azmi had said: "I hope you will let me know," to which the woman had replied: "Absolutely, if he authorizes it."

Remembering the photographs he had studied in Boston, Tehlirian believed the woman to be Enver Pasha's wife. Her appearance here seemed to confirm the report of Enver's imminent arrival. Since the

*Hrap is believed to have been *Hra*tch *P*apazian, a law student.

other Armenian's normal task was to keep an eye on Azmi's shop, it was agreed that he should remain while Tehlirian followed the woman.

In her black fur and plumed hat, she was easy to detect in the crowds. The snow had stopped and she seemed to be walking aimlessly. But suddenly she changed her pace and at the same time grew more cautious, looking up and down the street. He followed for an hour until she reached a residential area filled with villas. Stopping in front of a magnificent residence, she opened the gate to a snow garden, ran up the stone steps, opened the door with her key, and went in.

The next morning he returned and watched the villa. At noon a young man entered through the gate, rang the doorbell, and was allowed in. Tehlirian was annoyed that he had not scrutinized the man as he passed. From a distance he had resembled Enver, and Tehlirian berated himself for his inattentiveness. Looking down the street he saw someone lurking on the corner, watching him. But when the stranger lifted his head, he revealed himself to be Hazor. Coming close, Hazor identified the young man as an inconsequential Turk. Then he departed, leaving Tehlirian alone. One hour later, the young man emerged and rushed off, Tehlirian behind him, convinced that he was going to meet Enver, cursing the fact that he did not have his revolver. The Turk crossed the boulevard and entered Uhlandstrasse, disappearing into Number 47. Soon it began to snow again, and after half an hour Tehlirian began to feel chilled. He was also hungry but instead of looking for a restaurant he decided to return to the Tiergarten Hotel.

Toward evening, Hazor arrived and Tehlirian told him what had happened. Hazor became excited. He clapped his hands and said he would bet anything that Number 47 Uhlandstrasse was where Talaat lived. At ten o'clock that morning, he had seen the man whom Tehlirian had observed three days ago entering Azmi's shop. Hazor had recognized him as Behaeddin Shakir.

Hazor now introduced Tehlirian to two new colleagues. The first was called Vaza.* The other was Haigo, a student. Hazor reported what Hrap had learned at the Turkish Student Club: although Enver had not yet arrived in Berlin, he was expected. The Armenians therefore decided to maintain the closest possible surveillance of the

*Again a cover name, it invited speculation that Vaza was *Va*han *Za*chariantz, who later served at the trial as an interpreter.

two abodes—the Uhlandstrasse apartment and the villa inhabited by the woman who, all seemed to agree, was Enver's wife.

But from other sources it was learned that while the Turkish press had reported a number of times that Enver might go to Berlin, it was not to happen. These reports turned out to be nothing more than trial balloons. This lack of progress caused Tehlirian to see with disillusionment that he was no closer to the fulfillment of his mission. Toward the end of December, a recurring illness—first suffered after the massacre of his family—put him in bed and out of commission. As on previous occasions, he suffered a temporary loss of vision and dizzy spells. As soon as he recovered, he moved from the Tiergarten Hotel to a room at Augsburgerstrasse 51 where Yerevand Apelian, a friend employed by the Armenian Republic's consulate-general in Berlin, also lived.

Their landlady was a sixty-year-old woman named Elisabeth Stellbaum, who struck Tehlirian as the typical German *hausfrau*—meticulous to a fault, she kept the room immaculately clean and even wanted to personally shine his shoes. Their relationship was strained at first but slowly mellowed as he made her understand that in his society elderly women did not serve the young. That was noble, she replied, but he was a paying tenant and she had an obligation to him. These conversations, conducted largely through gestures and expressions, nevertheless helped him improve his German.

Apelian also introduced him to Levon Eftian, with whom he became very friendly. But neither knew of his mission, believing instead that he had really come to study in Berlin. They were critical of his German and raised the matter with him constantly, cautioning him that without improvement he could not possibly enter the university. Eftian remarked that the best way to learn was through a romantic attachment and that a charming teacher had to be found.

He was therefore introduced to Lola Beilinson, a twenty-one-year-old teacher of German who struck him as attractive and unassuming. Because she came from the Baltic area, they were able to communicate in Russian. And so it was arranged that there would be two lessons a week at her apartment. Meanwhile, Eftian introduced him to his sister and brother-in-law, the Terzibashians, and also to Kevork Kalustian. They spent many cordial evenings together, which brightened Tehlirian's otherwise somber existence. He was impressed with the way they all seemed to have transcended the tragedy in Turkey and established a new life in Berlin, where they now apparently felt at home in every way.

Shortly thereafter his two friends urged him to enroll in a dance class. Despite his reluctance, Apelian pressed him, saying it would help him go beyond his present German capability, which was limited to *"Was ist das?"* Tehlirian enrolled but was bashful with the German girls, who appeared forward to him. During an early lesson while he was dancing with one young woman, he felt his vision fade, his head began to spin, and he held her tightly so as not to fall. He heard her scream as he passed out.

This recurrence of his illness frightened him. But the next day, feeling better, he went to his language lesson. Fräulein Beilinson noted a change in him. After some gentle questioning she said she had observed that he was troubled. He said he could not talk about it. Did he want to talk about his homeland? He said he did not have a homeland.

Two days later he again took up observation of the Uhlandstrasse apartment. Toward noon he saw one of his colleagues following two men who were approaching the flat. He recognized one of them as Behaeddin Shakir. Catching up with his colleague, Tehlirian learned that the other was Dr. Nazim. He and Shakir were coming from Jemal Azmi's tobacco shop.

Shakir and Nazim disappeared into the doorway of Number 47, and the two Armenians waited on the corner. Fifteen minutes later Shakir emerged, and Tehlirian was instructed to follow while his colleague waited for Nazim.

Shakir walked very rapidly, making it difficult for Tehlirian, still weak from his attack, to keep up. The Turk traversed several of the main arteries of Charlottenburg—Tauentzienstrasse, Kantstrasse, and Kurfürstendamm.* At Wilhelmstrasse, where the diplomatic missions were located, Shakir stopped at the British Embassy.

His visit was brief and when he came out, he first looked up and down before setting off at an even faster pace, turning into side streets and making quick turns, as though he knew he was being followed. He went on to Jerusalemstrasse at a furious pace, and as Tehlirian made a greater effort to keep up with him, his vision darkened, and he felt a weakness come over him. The buildings spun and, as he tried to hold on to a wall, he fell.

---

*In present-day terms, Shakir was walking from downtown Berlin near the Kaiser-Wilhelm (Gedächtnis) Kirche toward what between 1961 and 1990 was known as Checkpoint Charlie, the former Allied point of entry through the wall into East Berlin.

When he came to, he was on the ground surrounded by a small crowd. Someone asked him his address, and somehow he got back to his room at Augsburgerstrasse. He was distraught because the illness was interfering with his mission, and Vaza recommended that he see a nerve specialist named Dr. Richard Cassirer.

After a week of mulling over his problem, Tehlirian came to the conclusion that his health would not allow any further delay. He could no longer postpone his mission. He would settle his score with Azmi, Shakir, and Nazim. None of them was the true object of his pursuit, but in the long run what difference did it make? All four were criminals. But Vaza and Hazor were opposed to this idea and advised against it. In the end it was decided to refer the question to "more senior levels," which they all understood to mean the ARF Bureau in Boston, and continue the surveillance.

In mid-February, Hrap reported that a Young Turk party conference of top leaders was to take place either in Berlin or Rome. Two days later Hrap reported that the news had been confirmed in the Italian newspaper *Lavoro Fascista*. Convinced that Talaat Pasha would most certainly be there, a Nemesis agent applied for an Italian visa. He was expected to leave on a moment's notice and, when he had confirmed Talaat's presence, to cable Berlin so that Tehlirian could go to Rome and carry out his mission. Meanwhile, every train departing from Charlottenburg was scrutinized from early in the morning until late at night. It was assumed that the delegates would be departing on one of the trains in that district because they all lived there.

One evening toward the end of February, just before the departure of an express train, Tehlirian and the other spotters saw a familiar figure, a gloomy-looking Turk whom they had often seen at Uhlandstrasse and believed to be a guard. Five minutes later three Turkish students joined him at the gate.

Almost immediately Behaeddin Shakir walked through the gate with a piece of luggage, shook hands with the students, and climbed aboard the train.

Then, just five minutes before the scheduled departure, there suddenly appeared another figure—stocky, rotund, with a bloated face—well-dressed and sporting a cane. Tehlirian felt a shock go through his body. This man bore a remarkable resemblance to photographs of Talaat, although he did not have the thick mustache and instead of a fez he wore a European hat. He quickly approached the gate. The students were visibly excited at his appearance and stood in line like soldiers to receive him.

Tehlirian went close, watching and listening. The first student took the offered hand, kissed it and said: "They are already inside, my Pasha."

The "new man" immediately went to the car and rapped with his cane on the half-open window. It was not clear who spoke from inside, but a booming voice called out in Turkish: "Don't forget the Armenians!"

Tehlirian walked closer. Behind him, the colleague with the Italian visa said he was certain it was Talaat and that when the cable from Rome came, Tehlirian should depart immediately.

But the new man did not leave. He remained behind with the others, told them something inaudible, and, as the train pulled away, walked out of the station.

Tehlirian heard a voice inside him repeating that the new man was Talaat Pasha. As he followed him out of the station, Hazor and Haigo caught up with him. They asked if it had been Talaat. Tehlirian said it was. But, they argued, he had not looked that much like Talaat. He was addressed as "Pasha," Tehlirian said, to which Hazor replied that in the émigré world, everyone was a pasha.

Barely twenty paces separated Tehlirian from the Turks, who assumed a respectful pace relative to the central figure. They walked one step behind him and came parallel only when he addressed one of them.

Tehlirian studied the man carefully—his powerful build, oxlike shoulders, and square back. Surely it was Talaat, but there was something different about his face. The group stopped near the Zoological Garden, and the three students performed a *temenna*—a low bow with fingers lifted first to the lips and then the forehead— and departed. Now accompanied only by his bodyguard, the man walked to Hardenbergstrasse 4 and entered the house. Tehlirian, Hazor, and Haigo stood watch for more than an hour but no one came or left. Tehlirian was struck by the fact that despite the previous surveillance, no one had seen this man before.

That night at their scheduled meeting, Tehlirian explained his reasons for believing that the new man was Talaat and said he wished to commence his mission. The silence that followed this announcement was broken by Hazor, who was still not convinced. He argued that although postponing the matter ran the danger of losing their man, even worse was the possibility that they were all in error. In that case they would lose Talaat for good. Tehlirian asked sarcastically whether they all thought the new man was his uncle. Nevertheless, the others appeared to agree with Hazor that the resident of Hardenbergstrasse 4 had to be identified beyond doubt.

Haigo pointed out that in Berlin every resident had to register with the district police. Even if Talaat had not registered in his own name, at least they might learn the identity of the man with the gloomy face and anyone else in the house.

Vaza seemed perturbed. He underlined that they were not murderers, and an error could be a catastrophe. Besides, he didn't have any ties to district officials and going to the police could be dangerous. In any case Talaat must be living under police protection. Instead, Vaza suggested that he should attempt to learn what he could from the landlady. Tehlirian reluctantly approved the plan. He had hoped for unanimous agreement on immediate action and was upset by the caution displayed by his colleagues.

The next morning he was met by snow and wind. Hardenbergstrasse was almost empty, and he had to keep moving to stay warm. After more than an hour, he was about to leave when suddenly the new man emerged from the villa, looked cautiously up and down the wide street, and began his walk. His steps were rapid and he hunched his neck inside his collar against the cold. He arrived at Uhlandstrasse and went into the apartment. Hazor was on duty, and Tehlirian sent him back to Hardenbergstrasse.

Tehlirian was almost totally convinced that it had been Talaat, but his colleagues were less certain. That night Tehlirian's head was filled with troubling thoughts. What if it was Talaat and he escaped? If he hadn't gone to Rome, he must regard his presence in Berlin as more important. If he had been cautioned not to forget the Armenians, then he might have other business.

Early the next morning the Armenians took up their posts: Haigo watching Jemal Azmi's tobacco shop, Hazor observing the apartment at Uhlandstrasse 47, and Tehlirian at Hardenbergstrasse 4. A short while later, the gloomy-looking Turk from the station came out carrying a basket and walked toward the shopping district, which implied that he lived at the villa and not the Uhlandstrasse apartment.

At 10 A.M., the new man appeared at the gate. Tehlirian again underwent an emotional upheaval at the sight of him. The man looked up and down the street and then, swinging his cane in a carefree manner, walked toward the center of town. He came to Uhlandstrasse and entered Number 47.

In half an hour, he emerged and returned to Hardenbergstrasse, where Hazor was stationed. It was now clear to Tehlirian that this visit to Uhlandstrasse 47 took place between ten and eleven o'clock every morning.

That night the Armenians gathered to hear Vaza's report on his talk with the landlady of Hardenbergstrasse 4. An elderly, talkative spinster whom Hazor found informative and pleasant, she lived in an apartment on Fasanenstrasse, not far from her villa and one block from Uhlandstrasse. Hazor passed himself off as a Swiss security official interested in renting the villa, which he understood would soon be vacant.

She displayed surprise because, according to the lease, which she consulted, there were still three months to go. Hazor apologized for his error and rose to leave.

The landlady seemed reluctant to release him and asked him how many rooms he required. Two or three, he said. In that case, she replied, perhaps he could come to an arrangement with the current tenants. The house was very large, and she would not object if he took over two rooms on the ground floor. Altogether, she said, there were nine rooms on the second floor with very little furniture, adding that as far as she knew, only three people lived there and that such splendor was not enjoyed even by German cabinet ministers.

She also revealed that the villa had been rented by an official of the Turkish Embassy named Zia Bey, whose name was on the lease.

Hazor ended his account and they all discussed the possibility that Ali Salih Bey was Talaat Pasha. Tehlirian found it hard to believe that the Turkish Embassy would rent a villa for an ordinary Turkish businessman. Besides, he knew Talaat's wife to be an uncommonly beautiful woman, as the landlady had observed.

Very early the next morning, Tehlirian went to the Tiergarten Hotel, gathered the photographs of the Young Turk leaders, and began scratching out Talaat's mustache. There was a knock on the door, and he quickly hid the picture. A hotel employee delivered a letter he said had arrived two days earlier from Paris. The letter was in code and said that in early February, Talaat had met with a British diplomat in Geneva. The letter was dated early February. Tehlirian became discouraged. Perhaps Ali Salih Bey was not Talaat after all.

Returning to his room, he locked the door and continued obliterating the mustache from Talaat's photograph. Again he was interrupted, this time by Levon Eftian, who invited him to dinner at his sister's home. When he returned that night, he resumed scratching out the mustache in Talaat's photograph. When he had finished, he sat back astonished at the resemblance to the new man, and when he penciled in a Western hat, he was certain.

He ran to the Tiergarten Hotel and revealed his discovery to the others. They were now convinced that the man they had seen at the station was Talaat Pasha. The time had come to act. It was decided that Tehlirian should move and rent a room near or opposite the villa, and on the evening of March 5, 1921, Tehlirian moved to Hardenbergstrasse 37 to embark on the final stage of his mission.

———

Tehlirian's new room was spacious, light, and airy, with large windows. His new landlady, Frau Dittmann, was a widow and younger than Frau Stellbaum, but like her kept the house immaculately clean. She also had a maid.

Once he was settled, he stood at the windows, which overlooked Hardenbergstrasse, and observed the activity on the broad street as workers and laborers returned home from work. Then he raised his eyes and looked beyond at the villa opposite, of which his windows afforded a clear view. Only twenty-five meters (about 80 feet) separated him from the man who called himself Ali Salih Bey. But was he really there?

Only two days before Haigo had reported that Ali Salih Bey had not appeared at Uhlandstrasse that morning but that Behaeddin Shakir had returned from Rome. What significance did Shakir's return have, coupled with Ali Salih's absence? If that absence were repeated in the next few days, would there be any point in having moved to Hardenbergstrasse?

Tehlirian passed a wakeful night tossing and turning, filled with the disturbing thought that after all this time, his mission might fail. Several times he arose and looked across the way for some activity, but all he could see was a light left on late into the night.

The next morning, Tehlirian sat at the desk and began to study German, though with an eye on the house opposite. It was a cold, bright day, and the sun reflected off the windows of the villa. Suddenly, after half an hour, the man known as Ali Salih Bey walked out to the garden gate. As was his custom, Ali Salih first looked up and down the street and then began to walk. Under his arm he carried a portfolio. This time, however, he walked not toward Uhlandstrasse but in the opposite direction, toward the beginning of Harden-bergstrasse, which let out on a large square called "Knie."*

Tehlirian grabbed his revolver, ran to the door, and tried to pull it open, but it wouldn't budge. He tried again; the lock was jammed. He became frantic and began to batter the door, frustrated and desperate. He turned and ran to the servants' entrance, but that door was locked. Ten minutes passed before he was finally able to force the lock and run out onto the sidewalk. But there wasn't a trace of the man he sought. He walked rapidly down to the Zoological Garden thinking that Ali Salih might have taken a roundabout way to Uhlandstrasse. Tehlirian waited there for an hour, fear mounting within him that he had missed his opportunity.

Eventually he decided to go to Jemal Azmi's tobacco shop; but there was no sign of anyone there. He stepped inside and for the first time looked at Azmi, who was reading a telegram. Tehlirian's fingers tightened around the gun in his pocket, and he briefly debated whether to kill him on the spot. But at that moment, Azmi's son appeared from the back of the shop. Tehlirian bought a pack of cigarettes and left.

On other days Ali Salih Bey had always left the villa by 10 A.M. and returned by 11. On this day, however, he had emerged before 9. He could, of course, have gone to several other places. None of Tehlirian's colleagues could account satisfactorily for the change in schedule, so he returned to his room where a locksmith was working on the door he had damaged.

The next morning he was again at his German studies, glancing through the window regularly to watch for activity at the villa. There was a knock on the door and the maid entered with tea; hovering behind her was Frau Dittmann. Tehlirian felt as though he had been caught in an illegal act, for they had come in as he had peered through a crack in the curtains. His landlady seemed vivacious this morning and made him understand by gestures that she was giving him a key to the new lock.

No one appeared across the way at either 10 or 11 A.M. Toward noon, one of his colleagues brought him another coded letter from Paris. It told him that hard information from Constantinople had identified the man living at Hardenbergstrasse 4 under the false name of Ali Salih Bey as Talaat Pasha.

---

*The square is known today as Ernst Reuter Platz, after the first postwar mayor of West Berlin.

Tehlirian was gratified by the official confirmation, although he himself had long since ceased to doubt the true identity of the resident of Number 4. He spent the rest of the day watching from his room, noting that even after dark there was no light in the villa. What did that mean?

When he awoke the next morning, he was feverish, dizzy, and in a generally debilitated condition. He was impatient, but at ten o'clock nothing happened and no one appeared. His earlier fears returned, and he was half convinced that Talaat had escaped for the second time—first from Constantinople and now from Berlin.

The next morning Tehlirian waited until eleven, and when no one appeared he was totally convinced that Talaat had fled again. He spent a miserable night tortured by nightmarish dreams and distressed at his fate.

He waited again until ten the next morning, feeling that the walls of his room were crowding in on him. He bemoaned his bad luck the morning the door lock jammed, preventing him from carrying out his mission. At noon he met Hazor, whose spirits were very high—and with good cause. He had spotted Behaeddin Shakir at Uhlandstrasse 47 again and predicted that Shakir's presence in Berlin confirmed that Talaat was still there—if Talaat had fled, Shakir would not endanger his own life by remaining.

That night Tehlirian dreamed of his mother and of happier times in Erzinga; toward the end of the dream, as she walked away from him, he cried out "Mother!" and she began to run until she disappeared. He awoke in a highly nervous state and wept like a child.

But as he lay in bed, feeling miserable and alone, he also saw the faces and heard the voices of his new companions, and he felt a warm stirring of reassurance. Once before he had felt this warmth within him, during those hectic years as a volunteer in the wilds of Anatolia, when he had fought, eaten, and slept alongside comrades whose will to avenge the slaughter of their loved ones was as great as his own. Now, once again, he was with comrades, united by singleness of purpose, on a very different mission—and this time, he was the key man. It was he who had been designated to strike Talaat down, he in whom the planners of the conspiracy had the greatest faith. It was he for whom Vaza, Hazor, Hrap, and the others toiled day and night to hunt down the quarry so that their nation might be avenged. To him they were like the family he had lost, and in the glow of their camaraderie he knew that he was no longer alone.

At eleven in the morning a taxi stopped in front of the villa. Leaping to the window, Tehlirian watched closely, his heart pounding. Out stepped two people, Dr. Rusoohi, who paid the driver, and a black-coated woman who walked up the steps, unlocked the door, and entered. It was Talaat's wife, he was certain.

He sat like a stone at the window for more than two hours waiting for further activity, but nothing happened the rest of the day. Nevertheless, he felt a renewal of hope. Now for the first time in several days, there were residents at Number 4.

The next day was March 13, and in the morning, Talaat's wife appeared and began to walk slowly toward Knie, Tehlirian following at a distance, recalling what he knew of her. In Constantinople he had heard that she was a highly intelligent and politically knowledgeable woman who had been engrossed in her husband's work and activities from his beginnings as a lowly postal employee to his ascent to minister of the interior and ultimately grand vizier. It was said that she had a great influence on him. She was widely respected among the Young Turks and would often walk in the public squares of Constantinople without a veil.

She arrived at the Botanical Garden, and Tehlirian followed her in. The sight of all the green plants and the fountains, which rose and fell as they played, had a strangely nostalgic effect on him. He recalled the hills and valleys of his native land and the muddy Euphrates River, which, kissed by the clouds, knifed its way down to the plains, and his heart was suddenly filled with a profound yearning for his Armenian homeland.

He was awakened from his trance by the proximity of Talaat's wife. He studied her and confirmed that she was indeed beautiful, as the villa's landlady had attested—shapely and charming, with a lovely complexion; large, pretty eyes; rich, black hair; and a small mouth— much like an Armenian woman, he thought.

The next day at noon he learned from Hazor that the apartment at Uhlandstrasse 47 had seemed that morning to be the focal point of a general pilgrimage. Hazor named Behaeddin Shakir, Dr. Nazim, Dr. Rusoohi, Jemal Azmi, and six or seven unidentifiable others. Surely Talaat would also appear, he surmised.

That night Dr. Rusoohi came out into the street with a basket but returned quickly after some brief shopping. The door did not open again. A light appeared in one of the rooms but was soon extinguished. The night passed without further ado.

The next day, March 15, was destined to be the most fateful day of Tehlirian's life. Fifteen minutes after Talaat Pasha left the villa, the life of the former grand vizier ended violently on a Berlin street—retribution for the fate he had visited on more than a million Armenians. For Tehlirian it would be a beginning. Purged of his obsession to avenge the Armenian holocaust, he was faced now with the judgment of German law.

4

The Trial Begins

*O*n Thursday, June 2, 1921, the Court of Assizes of the Supreme Court of Berlin was packed well before 9 A.M. Sitting in the crowded courtroom, many Berliners found themselves next to dark-haired, dark-eyed visitors speaking intently in foreign tongues. But the most animated attendees were the innumerable journalists, who filled the section reserved for the press. From the moment the courtroom doors were opened, the attendants realized with dismay that the section reserved for the press was far too small, as journalists poured in and scrambled for seats. Their babble of foreign tongues made it immediately obvious that editors far beyond Germany's borders were eager for news of this trial.

By 9:00 the courtroom (and every auxiliary bench) was jammed, and at 9:15 the first session began, as the presiding judge, County Court Director Dr. Lehmberg, two associate judges, and the Court Reporter entered. They were followed by State Prosecutor Gollnick and three defense attorneys, Privy Counselors von Gordon, Werthauer, and Niemeyer.

When the twelve jurors filed in, it seemed as though a cross-section of Berlin society had been handpicked to serve. The all-male jury included two locksmiths, a jeweler, housepainter, roofer, druggist, wall polisher, landlord, retired man, merchant, brickyard owner, and carpenter who served as foreman. All came from different areas of Berlin. Two alternates were also seated.

Now all eyes turned to the doorway through which entered a shy, nervous young man—the accused, Soghomon Tehlirian, seen for the first time by the representatives of the world press. Clad in a black suit, he calmly walked to his place at the defense table. Slight of figure and with slender features, the youth, though pale, seemed in control of himself. Now and then he looked around with what the press would call "the eyes of a fanatic," but his demeanor was gentle and restrained.

He seemed in awe of his surroundings—the crowded courtroom, the semicircular judges' bench, the tall columns leading to a high ceiling, and the crystal chandelier whose dangling ornaments refracted the rays of the morning sun. Turning around he caught the eyes of a woman dressed in black, whom he recognized as Talaat's widow. She stared steadily at him and he turned away, looking at the many people who were standing for lack of seats.*

Close behind were two Armenian interpreters, Vahan Zachariantz and Kevork Kalustian, and a host of witnesses, among them five medical doctors, including two psychiatrists.

After swearing in the jury, Judge Lehmberg addressed the witnesses and experts, informed them of the penalty for perjury, and asked them to leave the courtroom. He then announced that the trial would last two days, that there would be a lunch break at 1:30 and that nineteen witnesses in all would be heard this first day. Finally he underlined the need for thoroughness, and described the procedure that would follow, namely that he would conduct the initial examination of the accused and then proceed to witnesses.

The accused was then informed of the official charge against him:

The alleged student of mechanical engineering, Soghomon Tehlirian, of Hardenbergstrasse 37, the Dittmann Boardinghouse in Charlottenburg, born on April 2, 1897, in Pakaritch, Turkey, a Turkish citizen, Armenian Protestant, under arrest since March 16, 1921, is charged with intentionally having killed the former Turkish Grand Vizier Talaat Pasha in Charlottenburg on March 15, 1921, and of having carried out the killing with premeditation. A crime according to Paragraph 211.

As he was to do throughout the trial, Judge Lehmberg instructed the interpreters to inform the accused of the content of his procedural

---

*Initially present as a witness, Talaat's widow was later excused when it was established that she had not been at the scene of the crime.

comments, and specifically of the official charge, namely the premeditated killing of Talaat Pasha.

When the interpreters had finished, Judge Lehmberg turned to the accused: "How do you plead? Would you say yes or no to this accusation?"

"No."

"On earlier occasions you have said otherwise. You must admit to having carried out the deed with premeditation."

"When did I say that?"

"You would not say that even today? On different occasions, at different times, you have admitted that you reached a decision to murder Talaat Pasha."

Defense Attorney von Gordon intervened and addressed the court: "I request to ask the accused how he does not regard himself as guilty."

"I do not regard myself as guilty because my conscience is at peace."

Judge Lehmberg immediately pursued that with a question, only to receive the kind of paradoxical reply with which the accused was to intrigue the court and the public.

"How is your conscience at peace?"

"I have killed a man but I am not a murderer."

It may be useful to digress with a brief description of the four relevant sections of the German Penal Code of 1870, which were often cited during the trial, concerning how they differed from one another and the punishments they recommended.

Paragraph 211, mentioned in the official charge, referred to killing *with premeditation,* punishable by death. Paragraph 212 referred to killing *without premeditation,* punishable by no less than five years in prison. Paragraph 213 acknowledged that if the perpetrator had been *driven to anger or insulted by the murdered,* the punishment would be at least six months' imprisonment. Finally, there was Paragraph 51, quoted here in full: "A punishable deed is not in question if the culprit, at the time of the deed, was in a condition of unconsciousness or mental disturbance, through which his *exercise of free will was excluded.*"

A word also about German court procedure during this trial. Unlike American courts—where lawyers engage in direct examination, cross-examination, and frequently redirect examination, with the judge sitting as arbiter in instances of raised objections or for consultations at the bench—in this trial the judge played a different role, often acting as the chief interrogator, interrupting at will during a lawyer's examination to ask a question or to admonish a witness. Similarly, lawyers on both sides had the liberty to interrupt proceedings with a question in the interest of illuminating an obscure point. The same held true of expert witnesses and jurors.

Judge Lehmberg called Soghomon Tehlirian to the witness stand and began his interrogation. Always considerate, but demanding details and specifics, Lehmberg showed occasional impatience with interruptions from attorneys on both sides. As everyone in the courtroom was to learn, the judge was methodical, precise, and no sufferer of fools. It was also evident from the outset that he recognized the import of the trial.

His examination covered the facts of Tehlirian's family life and background, the suffering he and his family experienced, his escape from Turkey into the Transcaucasus and travels in Europe, his arrival in Berlin, and his discovery and murder of Talaat. Lehmberg thus established the motive and the execution of the crime. The accused, speaking through an interpreter, responded to all questions in a mild, almost apathetic manner.

"Were you totally surprised by the massacres in Erzinga or had there been indications earlier?" the judge asked.

"We were of the opinion that the massacres would happen because news was circulated that people were being killed."

"Were there any theories about these massacres? What did people say? Why did they take place?"

"Massacres have always taken place, from the very beginning when I was born and we moved to Erzinga. My parents told me that massacres always took place."

"Even before? When did the earlier massacres take place?"

"There were massacres in 1894."

Lehmberg asked if the youth knew the causes of the 1915 massacres; had the Turkish government been motivated by military necessities? Tehlirian replied that he had always heard only of religious and political reasons. At this point, the judge decided to hear, as he put it, "the prehistory to the deed in connection with the personal relations of the accused."

Tehlirian began his recital calmly, speaking in the strange, ancient tongue of his forefathers, stopping occasionally for the Armenian translator to put his words into German for the court.

When the war began in 1914, he said, Armenian soldiers, including his brother, were recruited into the Turkish Army. Early in 1915, however, most were stripped of all arms and employed as pack animals to transport army supplies, after which they were shot. In the villages posters announced that everyone had to surrender arms, but the Muslims were allowed to keep theirs while Armenians, when they complied, were charged as revolutionaries and tortured. Churches were desecrated and Christian symbols defiled. But these were only the initial moves by the Turkish authorities. In May news came that all Armenian schools had to be closed and the teachers, together with the community leaders, were sent to special camps. Shortly thereafter rumors spread that those who were taken away had already been killed. They had been given the alternative of renouncing Christianity, converting to Islam, and assuming Turkish names, but none had. In the months that followed only a small number of Armenians converted, for survival and to protect their families. At the beginning of June an order came—from Constantinople, everyone believed—that the entire Armenian population should prepare to leave Erzinga. Money and other valuables had to be delivered to the Turkish authorities for safekeeping. Three days later the Armenian population of around twenty thousand was led from the town early in the morning. They were not permitted to take goods and personal belongings, only what everyone had on his or her person. The Tehlirians were allowed only a donkey.

The deportees were formed into a long caravan of five or six columns, thereby evacuating virtually every Armenian in Erzinga. Turkish soldiers and gendarmes were present on all sides. Everyone was very tired, and it was difficult to count the hours of the march. On the very first day, members of Tehlirian's family were killed.

Lehmberg asked the accused to describe the death of his relatives.

When the column had marched for several hours, Tehlirian said, the Turkish soldiers ordered it to stop. The gendarmes began to plunder the deportees, looking for money and valuables they had not turned in.

"The guardians exploited the deportees? Why?"

"The Turks deal that way with Armenians."

As the plundering began, gunfire was heard from the front of the column, and when one of his sisters was dragged away by the gendarmes, Tehlirian said, his voice rising, his mother screamed: "May I be struck blind!"

Tehlirian now displayed great agitation. Breathing heavily and waving his arms, his voice reverberated in the courtroom as he shouted: "I cannot, I do not wish to remember anything further. I prefer to die rather than describe that black day!"

Judge Lehmberg tried to calm the accused and pointed out that the court gave the greatest weight to precisely the experiences he had undergone because he was the only one who could describe them. He advised the accused to control himself. Heeding the judge—behind whose stern demeanor, as he was to learn, there was a genuine compassion for his plight and a strong sense of justice—Tehlirian continued his description.

Several gendarmes dragged his sister off and raped her, while another split his brother's head with an ax. His mother lay dead nearby, killed, he thought, by a bullet. Panic stricken at the screaming and pandemonium in whose midst he stood, Tehlirian suddenly felt a blow to his head and fell unconscious. He didn't know how long he lay there—one or two days, he thought.

When he awoke it was dark, and he felt a great weight on his body. To his horror he discovered that the burden was his brother's corpse. Tehlirian struggled until he was able to push his brother's body aside and stand up. Despite the darkness he could see the corpses all around him, and he realized that the entire caravan had been killed. He was the sole survivor, left for dead by the Turks.

Standing unsteadily because of injuries to his head, arm, and leg, he viewed the sepulchral scene. Looking at the mutilated bodies surrounding him, including those of his mother and brother, the youth was overwhelmed with despair.

"Now you were helpless and without means. What did you do?" the judge asked.

Tehlirian found his way to a village in the mountains, populated by Kurds. An old woman gave him shelter and old Kurdish clothing, burning his own bloodstained garments. Several villagers advised him to go to Persia. Tehlirian spent two months with the Kurds and was later joined by two other Armenians who had fled another massacre in Harput. All three now left the Kurdish village for the long journey to Persia.

En route, once their meager provisions gave out, they ate only grass. One of them died on the way. The other, whom Tehlirian described as an intelligent man whose counsel he respected, advised that they continue on to Persia and then to the Caucasus.

They slept in the day and walked by night to avoid detection. Tehlirian thought the journey had lasted for about two months, until one day they came upon Russian Army units, to whom the two refugees, in their Kurdish clothes but without boots and head coverings, were an odd sight. The other Armenian was able to communicate with the Russians and related everything about the massacres he and Tehlirian had survived. The Russians found no reason to hold them and allowed both to go, but refused Tehlirian's request that he be allowed to go to the Caucasus. The two were released and found their way across the border to Persia.

Tehlirian arrived in the town of Salmas and there became ill, while his comrade went on to Tiflis, the capital of Georgia. Exhausted by his ordeal, Tehlirian found an Armenian church, where he was given food, clothing, and money. Eventually Tehlirian found a job with a merchant, for whom he worked for about a year. Then word reached him that the Russian Army had captured the part of Anatolia that included Erzinga. Tehlirian decided to return to his village to search for any family survivors. He also had a secondary purpose. His father had once imparted to him and his brothers a family secret: a cache of gold was buried under the house. Now he desperately needed money, but would the gold still be there? Toward the end of 1916 the youth began his return trip to Erzinga.

Tehlirian found the family home in ruins. All the doors had been torn off, and a large section of the house had been destroyed by fire. Overcome by emotion, Tehlirian collapsed to the floor. When, after some time, he came to, he toured the village and found two Armenian families who had survived by adopting Islam rather than being killed.

Returning to the house, Tehlirian began an earnest search for whatever he could salvage before focusing on his main objective. All that was left were some tools, but these at least gave him the means to dig for the family treasure. Recalling his father's instructions, he pinpointed the spot and began to dig. To his joy, he struck a hard object. Bending down, he dug his hands into a large mound of coins. He scooped up the Turkish gold pieces and began to count. They added up to 4,800 Turkish pounds.

Tehlirian remained in Erzinga for about six weeks, hoping for the return of deportees or members of his family. Eventually he went to Tiflis, where he began to study Russian and French at Nersessian College, which had opened its classrooms to Armenian émigrés and survivors of the massacres.* Although he studied there for five months, he said his thoughts had been so jumbled that he could not concentrate.

In February 1919 he went to Constantinople and, after a brief stay, visited some relatives in Greece. He also went to Serbia, then back to Salonika, and from there, in early 1920, on to Paris. Asked about the purpose of so much movement, Tehlirian said that he wanted to study but that his mind was confused, and he was not inclined toward any profession.

Further questioning extracted the information that while in Salonika he had undergone medical treatment for painful attacks, the first occurring in his parents' home in Erzinga, brought on by memories of the massacre. Tehlirian also admitted that he had suffered similar attacks while in Serbia and Constantinople.

"When did you become convinced that Talaat Pasha was the author of those massacres?" Judge Lehmberg asked.

"When I was in Constantinople, I saw things in the newspapers."

"Did you learn then where Talaat Pasha was?"

"I thought he might be in Constantinople in hiding."

"Did you entertain thoughts at that time of taking revenge on this man who, in your view, was guilty of the tragic loss of your family?"

"No."

Defense Attorney von Gordon interrupted to ask whether the accused had read in the newspapers that Talaat Pasha had been found guilty of the massacres and condemned to death by a military tribunal in Constantinople.

"I had read that and was in Constantinople when Kemal Bey (a Young Turk governor) was hung on the gallows," Tehlirian answered. "The newspapers reported that Talaat and Enver had been condemned to death."

Asked to continue the story of his travels, Tehlirian said that in Paris he spent most of his time studying French. But in November of

---

*Founded in 1824 by Archbishop Nerses Ashtaraketsi, after whom it was named, the college served as an Armenian institution of higher education until the 1920s, when it ceased to function.

the same year he had gone to Geneva, where through an Armenian friend, he had obtained a visa to go to Berlin for the purpose of studying German and mechanical engineering.

On his eighth day at the Tiergarten Hotel, Tehlirian received a residence permit from the Charlottenburg police and moved to a furnished room at Augsburgerstrasse 51. He told the judge that he had lived there for three months until moving once again, on March 5, to Hardenbergstrasse 37.

"Is it true that you had already established before then that Talaat Pasha was in Berlin?" Lehmberg asked.

"Yes. About five weeks before." Tehlirian described the circumstances under which he had seen Talaat at the train station.

"Did the idea of killing Talaat surface when you had this encounter?"

"The idea did not surface. I only felt ill, and it seemed to me as though the images of the massacre reappeared."

That night, Tehlirian testified, he had been tortured by the thought of being in the same city as Talaat. He spent the next three weeks in mental turmoil, trying all the time to continue his German-language studies and socializing with the handful of Armenian friends he had made. Until one night: "I was not feeling well and the images of the massacres were constantly passing before my eyes. Then, suddenly, I saw the corpse of my mother. The corpse rose up, approached me, and cried: 'You have seen that Talaat is here and you are totally indifferent? You are no longer my son!' "

Although the interpreter had translated this for the court, the judge, apparently impressed, repeated it to the jury.

"What did you do then?"

"I suddenly awakened and decided to kill that man."

"You had not made that decision when you were in Paris and Geneva and when you came to Berlin?"

"I had made no decision."

"Did you know that Talaat was in Berlin?"

"No."

Tehlirian related the self-doubts he suffered as a result of his decision to kill Talaat. He asked himself how he could kill a human being, and answered that he couldn't.

"I don't understand that. You said before that you had decided to move to Hardenbergstrasse. You knew that Talaat Pasha now lived opposite you . . . and you wanted to be nearby."

"Yes . . . as my mother said to me."

"Did you resolve from that time on to observe Talaat Pasha's every movement so that you would be in control?"

"No. When I moved to my new quarters I wanted only to go about my usual daily business."

His daily business involved classes with Fräulein Beilinson, his German teacher, and seeing his Armenian friends. But at night he was troubled by images of the massacre and by the vision of his mother. His mental state worsened, until one day on Jerusalem-strasse, he suffered another attack. He decided then to visit Professor Richard Cassirer—a neurologist—for treatment. By this time his condition no longer permitted him to continue his German studies.

"Besides your language studies with Fräulein Beilinson, how else did you spend your time?"

"I visited Armenian families, such as my friends the Ter-zibashians, Eftians, and Apelians. I read Armenian newspapers they gave me, and some Russian papers occasionally. I went to the theater, often to movies and to dances."

"You had enrolled in a dance class. . . . Is it true that in one of those classes, you had an epileptic seizure?"

"Yes, and at home too."

Judge Lehmberg established through his questioning that Tehlirian had had many epileptic seizures since arriving in Berlin.* He now addressed the specific facts of the crime and, by persistent and detailed questioning, drew from the accused a precise picture of what had happened.

———

In view of what is now known about Tehlirian's activities before the murder, it is evident that his testimony at the trial contained a number of discrepancies. They appear to have been deliberate sins of omission.

When relating the events following the Erzinga massacre, for instance, Tehlirian did not mention his service as a volunteer with the Armenian partisans. Could he have wished to hide his participation in these activities because they involved killing? It is conjectural whether he himself ever killed or even knew that he killed anyone during his partisan days, inasmuch as the raids on Turkish field units

---

*Contemporary research has established that the most frequent cause of the onset of epilepsy in people of Tehlirian's age group is a head trauma, such as he apparently suffered from an ax during the massacre.

often occurred at night, with heavy exchanges of gunfire but no hand-to-hand combat.

Possibly for the same reason, Tehlirian made no mention at the trial of his assassination of Harootiun Mugerditchian, the Armenian traitor who had collaborated with Talaat. To have done so might have given the impression that he was a professional assassin instead of a desperate young man avenging the murder of his family.

If the reason for these two omissions is open to conjecture, there can be no doubt about why in the court and earlier during his police interrogation Tehlirian misrepresented two vital matters concerning the crime. In response to questions on whether he acted alone and whether there was an organization supporting him, his replies were in contradiction of the facts, though the reason in both instances was clear.

Both questions involved his ties to the ARF and its role in the assassination. In fact, that role began when he was summoned to the United States, briefed at ARF headquarters in Boston, and recruited as an agent of Nemesis for the sole purpose of killing Talaat Pasha.

His failures to mention the trip to Boston, the existence and support of Nemesis, and the collaboration of a number of confederates—one of whom, Vaza, was an interpreter at the trial—were all for one and the same reason: to have admitted them would have compromised the Nemesis network and jeopardized its plans to carry out a series of assassinations against former Turkish officials like Talaat, who had taken refuge beyond Turkey's borders. Tehlirian's silence was also a measure of the discipline exercised by the ARF over all its members at this critical time.

Finally there is good cause to believe that Tehlirian had begun to understand the legal distinctions first explained to him by Levine—namely, the difference between a premeditated political crime and personal vengeance. Thus, by the time of the trial, Tehlirian had apparently made the decision to eliminate any references to political organizations, conspiracies, and accomplices and instead to assume sole responsibility for the crime.

On March 15, Tehlirian testified, he was in his room engrossed in his German lessons when he happened to notice movement at the house across the street. He went to the window and saw Talaat Pasha come out. He watched Talaat reenter his house, then emerge again from the building's ground-floor entrance.

"When he came out, my thoughts turned to my mother, and as they did, her image appeared again before me, and I realized that I was looking at the man who was responsible for the murder of my mother, my sisters, and my brothers," Tehlirian said.

"You saw the spirits of your loved ones and believed that Talaat was responsible not only for the bloodletting of your family but [for that] of your countrymen," the judge suggested.

Asked how long he had owned a gun, Tehlirian replied since 1919, when he had first gone to Tiflis. He had heard that if the Turks returned to Georgia, another Armenian massacre would take place. Consequently he had kept the revolver with him, always loaded.

Seeing Talaat begin his walk, Tehlirian said, he had taken the gun from his suitcase and run out after him. Closely questioned by the judge, the accused described how he crossed the street behind Talaat, passed him to make sure of his identity, then walked back behind him, put the barrel to his head, and fired. He did not recall every detail of what followed. While he did admit to running away, he said it was not because of the deed but because of the threatening crowd that quickly gathered.

"What did you feel, what did you think, when Talaat Pasha lay dead?" asked the judge.

"I felt a satisfaction of the heart."

"And how is it today?"

"Today I am still very content with the deed."

"Do you know, however, that under normal circumstances, no one may be his own judge, even if so much has happened to him?"

"I don't know. My mother said I had to kill Talaat Pasha because he was guilty of the massacre, and my soul was in such turmoil that I wasn't aware that I should not kill."

"But you know that our laws forbid murder, forbid killing a human being?" the judge admonished.

"I do not know the law," Tehlirian said simply.

"Does the custom of blood revenge exist among the Armenians?"

"No."

State Attorney Gollnick rose to note that in response to a question from Defense Attorney von Gordon, Tehlirian had said that Talaat had been condemned to death in Constantinople. "It is true that there was such a sentence of death," Gollnick said. "I must, however, point out that that happened after an entirely new government had taken over in Constantinople following the collapse of Turkey, and Constantinople found itself under the shadow of British naval cannon. I leave it to the court to judge what significance this sentence of death carries.''

Judge Lehmberg appeared to dismiss Gollnick's oblique attempt to dissuade the judge or jury from any opinion that by killing Talaat, the Armenian student was merely carrying out the sentence imposed by a Turkish court. Accordingly Gollnick introduced a different line of questioning:

"It has been stated that the massacre took place at Erzinga. But I have been informed that the caravan that moved from Erzinga was attacked by Kurdish bandits and that Turkish gendarmes were also killed. I ask the accused whether Kurdish robbers did in fact do so.''

"It was told to me that the Turkish gendarmes did the shooting.''

Defense Attorney Niemeyer intervened with an explanation: "It is a principle in the Turkish massacres that the Kurds are the arch-enemies of the Armenians; they live in the mountains and had been hired as gendarmes by the Turks to protect the Armenians.''

"The Kurds vary,'' Tehlirian explained. "Some are enemies of the Armenians, but many are good people to the Armenians.''

Niemeyer added that Tehlirian had taken shelter with some Kurds. On the other hand, there were also Kurds who were friendly to the Turkish government.

"Most of them,'' Tehlirian interposed.

The direct questioning of the accused now drew to a close as the third of Tehlirian's lawyers, Defense Attorney Werthauser, filled in some bits of testimony. When the massacre took place, he said, his mother had been fifty-two, his brothers twenty-eight and twenty-two, his married sister twenty-six, another sixteen and the youngest fifteen. Werthauser also refreshed the accused's memory by reminding him of pretrial testimony, wherein he had said that his married sister and her husband and children had all been dragged away and killed, that he had found another sister's corpse in a clump of bushes as well as the others, and that he had witnessed his mother's death.

On the morning of that day, Tehlirian now said, a Turkish Army official had announced that the village had to be evacuated of all Armenians, and that the order came from Constantinople. Tehlirian added that everyone had heard the widely circulated rumor that the signer of that order was Talaat Pasha.

Judge Lehmberg announced that the questioning had been completed and that eyewitnesses to the crime on Hardenbergstrasse would be examined. Two now testified, and while minor discrepancies were noted, both appeared to confirm the established facts. Two police officers, two medical examiners, and a firearms expert—who identified the murder weapon and said it was relatively new and well maintained—also testified.

Three women followed: Tehlirian's two landladies and his German teacher. Judge Lehmberg's questioning was crisp, and he was sometimes impatient with their loquacious and yet seemingly evasive answers. Frau Stellbaum, at whose boardinghouse Tehlirian had lived for two months, described her tenant as modest, polite, fastidious, and undemanding. "For example, he did not assume I would polish his boots," she explained. She also said, however, that she found her tenant very nervous, unable to sleep—she could hear his restlessness through her wall—and that she knew he was seeing Dr. Cassirer. He spent much time with Apelian, who also lived there, and with Eftian. Often they sang mournful songs together while he played the mandolin—in the dark, she said, because they thought it sounded better. The gas lamp seemed to bother Tehlirian and, in fact, although she had expected him to stay until May 1, he announced that on March 5 he would move because the doctor had suggested the gas was affecting his nerves.

Psychiatrist Dr. Liepmann interrupted to ask Frau Stellbaum what she meant by "nervous": "Do you mean distracted?"

She replied in the affirmative, noting that at night Tehlirian often talked to himself so that she thought there might be someone with him.

After Judge Lehmberg established that she had not noticed any change in Tehlirian's demeanor during his stay with her, Defense Attorney von Gordon asked Frau Stellbaum if Tehlirian had ever spoken of his past.

"No, only when he moved," she replied. "He came back after a few days to pick up his *Abmeldung*.* Then I asked him about his past, and he told me how he had returned to his home and found his house in ruins. His sisters, an older brother and his mother had been killed and only he had remained alive. Then he stopped, and I saw he did not want to speak further about it." He said all this, she concluded, with a certain intensity of emotion.

Frau Dittmann, Tehlirian's last landlady, was sworn in, and although she confirmed the virtues described by the preceding witness, she provided some new information concerning the day of the murder:

*Notice to the Berlin police of a change of address by a foreigner.

On the morning of March 15, the maid said to me that I should come for a moment because the gentleman was crying in his room. I said perhaps someone close had died, that she should leave him alone, that I could not help because he couldn't understand me. Soon thereafter, he left. Earlier I had been in his room. He had drunk some brandy. That surprised me.

Pointed questioning brought out that the accused had purchased a bottle of French cognac the day before because he felt weak, and had poured a little into his tea that night and the next day as well. He also said that he had neither cried nor sung. After this testimony, there was now some irritation with Frau Dittmann. She claimed at first, for instance, that Tehlirian left his room after 9 A.M. and did not return; then she agreed that he had left around 11 A.M. She also said that her initial understanding was that it was he who had been shot.

Now, in trying to pinpoint information concerning the revolver, the judge became vexed with both landladies. After learning from Tehlirian that he had kept the gun in his suitcase, Judge Lehmberg—apparently familiar with the nosiness of boardinghouse landladies—asked Frau Stellbaum if she had ever seen the weapon.

"I never saw it."

"I find it striking that you often looked in his suitcase and did not see the revolver."

"I do not wish to maintain that I often looked in his suitcase."

"Frau Stellbaum, you are giving testimony under oath! You never saw the revolver?"

"Not even once."

Fräulein Beilinson, questioned next, stated that she had begun teaching the accused German on January 18. She said he was a good student but later became so distracted that by February 20 the regular lessons stopped. The young teacher had noticed a general sadness in her pupil. But she knew that he was seeing Dr. Cassirer and ascribed it to a "spiritual malady."

"Once when I asked him about his homeland, he replied that he no longer had a homeland," she testified. "All of his family had been murdered. It was so pitiful that I asked no more. He visited me on February 27 or 28. He had studied well earlier but now he was distracted and said to me that he understood nothing."

"Is it possible that the lessons stopped at the beginning of March? Perhaps shortly before March 5?"

"Yes. Once he moved he did not come to me any more."

Both she and Tehlirian testified that he had told her he would continue his German lessons once his health improved. Asked whether he tried to educate himself in German, the accused said he practiced every morning in his exercise book. Concerning his progress, Tehlirian said he had difficulty reading handwritten script but less with print.

As the focus of the trial began to sharpen, the attention of the court now turned to Tehlirian's Armenian friends and contacts in Berlin.

Yerevand Apelian took the witness stand and testified that he had befriended Tehlirian because he was a countryman who knew no German. The young diplomat had persuaded him to socialize more and made him sign up for the dance class in which Apelian was already registered. The classes took place every Tuesday, Friday, and Sunday, and the two Armenians were joined by Eftian, another countryman. In the class, which consisted of sixty to seventy persons, Tehlirian had no special partner and danced with a variety of women because he wished to practice his German. Apelian found him to be introverted and "no daredevil with the women."

Responding to specific questions put by expert witness Dr. Cassirer, Apelian gave the court a vivid description of one of Tehlirian's epileptic attacks. During a dance class Tehlirian suddenly emitted a shrill scream and fell to the floor. He lay unconscious for ten minutes, then came to, and afterward went home. Asked by psychiatrist Edmund Forster if the attack had been brought on by some reference to the massacres, Apelian said: "No. But he had once told me that whenever he had an attack, he would first experience an odor in his nostrils."*

Tehlirian had not spoken of his former life except to say that he had lost all of his family, and also that he had suffered a head wound. During the three months they lived in the same building they spoke less and less, and Apelian noted that Tehlirian became moody when they disagreed, often declining to discuss personal matters. Pressed by Lehmberg, Apelian said that Tehlirian never mentioned having seen Talaat in Berlin, or that he knew of his whereabouts, or even that he owned a revolver.

Apelian was followed by Levon Eftian, a young man of twenty-one who had come to Berlin from Paris one year earlier. He lived with his

---

*The sensation of a strange smell is one of several phenomena accompanying a seizure.

sister, Christine Terzibashian, and her husband, a tobacconist who had lived in Berlin since 1914. Eftian described Tehlirian as a sad person who visited the Terzibashians once a week but never seemed eager to discuss his past.

"Did you lose a large number of relatives in the massacres?" the judge inquired.

"My parents were killed in the massacres. In 1912 I went from Erzerum, our home, to Constantinople and attended school for three years, until 1915. Then the war broke out and I could not travel back home. We learned that the deportations had already begun. Later I found out that my parents and relatives had been killed and that only two brothers and my sister were alive."

As he had with other witnesses, Judge Lehmberg pressed the question of how aware the Armenian community was of the presence in Berlin of Talaat Pasha. But Eftian said it was only a rumor he had heard in Constantinople, without any confirmation.

Defense Attorney von Gordon intervened, asking Eftian: "In your circles, is Talaat Pasha the only one responsible for the Armenian horror? I do not understand that none of the Armenians here seemed preoccupied with establishing with certainty that the author of this horror was in Berlin. Didn't anyone concern himself with that? There must have been great interest. The rumor that Talaat Pasha might be in Berlin must have enjoyed wide circulation. Did the possibility of his presence in Berlin originate only in news from Istanbul?"

Eftian—and Tehlirian, when asked again—reaffirmed that he had not known of Talaat's presence.

"Accused," said the judge, "you encountered Talaat. Why after this encounter of such import did you not tell your countrymen?"

"I thought they would laugh at me."

"Why so, when Talaat is considered the originator of the massacres?"

"If I had spoken about it, I would have been closely questioned."

"You didn't want to disquiet your countrymen who would have overwhelmed you with curious questions?"

"I was in such a state that I didn't want to speak of it."

At this point, State Prosecutor Gollnick called Privy Councillor Schulze—the same official who had questioned Tehlirian on March 16, the day after the killing—to testify. Lehmberg, evidently preoccupied with the issue of intent, followed Schulze's testimony closely, often interrupting with questions of his own. What transpired was an unusual exchange that brought matters into sharper focus. Gollnick, who until now had seemed somewhat casual, began to take notes and to show greater interest. The spectators also sensed that something was happening and strained to hear every word. For his part, Tehlirian realized that the issue first raised by his prison colleague Levine, the question of intent, was becoming central to his case.

Schulze recounted the major points of his examination, noting that Tehlirian had "admitted without hesitation" to having killed Talaat with premeditation and forethought. Tehlirian, he said, held Talaat responsible for the murder of his family, had made the decision to avenge them, and therefore had come to Berlin. Schulze repeated the specifics of the killing as told to him on March 16—Tehlirian's pattern of observation from his room, Talaat's appearance on the street, and the details of the shooting.

Lehmberg then turned to one of the two interpreters and asked if Schulze's testimony was correct. The question was directed to Kevork Kalustian, the same interpreter who had translated for Schulze on March 16.

"Yes," Kalustian replied, "but the accused was not at that time in a position to consider what he was saying. His head was still bandaged."

"Accused, on March 16 you admitted that [as early as] 1915, when you had to flee Erzinga, you had decided to kill Talaat."

"I do not recall having said that."

"But you must have testified so at the time. Weren't you questioned through an interpreter?"

"It is possible that I testified so because my head was injured."

"There is, however, an essential difference whether I reach a decision fourteen days earlier or carry it around with me for years, years before having purchased a revolver and years before coming to Berlin. A big difference. Were you not aware of the significance of your testimony?"

"I know nothing more than what I testified on that day. I simply and always said yes."

With the noon hour at hand and the lunch break imminent, the judge, Schulze, and the defense attorneys engaged in a rapid exchange. Schulze stuck to his claim that on March 16 Tehlirian had said he had come to Berlin to satisfy his passion for revenge. Judge Lehmberg wondered if the transcript of that examination should be read to the court. Von Gordon said it was not necessary and put the question directly to the accused: Did he say that he had planned the murder for years and was happy that he had done it? Tehlirian replied that he didn't know.

Niemeyer, observing that translations normally take place either through a voluntary flow of information or in response to specific questions, asked Schulze how Tehlirian's examination was conducted. Schulze replied that both methods were employed but that he had specifically put the question of motive into his inquiry.

Asked by von Gordon about the interpreter's state of mind, Schulze described Kalustian as very calm. He had brought chocolate and other sweets for the prisoner and became excited only when Schulze referred to Tehlirian as a murderer, saying: "What do you mean, a murderer? This is a great man whom we all admire." Von Gordon noted the importance of this testimony, and Judge Lehmberg recessed the court.

The proceedings resumed after lunch with what proved to be the most gripping testimony of the two-day trial. The audience and jurors were held spellbound by several Armenian witnesses, some of whom were survivors of the massacres, and two prominent Germans who, beyond being highly knowledgeable about Turkish policies toward the Armenians, had also played personal roles in the tragedy.

Judge Lehmberg opened the session with the unusual step of calling as witnesses the two interpreters, since both had also served in that capacity prior to the crime and at Tehlirian's examination the day after.

Vahan Zachariantz was an Armenian who worked at the Persian Consulate in Berlin, where he had first met Tehlirian in helping the latter to extend his visa. He testified that he had befriended the student and once went with him to visit Dr. Cassirer for his treatment. Cassirer had determined that Tehlirian was an epileptic, and during that visit, Tehlirian told the doctor that his first attack occurred after he had visited the ruined house in Erzinga.

Not wishing to overexcite his newfound friend, Zachariantz refrained from discussing the massacres because, as he testified, "I knew what he had suffered and did not wish to remind him of his pain."

Asked whether he knew that Talaat Pasha was in Berlin, Zachariantz said he did not personally know but had learned from one of the several newspapers he read daily—German, French,

Armenian, Russian, and Persian—that Talaat was rumored to be somewhere in Germany. In any case Tehlirian did not tell him he had seen Talaat. Besides, Zachariantz testified, he spoke less and less with the young man, noting that Tehlirian "was often depressed and simply stared ahead of him."

The second interpreter was Kevork Kalustian.

"Did you say, as another witness has testified, that the accused is a great man?" the judge asked.

"In my eyes, he is a great man."

Responding to questions about his family, Kalustian said that his parents had been killed in Aintab (now Gaziantep) in 1896 during the first large massacre, along with his uncle, a brother, and his grandfather, whose murder he had witnessed as a five-year-old. He said that constant repetition of those events in his mind kept them alive. The judge now addressed the question of the transcript of the March 16 examination.

"Do you regard the confession that the accused made to the examining magistrate as correct and true?"

"At the time I did not regard it as correct on the simple ground that it was not pleasant for the accused to be examined when his head was still in bandages. He said: 'I did this and that, I killed him.' To the question whether he had thought about the deed, he said: 'Yes, I thought about it.' "

"You confirm, therefore, what is in the March 16 transcript? But you had the impression that the accused said what he did only to say something. Did you give expression to your doubt? Did you say anything?"

"I purposely did not sign the transcript."

After the judge had confirmed that the interpreter's signature was not on the paper, Kalustian explained further: "I said it was possible that this man was not in control of his senses, that he could not comprehend what he had testified to, that it was perhaps not the right time to examine him." He added: "One thing I did notice, however—namely that he enjoyed an inner peace. He said simply: 'I have killed him.' "

Lehmberg turned to the attorneys and asked whether in their view the transcript could be considered valid. Only Defense Attorney Niemeyer replied, observing that it could not be considered a transcript because it did not attest that the interpreter had translated the examination.

Kalustian was excused, and the judge called on Terzibashian, with whom there was a brief exchange, most of it confirming testimony already given. The tobacconist had not experienced any of the massacres, having been in Berlin since the beginning of the war. This was not, however, the case with his wife, who followed him to the witness stand.

Judge Lehmberg led Christine Terzibashian directly into the events of 1915. At that time she had been twenty years old. He asked whether deportations had taken place in her hometown of Erzerum and how the Armenians had been notified. She replied: "In July 1915 the inhabitants were brought together and told they had to leave the city. The wealthy people were told eight days before by officials and the gendarmerie, but we were told only one hour before about the deportation. It wasn't until later that we learned that this was a deceit, and that only the Armenian population was to be taken away."

"The entire Armenian population was then driven at one time out of the city?"

"No, four times."

"In four sections?"

"Four sections in eight days."

"Did those remaining behind learn what happened to the earlier columns?"

"No."

She said that her section, the second, consisted of five hundred Armenian families. Her own family included twenty-one persons. They heard they would be going to Erzinga so they rented three oxen and carts.

"When we left our city and were at the gates of the fortress of Erzerum, the gendarmes came and searched us for weapons. Knives and umbrellas were taken from us. Then, from Erzerum we came to Baiburt, and when we went past that town, we saw piles of corpses. I had to walk over corpses, so that my feet were covered with blood."

They arrived in Erzinga, and although they had been promised housing, there was none. They were not allowed to drink water, and the oxen were driven away into the mountains. The judge asked for details of the events that followed.

"Five hundred young males were selected from our section and led away. My brother was among them, but he managed to flee and came to me, and I dressed him as a girl. The rest were herded together, tied to each other, and thrown into the river.''

Judge Lehmberg's eyebrows shot upward in astonishment as he asked: ''How do you know that?''

''I saw it with my own eyes. They were thrown into the river, and the current was so powerful that everyone was swept away. We screamed and cried and didn't know what to do but were beaten with thorny sticks to keep us moving.''

''Who did this?''

''Thirty gendarmes and a unit of soldiers.''

The deportees arrived later at Malatya and were taken into the hills, where the men and women were separated, and from a distance of ten meters the women could see what happened to the men.

''What happened to the men?''

''They were hacked to pieces with axes and then thrown into the river.''

The judge spoke with difficulty. ''Were both men and women massacred in this manner?''

''Only the men were killed this way. When it grew dark, the gendarmes came and sought out the prettiest women and girls and took them for themselves. A gendarme came to me also and wanted me to be his woman. Those who didn't obey, who wouldn't give in, were stabbed with bayonets and their legs ripped off. Even pregnant women were chopped up and the infants torn out of them and flung away.''

The commotion and outrage that erupted in the courtroom were so vociferous that the witness, as though to add the fullest authenticity to her testimony, turned to face the spectators, raised her hand, and declared in a trembling voice: ''I swear it!''

Judge Lehmberg's next question was almost a whisper.

''How were you saved?''

''My brother was decapitated, and when my mother saw that, she collapsed and died on the spot. Then a Turk came to me and wanted to make me his wife, and when I refused, he killed one of our children.''

Of the twenty-one people in her family who had begun the journey, only four were then still alive—her father, two brothers, and herself. Her father became ill, was thrown into the river, rescued by one of his sons, but died anyway. The deportees reached Samsek, then were forcibly moved on to Surich and into the mountains.

''Whom do you hold responsible for these atrocities?''

"These things happened on the orders of Enver Pasha. The soldiers forced the deportees to go down on their knees and cry out: 'Long live the pasha!' because the pasha had allowed them to live."

The spectators reacted again, and when their agitation had subsided, Defense Attorney Niemeyer rose and said:

It has frequently been recognized here, with understandable reaction, that the witness's testimony appears almost incredible. There are, however, thousands of such reports, all confirmed. I should like to request, in order not to allow the slightest doubt of the witness's credibility, that the two experts, Professor Dr. Lepsius and His Excellency Liman von Sanders be questioned about the connection between the Turkish police and the Turkish military, as it was then.

His colleague von Gordon added his voice to this request:

After this shattering description of the affair—of which I, to this day, had no knowledge, at least so comprehensively—I, too, must believe that we can dispense with the examination of further witnesses who wait outside [the court]. We agree to hear the two experts, and I request further that we examine a very prominent personality who has come to Berlin from Manchester, Bishop [Krikoris] Balakian. He has experienced all . . . these terrible things, and we can hear from him whether the entire Armenian people holds Talaat Pasha guilty. Whether he truly is, is another question.

State Prosecutor Gollnick had no objection to the request by the two defense attorneys; in fact, he said it would be desirable to hear the two experts. Judge Lehmberg then called the next witness, Pastor Johannes Lepsius. The courtroom buzzed with anticipation at the testimony to come from this widely known German author, theologian, and humanitarian, whose tireless struggle on behalf of the persecuted minority in Turkey had earned him the title "advocate of the Armenian people." Lepsius's struggle had not, however, begun with the massacres of 1915 but with the massacres two decades earlier.

5

Behind the Curtain of War

When he was twenty-six years old, Johannes Lepsius had gradu-
ated from the University of Munich, completed theological
studies in Berlin, and fulfilled his compulsory military service. He
was ready for a career dedicated to ecclesiastical life, and his first
posting took him to Palestine as an assistant preacher and teacher at
the Protestant School in Jerusalem. It was during his three years
there that he first encountered the problems of the many nationalities
contained in the Ottoman Empire—Greeks, Bulgarians, Assyrians,
Arabs, Jews—and above all, Armenians. But this was 1884, and
while discontent ran high within the empire, it could not compare
with the violence that erupted shortly, or with the horrors concealed
behind the curtain of the world war to come.

Before this assignment, Lepsius's familiarity with the Middle East
had come largely through his father, Richard Lepsius, a renowned
archaeologist who went to Egypt in 1842 and founded German
Egyptology, in 1869 participated in the opening of the Suez Canal,
became president of Rome's Institute of Antiquity, and established
Egyptian Studies in Greece.

In 1887, together with his bride, the daughter of a German pastor
in Jerusalem, Johannes Lepsius returned to Germany to become a
Minister in Friesdorf, a poor village in the Harz Mountains. There,
the same feelings that had prompted his compassion for the oppressed peoples of the Near East led him to found a small rug factory
to provide work for the Friesdorfers. This was the first of his ac-

tivities to arouse the animosity of his church elders in Berlin, who viewed his social concerns as evidence of neglect for parishioners' spiritual life. Undeterred, Lepsius tended to his flock both materially and spiritually, concentrating on little else—until the tensions he had sensed within the Ottoman Empire broke out in shocking violence late in 1894.

This took place in the mountainous areas of Sassun in Anatolia, when Armenians, taxed beyond their ability to pay and jailed by a corrupt Ottoman governor when they refused, arose in revolt. The brutality with which their resistance was suppressed—the first major massacre of Armenians—aroused a huge public reaction in Europe. A European Commission of Inquiry in 1895 identified gratuitous acts of cruelty and accused Ottoman officials of reprehensible and irresponsible conduct.

Johannes Lepsius was thirty-six years old when news of the massacre that had taken place in Sassun reached him. He was troubled by the minimal coverage in the German press of this massive crime against the small Christian nation he had come to know while in Jerusalem.

Lepsius was even more dismayed by the journalistic indifference when news of the second massacre in Trebizond and the massive destruction that followed reached him. Germany and Turkey enjoyed a close relationship, and the press, which largely supported the kaiser, published nothing that might have aroused the displeasure of the Sublime Porte. Lepsius decided to go to Turkey on a fact-finding trip and see the situation for himself.

Posing as a rug expert making a journey to study manufacturing techniques, Lepsius went to Turkey in the spring of 1896—the first of seven visits. He traveled extensively through Turkish villages and cities, collecting information from eyewitnesses. While most of the German press remained silent about the massacres, the largest Christian daily, *Der Reichsbote*, ran a series of articles between April and June by an unnamed German pastor on the true situation in Turkey. The series, which bore the title "The Truth About Armenia," infuriated not only Ottoman diplomats in Berlin but the nationalistic press of Germany.

Sultan Abdul Hamid II, certain that the author of these articles was Lepsius, declared him persona non grata and expelled him from Turkey in 1896. Back in Germany, Lepsius compiled his articles and other information in a book, *Armenien und Europa*, published a year later. He subtitled this work *An Accusatory Document Against*

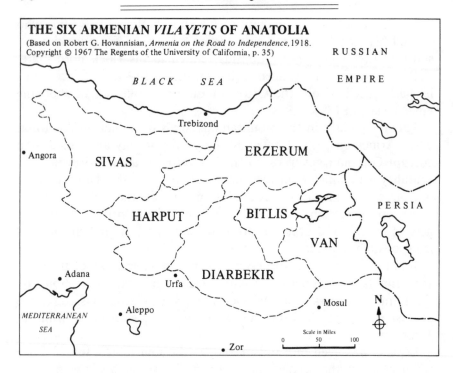

THE SIX ARMENIAN *VILAYETS* OF ANATOLIA
(Based on Robert G. Hovannisian, *Armenia on the Road to Independence*, 1918.
Copyright © 1967 The Regents of the University of California, p. 35)

the Christian Powers and an Appeal to Christian Germany. The book was soon translated and circulated widely throughout Europe in French and English editions.

Lepsius wrote:

> During my travels through Anatolia, I never once met a Moslem who was not convinced that . . . the annihilation and pillaging of the Armenian people was arranged by the government in conformity with the Sultan's will. . . . The mullahs in the mosques announce that the Armenian massacres have been ordered by the highest Moslem spiritual authority. . . . The German press is filled with stories from sources so one-sided that it is clearly the intention to fool Europe. That is the reason why today in Germany, nothing is known of the mass slaughter, plunder and forcible change of religion of a great Christian people.

Determined to correct the imbalance and become the voice and instrument of the Armenian people in Germany, Lepsius made a decision that would bring him into direct confrontation with the policies of Kaiser Wilhelm II, isolate him from most of the intellectuals of Germany, and lead eventually to persecution and exile.

Lepsius had two objectives: first, to provide assistance to survivors of the massacres in Turkey through a chain of relief missions; and second, to begin a public campaign in Germany to inform the German people of the events in Turkey.

To accomplish his first objective he began by transferring his factory, with all its machinery and personnel, to the city of Urfa in south-central Turkey and by beginning to recruit doctors, nurses, and teachers to work in the orphanages that he founded for Armenian children who had lost their parents in the massacres. Although not wealthy, he used what funds he had and was grateful for contributions from supporters in Germany. He also asked the Berlin Church Council for leave to go to Turkey in order to organize his German Orient Mission. When the council refused, Lepsius made another important decision. He resigned his pastoral office, severing relations with his clerical superiors, and embarked on what would become the main work of his life.

His second objective, although seemingly less daunting, proved to be almost as difficult. Informing the German public about the Turkish persecution of a Christian minority, in all its gruesome details, aroused the animus of many official bodies of the kaiser's government, not least the Foreign Ministry, the Interior Ministry, and police chiefs from Berlin to smaller jurisdictions, where Lepsius often addressed local audiences.

He found a valuable collaborator in Garabed Toumayan, a forty-four-year-old survivor of the massacres, who had been imprisoned and condemned by the Turkish government but freed through Swiss and British intervention. After that he had found his way to England. In September 1896 Lepsius invited Toumayan to deliver an account of his experiences at a series of mass meetings he had organized throughout Germany. Speaking in French through a translator, Toumayan whipped his audiences into a frenzy. Every massacre began and ended with a bugle call, he said, and the sound of that bugle early in the morning struck terror into every Armenian villager just as the final notes in the afternoon heralded a temporary respite.

In Berlin people arose from their seats with angry shouts of "Shame!" as he described the grisly terrors they had suffered— young girls raped before the eyes of their parents; women bound by their hair to the tails of horses, dragged through the streets, and then hacked to pieces with axes; parents decapitated as their children were forced to watch; or in one harrowing description, how Turkish soldiers bound children together and, with their parents looking on, vied to see how many throats they could cut with one stroke of a knife. Hundreds of others took refuge in churches only to have the Turkish soldiers pour gasoline on them from the adjoining roofs and be burned alive.

"They had only to repeat the Mohammedan articles of faith to save themselves, but they didn't," Toumayan said. "They remained faithful to their Christianity. It is not the Turkish people who are annihilating the Armenian Christians, but the Turkish government."

After one such speech, Lepsius addressed the mass meeting: "When I made my trip to the sites of the massacres, I was not well informed. But it was the Turkish population itself that informed me. I am not Armenian. I am a German, and I say to you that what this man has told you is only the smallest part of the whole truth."[1]

Inspired by Lepsius's campaign, other German intellectuals and clergymen took to the podium, holding similar mass meetings in various parts of Germany. In Düsseldorf a Pastor Keller attacked the passive attitudes of the major powers "which allowed the dying man of Europe to perpetrate these disgraceful deeds." But he saved his biggest blasts for the German press and singled out the influential *Kölnische Zeitung*, asking what position that paper would have taken if, instead of two hundred thousand Armenians, ten rich families from Düsseldorf or Cologne had been slaughtered.[2]

In Berlin, at the Tonhalle, a large auditorium, with Johannes Lepsius on the podium next to him, Pastor Wilhelm Faber told a packed audience:

Turkey is the showplace of Christian persecutions which are far bloodier and more horrible than those of Emperor Nero. The darkest pages of the 19th century have become blacker. This is not a political meeting. We are not interested in the political situation of the Armenians but only in their misery. These persecutions are a disgrace to our century. The press must perform its duty and its obligation. European journalists must go there and see for themselves. Public opinion must rise up and be heard. This concerns the voice of humane Europe.

This statement was greeted by extended thunderous applause.[3]

Mass meetings such as these were attended by plainclothesmen and local police chiefs, who reported in detail directly to Berlin on their substance and composition. But even though the German government took extraordinary steps to prevent embarrassment to its Turkish ally, it could not curtail Lepsius's German crusade to recruit support and collect money for Armenia.

By the end of 1896 Sultan Abdul Hamid's persecution of the Armenians—which had taken almost two hundred thousand lives in barely three years—was on the wane, and concomitantly, the German government's interest in Lepsius's activities declined. He now enjoyed a greater freedom to establish his orphanages, schools, and medical stations in Turkey, tending to the needs of a battered and brutalized nation.

Why in the second decade of his reign did this sultan turn his wrath on the defenseless Armenians—among the hardest-working and most reliable taxpaying elements of the country—a people who had been hailed throughout successive Ottoman regimes as the "most loyal nation"?

The answer to the question is complex. It oversimplifies the case to attribute the turnabout to religious differences, although undoubtedly the fact that the Armenians—like the Greeks and the Bulgarians —were Christians played a role in sparking the sultan's fanaticism. On assuming power, he had announced that all his subjects were to be known as Ottomans, that Islam was the state religion, and that he was appointing himself the Ottoman Empire's caliph, or spiritual head.

With the breakup of his multinational domain increasingly imminent, the sultan seemed to be presiding over an ever-shrinking empire. Greek and Bulgarian partisans fought Ottoman forces in Macedonia; a rebellion had to be suppressed in Crete; Christian peasants in Bosnia and Herzegovina revolted against Ottoman landlords. Nationalist movements seeking independence from repressive Ottoman rule were in wide evidence, and the Armenians were developing a particularly strong political consciousness, derived largely from progressive Western ideas. The extreme measures adopted by Abdul Hamid appear to have been the only way he knew to check the progress of the most rapidly developing nation still under his rule. This progress was being encouraged by European reform proposals, which he viewed as intervention in the internal affairs of his empire. When the European powers—reluctant to destabilize Ottoman rule and thereby damage their own economic interests—refrained from pursuing their proposals by means more forceful than words, the sultan showed his contempt by instituting the severest repressive measures yet against his Armenian subjects.

Abdul Hamid was an absolute autocrat, gripped by an irrational fear of everyone around him. His suspicions were so deep-seated that despite an existing wall surrounding his Yildiz Palace, he built a second wall and multiplied his Albanian Imperial Guards many times over. He viewed his courtiers as hypocrites and parasites, and ruled by what he considered divine right.

That the massacres he instituted were limited—in contrast to what followed under the Young Turks—may indicate that he did not intend "to exterminate the Armenians but merely to teach them a lesson . . . to abort their renaissance, and to restore an old order."[4] That order consisted of total compliance with the sultan's authoritarian rule and the exclusion of liberal ideas and separatist movements. Despite the limited nature of his persecution, however, the slaughterof two hundred thousand defenseless people and the widespread destruction of homes and villages cannot be minimized. By any standards, Abdul Hamid II stands as one of history's cruelest despots.

A curious theory was suggested by a German journalist, Bernhard Stern, who served for many years as a Turkish correspondent for the *Berliner Tageblatt* and Vienna's *Neue Freie Presse*. Stern did not hide his pro-Turkish views either in his news reports or in the two books that he wrote about Abdul Hamid II. In one of these books, devoted to the sultan's family, Stern suggested that the sultan's massacres of the Armenians were an attempt to deny his own Armenian side. He wrote: "Abdul Hamid's biological mother, who is no longer alive, was an Armenian slave. A palace eunuch who had known her told me that the Sultan was, to an astonishing degree, the image of his mother."[5] Stern's theory is supported by the fact that among native Turks the sultan was popularly known by the Armenian name of Bedros, because of his Armenian features.[6]

These observations, however, do not bring us any closer to understanding Abdul Hamid's nihilistic compulsions. Now, almost a century later, there are still many unanswered questions about the motivations of the "Red Sultan," as the French dubbed Abdul Hamid II for his bloody reign. The definitive explanation for the madness that held him in thrall in those closing years of the nineteenth century has yet to be written, but it may lie in the secrets of the Ottoman Archives in Constantinople, to which Western scholars have sought access for decades.

A clear-eyed judgment of the Turkish monarch, however, can be found in an evaluation some two decades later by the German ambassador, who, in seeking to provide an historical perspective, cabled his superiors:

> In the final years of his reign, Sultan Abdul Hamid, with his infamous massacres of the Armenians, had gone to such extremes in his pitiless policy of annihilation, that even in the Orient which has long been accustomed to the shedding of blood, he sent a shudder through every soul.[7]

Meanwhile, other forces were beginning to uncoil within Turkey that would unleash a terror so unparalleled in history as to convince Johannes Lepsius that Abdul Hamid's atrocities had been merely the prelude to a greater and more barbaric drama.

While the Armenian nation huddled in fear and despair, abandoned to the mercies of a ruthless tyrant, a movement was developing among liberally oriented Turks that would at first inspire new hope but in the end create new traumas for the persecuted loyal nation.

Turkish émigrés had been gathering over the years in European centers such as Paris, London, and Geneva to discuss the despotism and corruption of Ottoman rule. While the initial character of the movement was theoretical and intellectual, it became increasingly political as the influence of Western institutions pervaded its ranks. In 1889 the movement took on sharper focus when four Muslim medical students in Constantinople conceived the idea of overthrowing Abdul Hamid II. Appalled by the sultan's excesses, especially by his policy of exterminating Armenians and other minorities, which had aroused widespread revulsion abroad, these four became the nucleus of a revolutionary organization that would eventually become the Committee of Union and Progress—in Turkish *Ittihad ve Terraki*—popularly known as the Young Turks.

The committee soon grew to twelve members, each identified by a number to maintain secrecy. This group elected officers and drew up a simple but straightforward program: to agitate for progress within the reigning dynasty, and to institute reforms for the entire empire "not in favor of a single nationality, but in favor of all the Ottomans." The movement grew rapidly as other like-minded Turks joined it, among them a young letter carrier from Salonika named Mehmed Talaat.[8] When large-scale arrests of the would-be revolutionaries were made three years later, the Young Turks withdrew and began plotting an attack on Yildiz Palace.

The sultan was now engaged in the duplicitous strategem of resuming the massacres throughout Anatolia while appearing to accept the European reform proposals. The European powers remained silent, realizing that nothing short of armed intervention would influence the sultan. But two events that took place in August 1896 did for a brief time stir Europe.

The first was a sensational incident instigated by a group of Armenians, desperate to attract world attention to the plight of their nation. Twenty-five members of the ARF stormed the Ottoman Bank in Constantinople and threatened to blow it up if their demands were not met. These demands included judicial and tax reforms; freedom of worship, education, and the press; supervision of the Armenian provinces by a European high commissioner; and an amnesty for all Armenian prisoners. After thirteen hours, their inexperience prevailed—their leader was only seventeen years old—and, losing their will, they gave in. Fifteen managed to escape. But what then transpired only confirmed the nature and scope of Ottoman ruthlessness. In the presence of Europeans and in full view of foreign embassies, bands of Turks dressed in turbans and robes and armed with clubs and iron bars suddenly appeared in the streets of Constantinople. An orgy of killing ensued that lasted for two days and took more than six thousand Armenian lives.[9]

The second event was the coup that the Young Turks had been planning for three years. Their plot was discovered by the sultan's spies and aborted. In contrast to the Armenians, however, they got off lightly—the conspirators were exiled to distant areas of the empire. Once beyond Turkey's borders, they continued to plot an eventual takeover of power.

In Europe agitation on behalf of the Armenians began to spread. The official English view was reflected in a series of Foreign Ministry publications called "Blue Books," describing the massacres, while former Prime Minister Gladstone, now an elder statesman, lectured throughout the country, telling large audiences: "To serve Armenia is to serve civilization." Shocked by the slaughter following the Ottoman Bank seizure, Gladstone emerged from retirement at eighty-six for a final speech in Liverpool, where he referred to "the unspeakable Turk" as "a disgrace to civilization and a curse to mankind."[10]

In Germany the official view was remarkably different. Kaiser Wilhelm II, within months of assuming the throne in 1888, had made a much-touted trip to Constantinople to cultivate Sultan Abdul Hamid II. The German monarch now made another high-profile visit, at a time when no other European statesman wished to be seen or associated with a tyrant responsible for the slaughter of almost a quarter of a million Armenians.

Working privately against the kaiser was Johannes Lepsius, aided by his Armenian colleague Toumayan and countless German clergymen and intellectuals. Lepsius was traveling back and forth to Turkey on behalf of his German Orient Mission, establishing his orphanages and medical stations—these already totaled seven—as well as a German hospital in Urfa.

The Ittihadists, as the Young Turks were called, had made Salonika their headquarters and plotted their moves in this city so as to be out of reach of the sultan's agents. Among their more prominent members now were the former postal clerk Talaat, who had become an official of the Salonika Post and Telegraph Office, and an imposing army officer, Colonel Enver. So promising was their proposed reform program that even the ARF joined with them in plotting the overthrow of Abdul Hamid. Not that the Armenians hadn't tried it themselves: Once in 1905 they had almost succeeded in assassinating the sultan with a dynamite-laden carriage as he said his prayers inside a mosque in Constantinople.

In July 1908 the Young Turks forced a bloodless revolution as Turkish troops and Christian insurgents joined the Ittihadists and helped bring them to power. A constitutional government was proclaimed and rejoicing broke out all over the country as Christians, Muslims, and Jews embraced openly. Nine months later prosultan Muslim reactionaries launched a bloody counterrevolutionary coup in which many Ittihadists were killed, including some parliamentary deputies when the sultan's partisans invaded the building. Ittihadist leaders went into hiding, among them Talaat, who was given shelter by one of the Armenian leaders.[11]

The sultan's brief return was marked by yet another massacre, in Adana, in southern Turkey, where some thirty thousand Armenians perished in four days. But his countercoup lacked broad support, and within weeks he was deposed again and exiled by his brother Muhammad V, who was formally invested as sultan. The Ittihad ve Terraki dissolved itself as a secret organization and became the ruling party of Ottoman Turkey, but it was still not in total control of the empire. Finally, in 1913, the Ittihadists—led by Colonel Enver Pasha, his close associate Talaat, and several hundred partisans—

invaded the Sublime Porte, murdered the war minister and forced out the grand vizier. Enver, thirty-one years old and known as the "little Napoleon," appointed himself minister of war; Talaat, thirty-nine years old, was named minister of the interior; and a third prominent Ittihadist, Jemal Pasha, became military governor of Constantinople and later minister of the Navy. Close to this ruling triumvirate was another figure who would play a major role in the coming events— the executive secretary of the Ittihad Committee, Dr. Nazim.

Although initially liberal, the Ittihadists included some fiercely chauvinistic elements that quickly came to dominate the party. These elements espoused an ideology called pan-Turkism or pan-Turanianism, which envisaged a super-Turkey unified with all the lost lands of the past in East and Central Asia (Turan)—a warlike empire harking back to the earlier Turkic glories of Attila the Hun, Genghis Khan, and Tamerlane. In its striving for racial purity, pan-Turkism was not dissimilar from the ideology the German National Socialists adopted only two decades later. Armed now with authority as well as ideology, the Ittihadists suspended the constitutional rights they had reintroduced, making it clear that they had no intention of mollifying the nationalities in Turkey or of meeting Armenian demands for reforms.

American Ambassador Henry Morgenthau, arriving later the same year in Constantinople, provided personal evaluations of the Young Turks and their system of government in his memoirs. Talaat, Enver, and Jemal, he wrote, displayed an "insatiable lust for personal power." Morgenthau saw Turkey as a nation governed "by a small, wicked oligarchy at the top . . . a determined band of adventurers . . . with Talaat as the most powerful leader," whose preferred techniques included "assassination and judicial murder."[12]

On the eve of World War I, the Ittihadist triumvirate began to lay plans for an expansionist conquest to the east, beginning with neighboring Azerbaijan, intended to achieve unification with Turkic peoples of the Crimea, Caucasus, and Central Asia. The Christian Armenians represented the single largest obstacle within Turkey to racial uniformity.

With most of Europe hostile to the Sublime Porte, the Ittihadist leaders could look for support to only one European power. Imperial Germany had always stood by Imperial Turkey—the kaisers and the sultans always on the best of terms, especially in military affairs. As far back as the 1830s, there had been German advisors to the Ottoman Army, such as Count Helmuth von Moltke; and in the 1880s under Abdul Hamid, Baron Colmar von der Goltz. This special entente was not compromised by the sultan's overthrow. Between 1909 and 1911 Enver Pasha had served as Ottoman military attaché in Berlin, where he was able to observe Prussian military tactics. Enver, the most Germanophile of the Ittihadist triumvirate, welcomed the arrival in December 1913 of a German military mission headed by General Liman von Sanders, who made it clear he was a personal representative of Kaiser Wilhelm II.

As Morgenthau later attested, in early 1914, even before the outbreak of war, Germans in the Turkish Army included a chief of staff (General Bronssart von Schellendorff), an inspector general (von Sanders), and scores of German officers who held high commands.* Further, two German warships, the *Goeben* and the *Breslau*, renamed the *Yavuz* and the *Medilli*, sailed into Turkish waters in August 1914 while German Admiral Wilhelm Souchon restructured the Ottoman Navy. But the alliance with Germany went beyond military needs. The importation of prized German technical skills and materials, together with desperately needed economic assistance, into a backward Turkey was deemed essential to the realization of the reformers' ideological dreams.

While Minister of War Enver Pasha was cementing military ties with Berlin, Germany was also playing a role in resolving Turkey's economic problems. European powers had long viewed Turkey as a profitable extension of their own interests; one of the most lucrative economic adventures had been the construction of railroads linking Europe with the Near East and its most valuable resource—oil.

Although Chancellor Bismarck had evinced little interest in the Ottoman Empire, Kaiser Wilhelm II, working through Bismarck's successors, had a very different view. Following the military infiltration that had already taken place, the kaiser sought economic and commercial penetration as well, and intended to achieve this by means of a railway linking Berlin with the Persian Gulf.

Until 1888 there had been a serious dearth of railways in the Turkish parts of Asia Minor because no capitalist would risk funds without substantial guarantees—guarantees the Turkish Government

---

*Walker notes that von Sanders brought forty-two German officers with him and that von Goltz had reorganized the Ottoman Army between 1883 and 1888 (Walker, *Armenia—The Survival of a Nation*, p. 197 [see note 9]).

could not provide. Eventually a way was found—actually a system of tithes through railway areas—which generated European competition for the concession. But despite the open spirit of the competition, Turkey's pro-German prejudice was the determining factor: When the contest was ultimately narrowed down to German and British banks, the Germans won easily. The plans called for the Berlin-to-Baghdad Railway to extend for 1,550 miles, its construction to be supervised by German engineers. By the time the Young Turks came to power, thousands of German engineers were dispersed throughout Anatolia, employing innumerable Armenian laborers for the formidable task.[13]

Meanwhile, individual Germans, such as Johannes Lepsius, traveled freely between Germany and Turkey. But the Ittihadists looked upon him and his staffs of doctors, nurses, schoolteachers, and missionaries as humanitarian do-gooders who could not be allowed to interfere in the government's larger plans. These were soon accelerated by drastic events taking place in the outer reaches of the empire. Within three years of the Young Turks' accession to power in 1908, the empire had lost all of its European possessions, totaling some five hundred thousand square miles and five million people. With the final departure of the Greeks and the Bulgarians, the Armenians remained the only large Christian minority. In the eyes of fanatic proponents of pan-Turkism, the Armenians were therefore not only infidels but obstacles to the achievement of the larger dream.

In preparation for that day, Enver took two major steps that were to impact heavily on the Armenian nation. On August 2, 1914, driven by his zeal for an alliance, he signed a secret agreement with Germany stipulating that if Russia entered the war against the Central Powers, Turkey would join them. By engaging Russia, Enver saw the means of expanding into Central Asia. (Three months later the *Goeben* and the *Breslau* attacked Russian warships and opened fire on Odessa. In consequence, Turkey entered the war on October 30, 1914.) Enver's second major step took place on August 5, when he ordered that a paramilitary "special organization" (*Teshkilat-i Mahsusa*) be set up under the aegis of the Ittihadist Committee, led by Behaeddin Shakir, whose function it was to carry out decisions of the Ittihad party.

On paper this was a routine administrative action. In actuality Shakir organized the Teshkilat-i Mahsusa by throwing open the prisons of Anatolia and releasing its worst criminals—murderers, thieves, and rapists. This "special organization" was then given the task of eliminating the Armenian nation—a final solution that would cleanse Turkey of its most troublesome minority in the quest for a racially pure Turanian empire.*

The curtain rose in Constantinople on April 24, 1915, when, over a three-day period, usually at night, some six hundred prominent Armenian intellectuals—writers, poets, editors, journalists, doctors, composers, and political and religious leaders—were arrested, deported to remote areas, and killed, except for a mere dozen who managed to escape.†

This action was taken on the authority of an order that had been circulated a week earlier to governors, provincial authorities, and mayors. The order speculated that following a possible defeat in the war, England and Russia might exploit the Armenian people "to serve their interests." Therefore, "to forestall the presentation of the Armenian Question . . . taking advantage of the freedom the war has granted us, the government has decided to end that Question once and for all by deporting the Armenians to the deserts of Arabia."

Branding as an enemy of Turkey and the Muslim religion anyone who protected the Armenians, the order announced that its implementation would be undertaken by local organs of the Committee of Union and Progress "at sunrise on April 24." The order was signed by three officials of the committee: Talaat, Enver, and Nazim.[14]

There is good cause to doubt that such long-range reasoning was the true motivation for the issuance of this order at this particular time. There were other more immediate concerns, some specious, some completely unfounded.

Only eight days before, the lakeside town of Van in southeastern Turkey, about one hundred miles from both the Persian and Russian borders, had erupted in what was to be known as the Van Uprising.

---

*Morgenthau, who saw Talaat almost daily and, as will be seen, objected vehemently to the measures taken against the Armenians, was also aware of Turkish actions against Greeks and Jews, but never to the degree employed against the Armenians.

†The list was drawn up by Talaat Pasha's Armenian agent, Harootiun Mugerditchian, whom Tehlirian killed later in Constantinople. One of the handful who miraculously survived was the composer Komitas (Soghomon Soghomonian), revered as no other Armenian by all his compatriots. He lost his sanity at sight of the massacre, was taken to Paris, and died in an asylum in 1935.

The governor of Van, Jevdet Bey, who happened to be Enver Pasha's brother-in-law, had organized a reign of terror in the guise of a search for arms, his gendarmes killing Armenians at the slightest sign of resistance (the Armenian population numbered approximately thirty thousand). On April 16 four leaders of the Armenian community, who had been asked by the governor to investigate a demonstration in a nearby village, were murdered on his orders. The Armenians viewed this bloody deception as the final outrage and took up arms to protect themselves. The Turkish Army besieged Van for a month, until, facing the threat of a rescuing force from the Russian Army, the governor bombarded the town one last time and withdrew all Turkish forces. The Ittihadists, totally ignoring the executions that had preceded and motivated the reprisals, claimed that the uprising had begun as an Armenian assault on Turks.

But even before Van, similar assaults had taken place in other towns such as Moush in eastern Anatolia and Zeitun in south-central Turkey, where Armenians had fought back against Turkish military excesses. These were among the first acts of terror inflicted on the Armenian communities in five years, since before the sultan's fall, and they were met by shock. Armenian political leaders had placed considerable faith in the Ittihadists, and for the first time they began to realize that the great promises in the Constitution of 1908 were mere words on paper. Thousands saw no future left in Turkey and fled east, to Russian Armenia, in the spring of 1914.

This massive flight aroused Turkish fears about Armenian collaboration with Russia, Turkey's age-old enemy. They became even more acute when several prominent Armenians joined the exodus. Among them was Armen Garo, one of the leaders of the Ottoman Bank seizure, who was later to mastermind Nemesis from Boston. Garo assumed command of the Second Battalion of the Russian Army, consisting of Armenian escapees from Ottoman Turkey.*

Another development compounded the problem for the Turks—the landing that same April weekend of Allied troops at Gallipoli in a vain attempt to capture Constantinople. Although the Turkish Army, led by Field Marshal Liman von Sanders and his deputy

---

*The number of Armenians who fought with the Russians in the czar's army is not precise but historian Richard G. Hovannisian has suggested between 100,000 and 150,000, with seven contingents of volunteers from Ottoman Turkey. An "Armenian Legion," which served under British General Allenby in Syria and Palestine, was also formed by Armenian volunteers from the United States. (*The Republic of Armenia*, University of California Press, Berkeley and Los Angeles, 1971, p. 14.)

Mustafa Kemal, later defeated the Allies, at that time, the landings aroused Turkish fears of an uprising in Constantinople, timed to coincide with the attack. These apprehensions added to the circumstances that prompted the Ittihadists to arrest, deport, and eliminate the leaders of the Armenian intellectual community on the night of April 24.

Three weeks later, Talaat Pasha, in his capacity as minister of internal affairs, accused the Armenian people of treasonous intentions and of being on the verge of a general rebellion. Armenian soldiers in the Ottoman Army, who had been disarmed and placed in labor battalions, were taken into isolated areas and shot. Talaat issued further orders that the general population be deported to "relocation centers." This seemed on the surface almost a benign administrative measure prompted by Turkish security fears. But these centers proved to be concentration camps in desert areas of Syria and Mesopotamia, at that time still part of the Ottoman Empire. Deir Zor—a name that has inspired the most tragic poetry in the Armenian language—was the final destination of the ever-dwindling caravans of deportees, which had traveled three hundred miles across mountains and deserts in peak summer heat.

During the march the men were massacred and women and girls stripped naked and assaulted. Many women killed themselves and their children; the rest were forcibly converted to Islam and enslaved in Turkish households and harems. Those who survived the long marches died of starvation, disease, and exposure. Charged with the organization and execution of this genocidal operation involving more than a million people was Dr. Behaeddin Shakir and his twelve thousand-man force of Teshkilat-i Mahsusa (special organization)—convicted criminals released from prison and dressed in the uniforms of Turkish gendarmes.

These shocking events, which began in 1915 and continued into 1916, were observed by hundreds of eyewitnesses.* Many who were employed on the staffs of Johannes Lepsius's orphanages saw huge caravans of women, children, and old people shuffling miserably through towns and villages, some left dying by the roadside.†

---

*The *New York Times* ran close to two hundred stories on the atrocities.
†That the brutality was practiced in areas outside Turkey was described by the director of one of Lepsius's orphanages in Northern Persia, where 850 headless corpses were taken out of wells—headless because the Turkish commander had promised his troops a reward for each head brought to him. Nearby, Turkish troops carried the head of the Russian consul on a bayonet as they marched by.

But most of the official accounts came from the many consular officers—especially those of Germany and the United States—stationed in Turkish cities. Both countries' archives still contain hundreds of diplomatic cables recounting the Armenian tragedy. Those cables were signed for the most part by those two countries' ambassadors, both of whom soon found themselves locked in a struggle of wills with the Young Turk government to which they had been accredited.

In 1913 President Woodrow Wilson had appointed one of his most ardent supporters, banker and developer Henry Morgenthau, as United States ambassador to the Sublime Porte.* Of German birth, Morgenthau quickly got to know his German counterpart, Baron Hans von Wangenheim, a career diplomat of thirty years' experience who had been personally selected by the kaiser. When Turkey entered the war in late 1914, Morgenthau discovered that he would be representing more than the United States, for, when the Allies severed relations with Turkey, the United States became the sole representative of the interests in Turkey of Great Britain, France, Russia, Italy, and other Allies. Wangenheim, as Morgenthau soon learned, was also kept busy; but with a quite different perspective. The German presence in Turkey was overwhelming, ranging from the Army and Navy to the troops and engineers who were omnipresent throughout Anatolia, not to mention the orphanages and hospitals and their German staffs, largely the creation of Johannes Lepsius. Thus when Turkey entered the war—to Enver Pasha's great pleasure†—Morgenthau beheld his German colleague behaving more like a proconsul of ancient Rome than an ambassador. The situation became even more trying when the Armenian deportations began and Morgenthau found himself pleading with the Turks to desist from such horrors and with the Germans to exert pressure on their Turkish ally.

The record that Morgenthau established in his four years in Istanbul, both as American ambassador and as a civilized human being, is exemplary. From the time of the Constantinople arrests until his departure in 1916 (to aid Wilson in his reelection campaign), Morgenthau documented every move of the Ittihad Committee and every

---

*Morgenthau was the father of Henry, Jr., who was secretary of the treasury under President Franklin Roosevelt and the author of the famous plan to convert Germany into an agricultural state after World War II—known popularly as the "potato patch" solution to the German problem.
†But not to Mustafa Kemal's, who represented the only opposition to alliance with Germany in Turkey's upper echelons. This so enraged Enver that he dispatched Kemal to Bulgaria as Turkish military attaché.

conversation with its leaders, especially Talaat and Enver. He was assisted and supported in his duties by his ten American consuls, stationed throughout the Ottoman Empire. Some of these consuls, especially those in Anatolia, were eyewitnesses to the deportations, and their reports present the most accurate account of the devastating events that engulfed the Armenian nation.

The reports to Morgenthau, which he forwarded to the State Department, from three consuls in particular—Leslie A. Davis in Harput, Oscar S. Heizer in Trebizond, and Jesse B. Jackson in Aleppo—constitute the most accurate documentation of the deportations and massacres from official American sources.

These dispatches began coming in after Turkey's entry into the war in late 1914 and, although initially fragmentary, they made Morgenthau aware that all was not going well with the Armenians in the provinces. He revealed even greater knowledge when he wrote: "Up to the outbreak of the European War, not a day had passed in the Armenian *vilayets* without its outrages and its murders." But after the Constantinople arrests, the Van uprising, and the initiation of mass deportations in 1915, the Turkish government forbade the use of cyphers in the messages between the American consulates and the embassy and also instituted censorship of mail. This only confirmed Morgenthau's suspicions that the Ittihadists wished to hide something genuinely terrible that was transpiring in the Ottoman Empire. But it did not put a halt to communications between the embassy and the ten outlying consulates, which—no longer able to send coded reports—found other means by which to communicate safely with Constantinople.

Excerpts will attest to the compassion of the American officers for the welfare of the Armenian minority in their consular districts. Thus, Davis on July 11, 1915, from Harput in central Turkey:

> It has just been announced that every Armenian, *without exception*, must go. . . . I have visited their encampment a number of times and have talked with some. . . . A more pitiable sight cannot be imagined. They are . . . ragged, filthy, hungry and sick. . . .
> That is not surprising in view of the fact that they have been on the road for nearly two months with no change of clothing, no chance to wash, no shelter and little to eat.
>
> I watched them once when their food was brought. Wild animals could not be worse. They rushed upon the guards who carried the

food and the guards beat them back with clubs, hitting hard
enough to kill them sometimes. As one walks through the camps,
mothers offer their children and beg me to take them. In fact, the
Turks have been taking their choice of these children and girls for
slaves, or worse. There are very few men among them, as most of
them have been killed on the road. . . . Many died of sickness and
exhaustion. By continuing to drive these people on in this way, it
will be possible to dispose of all of them in a comparatively short
time. . . . The entire movement seems to be the most thoroughly
organized and effective massacre this country has ever seen. . . .
On Monday, many men were arrested in Harput and put in prison.
At daybreak Tuesday they were taken out and made to march towards an almost uninhabited mountain. There were about 800 in
all and they were tied together in groups of fourteen each . . . they
were without food or water. All their money and much of their
clothing had been taken away. On Wednesday they were taken to a
valley . . . all made to sit down. Then the gendarmes began shooting them until nearly all were killed. Some who had not been killed
by bullets were disposed of with knives and bayonets. Among
those killed was the Treasurer of the American College. . . . The
same thing has been done systematically in the villages. . . . We
know too much about what is happening in the interior of Turkey
and the authorities do not intend to let any Americans leave here
alive to tell about it. . . . I do think the life of every American here
is in danger and the danger is increasing. If all of the missionaries
can get away safely, I shall feel greatly relieved.[15]

Heizer's reports from Trebizond, located in northern Turkey on
the Black Sea, included this message of June 28, 1915:

As I am not permitted to use the cypher code, it does not seem best
to send an open telegram to the Embassy . . . but I have talked
with my Austro-Hungarian colleague who has the privilege to use a
code . . . On July 1 (in three days), the entire Armenian population of Trebizond and vicinity including men, women and children
will be obliged to turn over to the government such property as
they cannot take with them, and start for the interior. . . . It is impossible to convey an idea of the consternation and despair that
this proclamation has produced. . . . I have seen strong, proud
wealthy men weep like children. . . . Many are providing themselves with poison. . . . All horses, wagons and vehicles have been
requisitioned for military purposes and the only way for these peo-

ple to go is on foot, a journey of sixty days. . . . At this season of the year in the heat and dust it is simply impossible for women and children and old men to start on such a journey.[16]

On July 28 Heizer wrote:

On Saturday . . . the proclamation regarding the deportation of all Armenians was posted in the streets. On Thursday all the streets were guarded by gendarmes with fixed bayonets and the work of driving the Armenians from their homes began. Groups of men, women and children with loads and bundles on their backs were collected . . . near the Consulate and when a hundred or so had been gathered they were driven past the Consulate on the road . . . toward Erzinga in the heat and dust by gendarmes with fixed bayonets . . . Three groups numbering some 6000 were sent from here during the first three days and the smaller groups from Trebizond and the vicinity sent later numbered about 4000. The weeping and wailing of the women and children was most heart-rending. . . . There were clergymen, merchants, bankers, lawyers, mechanics, tailors and men from every walk of life. . . . The whole Mohammedan population knew these people were to be their prey from the beginning and they were treated as criminals. . . . Many persons who had goods which they could have sold if they had been allowed to do so were obliged to start off on foot without funds and with what they could gather up from their homes and carry on their backs. Such persons naturally soon became so weak that they fell behind and were bayoneted and thrown into the river and their bodies floated down past Trebizond to the sea, or else lodged in the shallow river on rocks where they remained for 10 to 12 days and putrefied to the disgust of the travelers who were obliged to pass that way. I have talked with eyewitnesses who state that there were many naked bodies . . . in the river 15 days after the affair occurred and the smell was something terrible.

Heizer described some of the events preceding the deportations:

During the early days before the deportations commenced, a large caique . . . was loaded with men supposed to be members of the Armenian Committee and sent off towards Samsun. Two days later, a certain Vartan, a Russian subject and one of those left in the boat, returned over land to Trebizond badly wounded about the head and so crazy he could not make himself understood. All he could say was "boom, boom." He was arrested by the

authorities and taken to the municipal hospital where he died the
following day. A Turk said this boat was not far from Trebizond
behind another boat containing gendarmes who proceeded to kill
all the men and throw them overboard.

He reported grim details of the fate of the girls and young women:

> The plan to save the children by placing them in schools or or-
> phanages in Trebizond under the care of a committee . . . has been
> abandoned and the girls are now being given exclusively to
> Mohammedan families. . . . The best-looking of the older girls who
> were retained as caretakers in the orphanages are kept in houses for
> the pleasure of members of the gang which seems to rule affairs
> here. . . . A member of the Committee of Union and Progress has
> ten of the handsomest girls in a house in the central part of the city
> for the use of himself and friends. . . . The 1000 Armenian houses
> are being emptied of furniture by the police . . . everything of
> value is being stored in large buildings. . . . There is no attempt at
> classification and the idea of keeping the property in "bales under
> the protection of the government to be returned to the owners on
> their return" is simply ridiculous. . . . A crowd of Turkish women
> and children follow the police about like a lot of vultures and seize
> anything they can lay their hands on. . . . I see this performance
> every day with my own eyes.

And he provided further confirmation of the atrocities:

> The German Consul told me that he did not believe the Armenians
> would be permitted to return to Trebizond even after the war. . . . I
> have just been talking with a young man who has been performing
> his military service in the *inshaat taburu* (construction regiment)
> working on the roads. . . . He told me that fifteen days ago all the
> Armenians, about 180, were separated from the other workmen
> and marched off some distance from the camp and shot. He heard
> the report of the rifles and later was one of the number sent to bury
> the bodies which he stated were all naked, having been stripped of
> clothing. . . . A number of bodies of women and children have
> lately been thrown up by the sea onto the sandy beach below the
> walls of the Italian monastery here in Trebizond and were buried
> by Greek women. . . . Further details might be added of atrocities
> committed upon the Armenians but it is difficult to verify all the
> stories circulated and I have confined myself to those I believe to
> be correct.[17]

Jackson's reports are particularly piercing because Aleppo had become a focal collection point for the deportations. Located in Syria—then part of the Ottoman Empire—Aleppo was about 300 miles from the heart of Anatolia, where the caravans originated. But, more important, Aleppo was the main transit point for the caravans on their way through the Euphrates region to their final destination of Deir Zor. Having arrived at Aleppo, the survivors still had another 175 miles to march through the desert before reaching Deir Zor. Thus, Aleppo was in many ways the best-located consulate—American or German—from which to observe the deportations firsthand.

On June 5 Jackson reported to the embassy:

> There is a living stream of Armenians pouring into Aleppo from the surrounding towns and villages. They all come under a heavily armed escort and consist of old men, women and children; all the young and middle-aged men have been taken for military service . . . those not fortunate enough to have means of transport are forced to make the journey on foot . . . they are forced to continue the journey to some out of the way place where there is neither food, shelter nor means of possible existence . . . they are being scattered over the desert to starve or die of disease in the burning heat . . . more than 25,000 people have already been taken from here and scattered in various directions. . . . In the interior a perfect reign of terror exists, especially at Diarbekir . . . great numbers have been beaten to death. Such has been the situation here since about April 25 . . . outrages are being practised daily upon a defenseless and inoffensive people that demand nothing more than to be given a chance to eke out at best a miserable existence. . . . It is without doubt a carefully planned scheme to thoroughly extinguish the Armenian race.[18]

Again from Jackson, on August 3:

> On August 2 about 800 middle-aged and old women and children under the age of 10 arrived afoot from Diarbekir, after 45 days enroute and in the most pitiable condition. . . . The Governor of Deir Zor who is now in Aleppo says there are 15,000 Armenian refugees there. . . . As 90 percent of the commerce of the interior is in Armenian hands, the country is facing ruin . . . hundreds of prominent business men other than Armenians face bankruptcy. . . . The Germans are being blamed on every hand, for if they have not

directly ordered this wholesale slaughter . . . they at least con-
done it.[19]

On August 19 Jackson wrote:

Household belongings were left behind to be taken by the first
plunderer to arrive. Most of the merchants of the city being
Armenians, their stocks are likewise disappearing. It is a gigantic
plundering scheme as well as a final blow to extinguish the race.
. . . Since August 1, the German Bagdad railway has brought nine
trains each of fifteen carloads of these unfortunate people to
Aleppo . . . making about 20,000 that have so far arrived in
Aleppo. . . . They all relate harrowing tales of hardships, abuse,
robbery and atrocities committed en route. . . .

Travelers from the interior have related to the writer that the
beaten paths are lined with corpses of the victims. . . . Conservative persons well-informed on the questions place the total loss of
life up to August 15 at over 500,000.[20]

Finally, on September 29, taking stock of the overall situation,
Jackson wrote:

The deportation of Armenians from their homes by the Turkish
Government has continued with a persistence and perfection of
plan that it is impossible to conceive in those directly carrying it
out . . . at least 100,000 have arrived afoot . . . many having left
their homes before Easter, deprived of all their worldly possessions, without money, sparsely clad, some naked from the treatment by their escorts and the despoiling population en route . . .
So severe has been the treatment that careful estimates place the
number of survivors at only 15 percent of those originally deported. On this basis, the number of those surviving even this far
being less than 150,000 up to September 21, there seems to have
been about 1,000,000 persons lost up to this date.[21]

Ambassador Morgenthau did far more than merely relay these
reports to Washington. He often took the initiative with the State
Department, such as in this excerpt from a cable on July 10 to
Secretary of State Robert Lansing:

Persecution of Armenians assuming unprecedented proportions.
Reports from widely scattered districts indicate systematic attempt
to uproot peaceful Armenian populations and through arbitrary
arrests, terrible tortures, wholesale expulsions and deportations

from one end of the Empire to the other, accompanied by frequent instances of rape, pillage and murder, turning into massacre, to bring destruction and destitution on them. These measures are not in response to popular or fanatical demand but are purely arbitrary and directed from Constantinople in the name of military necessity, often in districts where no military operations are likely to take place. . . . Untold misery, disease, starvation and loss of life will go on unchecked. . . . There seems to be a systematic plan to crush the Armenian race. . . . The only embassy here which might assist in lessening these atrocities is the German. . . . The German Ambassador is about to leave on a six weeks vacation. I have impressed on him that he and his Government will have a considerable share in the odium. . . . I have repeatedly spoken to the Grand Vizier* and pleaded earnestly with the Minister of the Interior [Talaat] and the Minister of War [Enver] to stop this persecution. . . . Turkish authorities have definitely informed me that I have no right to interfere with their internal affairs.[22]

Conceding that the Turkish government was legally correct in that assertion, Morgenthau nevertheless continued to raise the subject of the treatment of the Armenians for, he wrote,

As the country which the Turks particularly wished to keep in ignorance was the United States, they resorted to the most shameless prevarications when discussing the situation with myself and with my staff.[23]

Ambassador Morgenthau sought to become involved at every opportunity, most of all when he had a new report, not just from his consuls but from unofficial sources as well. For he was armed with vast amounts of trustworthy eyewitness reports from schoolteachers, doctors, nurses, and missionaries. Two in particular were highly corroborative of the many reports he was receiving from his own consular officers.

The first was from an old and close friend, Dr. William S. Dodd, director of the American Hospital at Konia, who wrote to Mor-

*At that time the grand vizier was Said Halim Pasha, whose attitude to the Armenian plight was evident when a few days after the April 24 arrests he rejected the entreaties of two Armenian members of parliament, who were then killed, and of the Armenian Patriarch Zaven, who was exiled to Jerusalem. Said Halim was succeeded as grand vizier by Talaat Pasha in 1917.

genthau almost five months after the beginning of the deportations in April.

> The deportation is still going on in full force . . . The whip and the club are in constant use by the police and that upon women and children too. Think what it is for people, many of them cultivated, educated, refined, to be driven about in this way, like dogs by brutes. I have seen women black and blue from the beating they have received. The Vali [Governor] is a good man but almost powerless. The Ittihad Committee and the Salonika Clique rule all. . . . Hardly anything makes me so hot as the thought of the soldiers' families. The men, the fathers, brothers, sons, husbands are serving in the Turkish Army as loyally as any, and their families, their children with wives and sisters are driven off in this inhuman manner. . . . Oh, I wish you could see the abominable cruelty of the treatment and the diabolical ingenuity of the ways to strip them of their money before having them die. . . . I must add a report from Angora. . . . Some two or three weeks ago about 200 of the chief Armenians were imprisoned, then taken at night in wagons, 30 or 40 at a time, and killed . . . 18 employees of the railway and the director of the Ottoman Bank were among them. Within the last week, all the men have been taken, stripped to shirt and drawers, tied together and taken away and heard from no more. The women and girls have been distributed to the Turkish villages . . . one of the wealthiest men in Angora, whose wife and three daughters were taken away before his eyes, went crazy. . . . The saddest part of all this is our utter impotence to do anything to stay the awful deeds that are being perpetrated.[24]

The second unofficial report came from a Swedish woman, Alma Johanson, who had worked for thirteen years with the German mission in Moush. It is significant that she chose to send this report not to the German but to the American Embassy in Constantinople. She wrote in part:

> Harput has become the cemetery of the Armenians; from all directions they have been brought to Harput to be buried. There, they lie and the dogs and the vultures lick their bodies. Now and then some man throws earth over their bodies. In Harput and Mezre, the people have had to endure terrible tortures, such as their eyebrows being pulled out, their breasts cut off, their nails pulled out, their feet cut off or nails hammered into them just as they do with

horses. This is all done at night in order that others may not hear their screams and know of their agony, as soldiers stand near the prisons beating drums and blowing whistles . . . many died of these tortures. : . . The soldiers then cry—'Now let your Christ help you!' At the beginning of July, 2000 Armenian soldiers were ordered to leave for Aleppo to build roads. The people of Harput were terrified. . . . They had scarcely left when we heard that they had all been murdered and thrown in a cave. A few managed to escape who reported this to us. It was useless to protest to the Vali. The American Consul at Harput protested several times but the Vali treats him like 'air' and in a most shameful manner. . . . We knew in November that there would be a massacre. The Mayor of Moush, who was an intimate friend of Enver Pasha, declared quite openly that they would massacre the Armenians at an opportune moment and exterminate the whole race. Before the Russians arrived, they intended to first butcher the Armenians and then fight the Russians. . . . It is a story written in blood.[25]

Confronted by Ambassador Morgenthau with accusations based on reports such as these from American consuls and private eyewitnesses, Talaat and Enver became enraged, often with remarkable reactions. Once, when Morgenthau had made yet another verbal protest, Talaat retorted vehemently: "Why are you so interested in the Armenians anyway? You are a Jew, these people are Christians. Why can't you let us do with these Christians as we please?"

Morgenthau replied: "You don't seem to realize that I am not here as a Jew but as the American Ambassador. . . . I do not appeal to you in the name of any race or religion but merely as a human being."[26]

Morgenthau relates that one day Talaat made "what was perhaps the most astonishing request I ever heard." The New York Life Insurance Company and the Equitable Life of New York had done business for years among the Armenians. Talaat said: "I wish that you would get the American life insurance companies to send us a complete list of the Armenian policy holders. They are practically all dead now and have left no heirs. It of course all escheats to the State. The Government is the beneficiary now. Will you do so?"

Morgenthau lost his temper and stormed out of Talaat's office.[27]

On another occasion when Morgenthau asked why the Ittihadists would so deliberately impoverish the country by their continuing persecution of the Armenians, Talaat replied: "We care nothing about the commercial loss. We don't worry about that. . . . Our Armenian policy is absolutely fixed and nothing can change it. We will not have the Armenians anywhere in Anatolia. They can live in the desert but nowhere else."28

Although it had already become quite obvious to Morgenthau, this last statement made it eminently clear that deportation was merely a euphemism for annihilation, for report after report had indicated without any doubt that the Armenians were dying by the hundreds of thousands on the roads and in the deserts, and that the agents for this so-called deportation, the Teshkilat-i Mahsusa, were playing an infernal role.

By now the American ambassador had had his fill of Germans as well. However, one German, whom he looked on with favor and treated cordially, was Johannes Lepsius, who, in July 1915, went to Constantinople and asked Morgenthau for access to American Embassy files for information he wished to submit to the International Red Cross concerning the massacres. Morgenthau cabled Washington for permission and received a positive response. After a futile conversation with Enver Pasha, Lepsius departed for Berlin, where he continued working through his German-Armenian Society (founded in 1914), which counted among its supporters many European intellectuals, notably the German author Thomas Mann.

Remaining, however, was the omnipresent Baron von Wangenheim, on whom Morgenthau looked with far less favor. For the German ambassador, although a diplomatic colleague, was also a political adversary. Wangenheim was clearly in an unenviable position, caught between political expediency and moral truth. But just as Kaiser Wilhelm II had maintained cordial relations with Sultan Abdul Hamid, now again the kaiser's allegiance to his ally was vital to the execution of the war. Wangenheim made no secret of the fact that he had been selected for the post by the kaiser himself, so that, despite reports from his consuls describing the mind-boggling horrors being inflicted on the Armenians, on May 31, 1915, Wangenheim cabled Berlin that while the Turkish measures were "harsh," Germany "must not hinder them on principle."29

At the time Morgenthau viewed Wangenheim as a tool of Berlin who appeared indifferent to the horrors of the Armenian persecutions. And in fact, Wangenheim's early cables to Chancellor Theobald von Bethmann-Hollweg do reflect this attitude. Very soon, however, Wangenheim could no longer hide the truth from either himself or Berlin.

Official reports from the Anatolian interior reaching the embassy in Constantinople and the Foreign Ministry in Berlin were often as horrifying as those Morgenthau was sending on to Washington. The German consuls—primarily Walter Rössler in Aleppo, Max Erwin von Scheubner-Richter in Erzerum, and Dr. Bergfeld in Trebizond—no less than their American counterparts, were vivid in their descriptions of the atrocities being committed. And just as Morgenthau was receiving unofficial reports, Wangenheim too found himself reading harrowing accounts by responsible persons working in the *vilayets*.

One such report by two Red Cross nurses who had served in the German Hospital in Erzerum contained the following description:

At the beginning of June, the head of the Red Cross Mission at Erzinga told us that the Armenians had revolted at Van . . . and that the entire Armenian population of Erzinga and vicinity would be transported to Mesopotamia. . . . We heard subsequently how the defenceless Armenians had been massacred to the last one. The butchery had taken four hours. The women threw themselves on their knees. . . . They had thrown their children into the Euphrates. . . . Convoys of exiles were continuously arriving, all on their way to the slaughter . . . the victims had their hands tied behind their backs and were thrown down from the cliffs into the river. . . . This method was easier work for the murderers. . . . Twelve hours' distance from Sivas, we spent the night in a government building. For hours a gendarme sitting in front of our door crooned to himself over and over again: *"Ermenleri hep kestiler"* (The Armenians have all been killed).[30]

Another German nurse wrote that in Diarbekir six priests were stripped naked, smeared with tar, and dragged through the streets. After reporting that along the line of the Baghdad Railway, near Mosul, people were thrown alive down wells, she continued:

For a whole month corpses were observed floating down the Euphrates River nearly every day, often in batches of from two to six corpses bound together. The male corpses are in many cases hideously mutilated (sexual organs cut off, and so on), the female corpses are ripped open.[31]

Four German teachers in Aleppo wrote in a letter that was transmitted to the foreign minister in Berlin:

Our teaching work will in future lack a moral base and lose all authority in the eyes of the natives if the German Government is effectively unable to soften the brutality with which the expelled wives and children of the Armenians who have been killed are being treated. In the presence of the scenes of horror that are unfolding daily before our very eyes outside our school, our work as teachers becomes a challenge to humanity. How can we make our Armenian pupils read the story of *Snow White and the Seven Dwarfs*, how can we teach them to conjugate and decline, when next to the school their compatriots are dying of hunger? When almost naked girls, women and children, some lying on the ground, others huddled among the dying or the waiting coffins, are breathing their last breath?[32]

But if Wangenheim had any hopes that Berlin might mediate a change of Turkish policy, he was soon disabused of them by Talaat Pasha himself, who informed him, as Wangenheim reported in a cable to Berlin, that the Porte intended to make use of the war to deal with its internal Christian enemies and would not be diverted by diplomatic intervention from abroad. (In any case, there is no evidence that Berlin even tried.)

Together with his Austro-Hungarian colleague Johann Pallavicini, Wangenheim protested in a memorandum to Talaat that the mass deportations seemed hardly justified, but to no avail. Meanwhile, suffering from a worsening heart condition, Wangenheim planned a return to Berlin. But before doing so he arranged for Johannes Lepsius to visit Constantinople in order to see Enver Pasha—despite the Porte's and Berlin's hostility toward Lepsius for his humanitarian activities.

Lepsius did see Enver but despite impassioned arguments did not succeed in swaying the Turkish war minister or in obtaining permission to travel into central Turkey.[33] Profoundly disappointed, he returned to Berlin carrying—sewn into his luggage to protect his sources—the information provided by Ambassador Morgenthau (considered illegal by the German and Turkish military censors) with which he would later attack the policies of the German foreign ministry.

In 1916 he published this information in his *Report on the Situation of the Armenian People in Turkey*, later issued under the title *The Death Route of the Armenians.** The German government and the Turkish ambassador were furious when Lepsius, circumventing

*This courageous publication was undertaken by *Der Reichsbote*, the same Christian newspaper that in 1896 had published Lepsius's reports on Abdul Hamid's massacres.

the censors, circulated more than twenty thousand copies throughout Germany, a move that even caused his friends to fear for his safety.[34] In speeches and articles in the European press he called Germany "a slave of the Porte," once even making this charge in a lecture delivered to the Press Club in the Reichstag building itself. In September of that year the German Foreign Ministry forbade Lepsius to travel outside Germany, apparently unaware that he had already fled to Holland.

Before his hasty departure, however, Lepsius found the time and the means to publicize one other major event, news of which Turkish and German military censors had suppressed. This was the heroic resistance by a small colony of Armenians in the Gulf of Alexandretta to Turkish deportation orders issued in July 1915 to six villages surrounding Musa Dagh ("mountain of Moses"). When the Armenians refused to move, Turkish forces invaded the villages and the inhabitants fled, seeking refuge on Musa Dagh. For fifty-three days the Armenians repulsed intense attacks by the Turkish forces, until—learning from their scouts that French warships were in the region of the gulf—they raised flags on the mountain, one with a very visible red cross. Within hours more than four thousand Armenian men, women, and children were rescued. (This episode later became the subject of Franz Werfel's *The Forty Days of Musa Dagh*, a bestselling novel that fascinated audiences in Europe and the United States in the 1930s.)

Lepsius was too taken by the heroic nature of the Armenian resistance to allow the story to die at the hands of the censors. In 1916, in the April–June edition of his periodical *The Christian Orient and the Moslem Mission*, he published a long story with the misleading title "The Rescuing Cross: A Story of the Crusades." To deceive the military censors, he presented it in the guise of medieval history, although the title itself referred to the Red Cross flag the Armenians had raised atop Musa Dagh.*

Wangenheim left Istanbul in early July of 1915, on home leave, returned in early October, and died of a heart attack on October 24. During his absence Prince Ernst Hohenlohe-Langenburg had acted as chargé d'affaires and, after Wangenheim's death, was replaced by Count Paul Wolff-Metternich as ambassador. By late 1915 all three had been sending a barrage of cables reflecting alarm at the outrages being reported by the German consuls in the field, but the govern-

---

*I am indebted to Dr. Goltz for this little-known information.

ment in Berlin—in the persons of Chancellor Bethmann-Hollweg, Secretary of State for Foreign Affairs Gottlieb von Jagow, and his deputy Arthur Zimmermann—displayed no anxiety whatsoever about Turkey's monstrous excesses.

Berlin was far from blameless, but it is difficult to fault the successive German ambassadors—three in 1915—and their staffs, who were, after all, very much on the scene and perfectly aware that the Porte was giving them deceitful answers on the massacres. The embassy's position was stated clearly in a cable to Berlin on August 12, 1915, which began:

> The systematic slaughter of the Armenian population, expelled from their homes in recent weeks, has taken on a scope of such magnitude that it appears necessary for us to make a renewed, urgent representation that this forced march into the desert was not only tolerated but openly ordered by the Government.[35]

Although having earlier mendaciously agreed to take action and halt the measures against the Armenians, Talaat on December 22, 1915, sent a furious note that in effect rejected all German intervention, claiming that the measures were either dictated by military necessity or taken as a defense against subversion. The fraudulence of Talaat's argument was patently clear to the German Embassy. As for Berlin: "They [the German Foreign Ministry] realized that by raising the question of Armenian killings they were trespassing on the sacred precinct of Ittihadist fanaticism."[36]

The Porte then took the only remaining step regarding interference from the German Embassy—it demanded the recall of Ambassador Wolff-Metternich, which took place in September 1916. But by then the monumental catastrophe that had befallen the Armenian people was already irreparable. Wolff-Metternich's predecessor, Hohenlohe-Langenburg, had been told on August 31 by Talaat: "*La question arménienne n'existe plus.*"[37] And certainly no one can dispute the claim made by Talaat concerning the activities of the summer of 1915: "I have accomplished more toward solving the Armenian problem in three months than Abdul Hamid accomplished in thirty years!"[38]

While the Armenian deportations ceased after Talaat became grand vizier in February 1917, the persecutions continued, but at a diminished level, into 1923.

If what Henry Adams Gibbons has called "the blackest page of modern history"[39] had even one bright spot, it was the heroism shown by some Turkish provincial governors (*valis*) who, in revulsion at what the Ittihadists were ordering them to do, refused to comply.

Thus, the *vali* of Angora (now Ankara) rejected orders to deport and kill Armenians. He was supported by the police chief and the military commander. All were dismissed, and their replacements carried out the orders.[40] Elsewhere, the *vali* of Aleppo, Jelal Bey, informed Constantinople, "It is the most natural of rights to live." His successor agreed with him. Both were replaced.[41]

Many other Turkish officials disagreed with their government's policy of annihilation of the Armenians, some even organizing emergency relief and escape routes. Of these, perhaps the most courageous was the *vali* of Deir Zor. Eyewitness himself to the starved, dehydrated, and bedraggled survivors of the months-long marches through the deserts, Ali Suad Bey refused the orders to kill the Armenians. Instead, he himself cared for almost one thousand Armenian orphans whose parents had been murdered en route to this terminal destination. He was quoted as saying: "If the purpose is to slaughter them, I can neither do it myself nor have it done." The respite for these final survivors, however, was short-lived. The new *vali* proved to be both barbarous and cruel, and the atrocities resumed.

Even in the Turkish Parliament, voices of protest were sometimes raised. But dissent on this issue was hardly tolerated. A German political writer described one such incident:

> Recently . . . there arose in the Chamber and in the Senate such vehement protestations against the war . . . against the Armenian massacres, that the Minister of Internal Affairs Talaat Pasha, the civil alter ego of Enver Pasha, wished to order the arrest of 52 deputies.[42]

When some semblance of sanity returned after the near-total destruction of the nation, several estimates of the Armenian losses were made, based on prewar Turkish census figures as well as those kept by the Armenian patriarch of Constantinople. The losses were unparalleled in the annals of civilization, and some of those who made these estimates—famed British historian Arnold Toynbee,[43] for one, as well as Lepsius—conceded that they were conservative. In any event, of the two million Armenians in prewar Turkey, about one million were killed, two hundred thousand survived in their villages (some protected by Turks and Kurds), two hundred thousand women and children were forcibly converted to Islam and sold into harems, three hundred thousand crossed over into Russian Armenia, and two hundred thousand reached Deir Zor where they were driven into the Arabian desert and died of disease, exhaustion, exposure, or deliberate slaughter.[44]

Remarkably, much of this had been predicted by one of Wangenheim's own staff. Consul Max Erwin von Scheubner-Richter, stationed in Erzerum, was obviously ignored by the German embassy in Constantinople and the German government in Berlin. Scheubner-Richter's prophetic words are in his report of June 3, 1915, written barely six weeks after the Istanbul arrests and the onset of the deportations:

> The Armenian population at all levels are to be dispatched to Deir Zor in the Arabian desert. This deportation on such a large scale is synonymous with massacre because, owing to a lack of transportation, barely half will reach the final destination alive; this shall bring about not only the ruin of the Armenians but of the entire country.[45]

With Turkey's defeat on October 7, 1918, the Ittihadist regime collapsed and the three Young Turk leaders—Talaat, Enver, and Jemal—together with Drs. Nazim and Shakir, escaped from Turkey to Odessa in a German torpedo boat.

Two months later, the successor sultan, Muhammad VI, on his own initiative, issued an edict appointing an Extraordinary Military Tribunal before which all documents relating to the Young Turk government and the Armenian massacres would be examined.[46]

6

Judgment and Exile

*M*uhammad's edict was a fulfillment of the Allies' early pledge to bring to justice those responsible. That pledge had been made on May 24, 1915, exactly one month after the initiation of the Armenian holocaust, when Great Britain, France, and Russia charged that Turkish and Kurdish forces were carrying out massacres and that the Ottoman government was dealing ruthlessly with the defenseless Armenian population. In a joint declaration the Allies said:

> In view of this new crime of Turkey against humanity and civiliza-
> tion, the Allied governments publicly notify the Sublime Porte
> that they will hold personally responsible all the members of the
> Turkish Government as well as all officials who have participated
> in these massacres.[1]

Thus, while the atrocities ordered and organized by the Committee for Union and Progress were tolerated or overlooked by the kaiser's government, the Allies' outrage was certainly no secret to the Sublime Porte. Further, prominent intellectuals in Europe were firing up public sentiment on behalf of the desperate Armenians. Two of the best known, Joseph Marquart (a German and a close friend of Lepsius's) and Guy de Morgan (a French historian), demanded that the criminals responsible be brought to justice. In January 1919 Marquart even asked that his government help in the search for Talaat, Enver, and the others and hand them over to the Allies for a trial before an international court.

Actually, Talaat and a number of other Ittihadists had already arrived secretly in Germany. It is completely implausible that the German government was not aware of their presence, as the German press stressed after Talaat's murder. In fact, the Turkish ambassador in Berlin was dismissed by the new Turkish prime minister for not succeeding in having Talaat, Shakir, Nazim, and other Ittihadists arrested. Their refuge in Berlin was thus obviously known to Constantinople. Only later was it learned that the Germans had refused to act, claiming inadequate evidence.

Muhammad meanwhile expanded on his official edict in a *New York Times* interview, in which he promised to punish severely the instigators of the atrocities. The new minister of the interior, Mustafa Arif, was assigned the task of traveling through the provinces to collect evidence for the military tribunal. During that two-month period in December 1918 and January 1919, the newspapers in Constantinople erupted in an explosion of accusations and recriminations against the Young Turks and their national policies.

One important source of information at that time was *Renaissance*, a French-language newspaper published in Constantinople, which reprinted many articles from the Turkish press. Among them was an open letter to the former justice minister, which appeared in the Turkish newspaper *Sabah*, raising a series of devastating questions:

> Was it not the bandit chief Talaat who appointed you Prefect of Salonika and then took you to Constantinople to make you Justice Minister?
>
> Was it not at a meeting of the Young Turk Party that the decision was made to release from prison the worst criminals for the sole purpose of expelling the Armenians from their homes and despite their innocence barbarously destroying them?
>
> Was it not you who gave the order to release them from prison and who organized them?
>
> Was it not you who refused to have a physician examine these criminals to determine their competence?
>
> Was it not you who after agreement with your chief Talaat, gave the order to immediately dismiss Armenian officials from those areas where Armenian deportees were to be exiled and killed?
>
> And finally, was it not you who revelled in the barbarities visited on the Armenian people with axes and hatchets?[2]

Not a day passed that the Turkish press did not print an editorial or public statement acknowledging the culpability of the Young Turk regime. In the Ottoman Parliament, a cabinet member was quoted as saying that "the barbarous crimes against the Armenians have evoked all humanity's revulsion, as a consequence of which our country is now seen as a gigantic slaughterhouse."

The president of the Turkish Senate announced:

> From the time of our participation in the World War, October 30, 1914, until the fall of the government of Talaat Pasha, October 7, 1918, the crimes of the government—its errors, its slaughters, its confiscation of property, buildings and wealth, shall be refered to the Courts of Justice by me in order to expose all the crimes.[3]

The Turkish paper *Tasfir-i Evkiar*, in an editorial entitled "From the Palace to the Dungeon," commented on the former officials, "now in prison as common criminals": "It is difficult to understand why they did not realize that one day they would have to give account for the crimes committed by the government of Talaat Pasha, even if we were victorious."

Another paper wrote: "The Turkish people bow their heads in shame before the tragedy of the Armenian people."

Sixty-three Young Turk officials were arrested on January 30–31, 1919, when the investigation leading to the trial began—a trial ordered by the sultan and conducted under the aegis of the Allied Occupation Forces, primarily Great Britain. Unluckily, however, the major figures had escaped and were in hiding outside the country.

The first session of the military tribunal took place on February 5 in the Great Hall of the Ministry of Justice before five judges: The president of the tribunal was a corps commander, three others were generals, and the fifth was a colonel. The court was assisted by a bench of civil judges, among whom were a Greek and two Armenians, sitting as assessors. Its final session would take place some six months later. The main charge concerned the massacre and deportation of the Armenians.[4] The evidence consisted of eyewitness accounts and reports and papers gathered by the minister of the interior.

That first session produced an ominous phrase that would echo through the halls of another tribunal a quarter of a century later in Nuremberg. On trial was Kemal Bey, former governor of Diarbekir, who personified the Military Tribunal's first and most expeditious example of justice. His defense attorney argued that Kemal Bey, charged with having organized the killings, deportations, and robberies in the district called Yozgat, deserved a pardon because "he only carried out orders." The ministers and high-level officials should be punished first, because "the order to destroy the Armenians won approval in the Ministerial Council and became legal when the Sultan issued an Imperial decree."[5]

But the chief Turkish prosecutor of the Military Tribunal, Sami Bey, countered by saying: "It is true that everyone is obligated to carry out orders from the highest offices, *but he must judge and weigh in balance whether the issued order does not violate justice and the law, and whether one must obey it or not.* The fact is that some officials did not obey these orders and distanced themselves from them. The Vali of Ankara, for instance, responded to the order to kill the Armenians by pointing out he was a Governor and not a criminal. [author's italics]"*

The tribunal found Kemal Bey guilty and sentenced him to death on the basis of two sections of the Turkish criminal code: Paragraph 170, which deals with premeditated murder, and Paragraph 171, which concerns the pillaging and sale of goods.

As the *New York Times* reported on its front page, Kemal Bey was publicly hanged on April 12 in Bayazid Square in Constantinople in the presence of the military governor and other senior Turkish officials.

His former commander of the gendarmerie, Tefik Bey, was incriminated by many documents graphically describing the killing of 8,500 Armenians, the confiscation of their property, the burning of their houses and deportations of their survivors. These eyewitness accounts proved especially disastrous for Tefik. He was described as having a "psychopathic hatred of Armenians" and of personally raping Armenian women. According to one account appearing in *Renaissance*: "This bloodthirsty monster set fire to villages. The Armenian men pleaded with him not to kill the women and children, but he did, using his sword to dismember female prisoners. It is impossible to list the indescribable acts committed by Tefik."

On April 14 the *New York Times* reported that Tefik Bey had been sentenced to fifteen years' imprisonment at the fortress in

---

*Later in the trial, on March 19, the president of the tribunal, Hayret Bey, admonished a defendant from Kemal Bey's district of Yozgat with the following words: "The Constitution forbade carrying out upper echelon orders if they were illegal. You should have resigned your office."

Diarbekir. In view of the acts with which he was charged, his punishment seemed lenient. But Tefik's salvation was Paragraph 45 of the criminal code, which stated that "if the chief criminal gets the death penalty, his cocriminals should get no less than fifteen years of hard labor."[6]

By this time the trial had caught the world's attention, and the role of Turkey's wartime ally, Germany, also began to come into clearer international focus. On April 15 the *New York Times* commented:

> Before the hangings in Constantinople on account of Armenian and other massacres become numerous, they ought to include at least a few participants in the murderous work who were not Turks at all. All through the war the real rule of Turkey was in the hands of German military officers and diplomats . . . nothing was done without their permission and approval. They looked on coldly and calmly while helpless men, women and children were slain by the hundreds of thousands. These are the men whose guilt is at least as great as is that of the Beys and Pashas who gave the orders, and their only justification was "military necessity." That they all ran home before the Allies arrived explains why none of them now faces trial.

In the weeks that followed, considerable testimony concerning many lower-echelon Ittihadist officials was taken and all were found guilty and sentenced to varying terms of imprisonment. Slowly, however, the Turkish military tribunal was building its case against those who bore the ultimate responsibility—the Young Turk leaders. In order to make the case complete, the tribunal had to show that orders had originated with the Ittihadists to deport and massacre Armenians, and also hear testimony on the means and the methods of carrying them out.

In late April the tribunal made a lengthy statement accusing Talaat, Enver, Jemal, Nazim, Shakir, and other senior members of the Ittihadist Committee—all of whom had fled Turkey seven months before—of having issued the orders instructing provincial Turkish authorities to destroy Armenian villages and deport the inhabitants. Talaat, Enver, and Jemal were accused of "having used Turkey's entry into the war—when Europe's attention was diverted—as a subterfuge for the carrying out of this policy of annihilation." They were also accused of "resolving by violent means those issues which should have been painstakingly examined by legal processes, and by employing such brutal methods placed a tremendous burden on the population and unleashed massive lawlessness."[7]

A mountain of documents was heaped on the tribunal, including imperial decrees, orders largely signed by Talaat, and official telegrams to provincial authorities and Ittihadist agents in the field giving precise instructions on how to eliminate the Armenians.

Some of the incriminating messages reflected irritation that the Euphrates was clogged with bodies. Coded telegrams exchanged in July 1915 between Ittihadist leaders and local Turkish officials discussed improved measures for disposing of Armenian corpses. Talaat Pasha instructed the governors and mayors of Diarbekir, Harput, Urfa, and Zori not to throw the corpses into ditches, lakes, and rivers but to bury them and burn all personal effects. Jemal Pasha, in a telegram to the governor of Diarbekir, insisted that he have all corpses buried and not leave any in view. A reply pointed out that the Euphrates did not come near Diarbekir and that the corpses floating down the Euphrates were from Erzerum or Harput, adding: "Here, we throw the bodies either into caves or burn them, rarely burying any."[8]

One telegram revealed that the number of Armenians deported from Diarbekir alone exceeded 120,000; a second from the governor of Harput complained that the roads were blocked by the corpses of women and children and he was unable to bury them; a third from the commander of the Third Ottoman Army to the six governors of provinces under his jurisdiction reflected the degree of local Turkish resistance to Ittihadist policy by warning that "every Muslim who attempts to protect an Armenian shall be hanged before his house and his house will then be burned to the ground."[9]

The charges also focused on the special squads created to carry out the liquidation of the Armenian nation, namely the Teshkilat-i Mahsusa (TiM). Evidence was presented of the many telegrams signed by Young Turk leaders and sent to *valis* throughout central Turkey, where Armenians were most numerous, instructing officials to organize the TiM by releasing criminals from local prisons. Evidence was presented of close ties between the TiM and the Ittihadist Committee in Constantinople. The tribunal also established that the major part of the TiM files had disappeared.

Many relevant accounts were heard in testimony, especially from documents provided by current officials from those specific areas. From Arvas Prison, a notorious bandit named Mahir Bey and 123 other criminals had been released on the pretext that they would be sent to the front. Instead, they were absorbed into the TiM and assigned the task of killing Armenians. (Condemned to fifteen years imprisonment for murder on June 26, 1912, at the time of his release Mahir had served only two years and nine months.) Among Mahir's first victims was a priest who, having escaped from Erzinga, was passing through Arvas. The tribunal heard extensive testimony about the cruelties of the TiM, especially toward women and girls throughout Anatolia, where the deportations were ordered.

The chief culprit of these crimes was Dr. Behaeddin Shakir, who according to documentary testimony "had been dispatched for the express purpose of organizing bands of criminals to kill and rob the Armenians." Telegrams signed by Shakir were presented as evidence of his responsibility for the crimes of the TiM. As a young man, Shakir had studied medicine and worked in a hospital in Paris, eventually becoming a professor at the Constantinople Military Medical Academy, where the nucleus of the Ittihadists had first formed. Eyewitness testimony accused Shakir of having poisoned sick Armenians in the hospital in Trebizond.

Further testimony shed light on his accomplices in this little-known aspect of the atrocities. The new director of the Trebizond Health Welfare Department confirmed that his predecessor during the 1915 massacres—with the approval of Jemal Azmi, then governor of Trebizond—employed chemical poisons to kill Armenian children who had been orphaned, as well as Armenians and Greeks who had escaped the TiM and fled to Trebizond.

Experiments with typhus vaccines on Armenian soldiers were also described, administered by the Turkish Third Army's chief physician. Lengthy descriptions of these experiments, presented as evidence had already appeared in the Turkish press. When the sultan's decree appeared, one Turkish newspaper published an open letter to the new Minister of the Interior from a Dr. Haydar Jemal, who had apparently witnessed these experiments. Jemal concluded, "It is vile and horrible that not only political but scientific crimes were committed against the Armenians, about which I am prepared to give testimony."[10]

Another newspaper published a letter shortly thereafter signed by a Dr. Selaheddin, which said:

Conscience, morality and honor had no value in the crimes and cruelties against the Armenians. It was precisely because of this mentality that the medical experiments in Erzinga were performed. Just as those responsible for the deportation, massacre and robbery of the Armenians must be held to account, so too those who committed these vile medical crimes. The truth must be exposed not only in newspapers but in a court of law.[11]

It was exposed, and among the many who were condemned to death by the tribunal were Dr. Behaeddin Shakir and Governor Jemal Azmi: "Shakir for having organized and coordinated the activities of the TiM and Jemal for having formed the TiM gangs by releasing from jail criminals to kill Armenian women and children and having given them specific orders to massacre and plunder the Armenian deportees."[12]

As the verdict noted, these sentences were passed in absentia, Shakir and Jemal Azmi having long since escaped abroad with the triumvirate.

Talaat, Enver, and Jemal, together with Dr. Nazim and twelve other Ittihad ve Terraki leaders—"only three of whom are present," noted the president of the tribunal—were charged with having planned and executed the Armenian massacres. Noting that some of the Ittihadists had insisted that they had been informed of the massacres after the fact, the tribunal pointed out that they were then guilty of not preventing further massacres or punishing the instigators. These charges, which were made on April 28, comprised "a lengthy list of names, crimes, abuses and atrocities of all kinds, substantiated by documents which incriminate heavily Enver, Talaat, Jemal and other fugitives in the massacres and deportations of the Armenians."[13]

The tribunal spent two months examining witnesses and documents relating to these charges, specifically accusing Ittihadist leaders of unilateral decisions that contradicted the nation's interests and of activities reminiscent of those of Sultan Abdul Hamid II. It noted as well that all the accused and their lawyers rejected these charges and refused to acknowledge their guilt.

Finally, on July 11, 1919, the tribunal found that Talaat, Enver, Jemal, and Nazim were guilty and condemned them to death in absentia on the basis of Sections 45 and 55 of the Turkish criminal code, specifically for violations of the Turkish constitution. But, as was widely known and reported, all four had fled, their whereabouts unknown. The verdict was characterized by the *New York Times* as "the climax of a long series of prosecutions undertaken by the officials of the new regime to clear the skirts of the Turkish people from blame for joining in the war and for the Armenian, Greek and Syrian atrocities and deportations."[14]

The trials in Constantinople involving the Ittihad ve Terraki Committee finally came to an end, and while many were sentenced, only a few were punished. But those who escaped the justice of the Turkish Military Tribunal did not escape retribution.

Within weeks of the collapse of the Young Turk regime in mid-October 1918, Talaat, Enver, and Jemal had been spirited to Odessa through the benevolent intervention of the German Navy. When they reappeared it was not in Germany, however, but in the newborn Soviet Union. Still entertaining hopes for a return to power in Constantinople—the Ittihadists having remained entrenched and still active in the provinces—the triumvirate made a short-lived attempt to enlist Bolshevik aid for a resurgence of the Ittihad ve Terraki. But efforts to win the support of Lenin and Trotsky proved futile. Talaat surfaced in Germany, while Jemal lent his military talents briefly to the Red Army in Afghanistan.

Enver remained for the time being in Moscow, where his earlier Prussian experience won him, too, employment as an adviser to the Red Army. He particularly enjoyed the assignment given him on the Caucasian front to the south, where he supervised Tatars who were harassing the population in the Russian-controlled areas of Armenia.[15] Later he was transferred to the eastern sectors of Soviet and Chinese Turkestan, Kazakhstan, and Afghanistan—an area that had once figured in his pan-Turkic dreams of empire.

In Moscow Enver cut a dashing figure with his kaiserlike waxed mustache and handsome visage. Always vain, he wore a high black tarboosh, or fez, to detract attention from his lack of height. One of the frequent contacts he enjoyed was with Louise Bryant, the widow of the American revolutionary John Reed, whom he had first met in Constantinople. As honored guests of the Soviet Union Bryant and Enver had been allotted special quarters by the Foreign Ministry in what was known as "the little palace." Every day for six months she sat next to Enver at dinner and engaged him in conversation. Her comments in her memoir, *Mirrors of Moscow*, reveal much not only about Enver but about the mentality of which he was part. Bryant wrote of him:

> Enver Pasha certainly has charm, in spite of his obvious opportunism and the cruelty and lack of conscience which his fatalistic belief in Allah inspires. He is interested in himself above all things and leaves the future to Allah.

I learned much of Turkish character from him: friendship once given has no barriers; a friend is a friend through sorrow, dishonor, poverty; an enemy is beyond all consideration, he is spared nothing, forgiven nothing.

Enver said he could never understand why Americans were so sentimental about Armenians. "Do Americans imagine that Armenians never kill Turks?"

He lived as though there were no tomorrows. I remember when Talaat Pasha, his life-long friend, was murdered by an Armenian in Berlin. Enver read the message with no show of emotion and his only comment was, "His time had come." Thereafter, he slept with one eye open and carried a dagger and a loaded automatic.[16]

Still pursuing his pan-Turanic dream and thereby coming into conflict with his Bolshevik protectors, Enver became the leader of the Afghan insurgents known as Basmachis, who were fighting the Red Army. On the night of August 4, 1922, a Red Army patrol came upon a group of Basmachi leaders in secret conference. The patrol engaged them in hand-to-hand combat with scimitar and saber. When the corpses of the Basmachis were examined, all were found to be dressed in long, richly colored Bukharan robes and Central Asian headgear—all but one, who wore high military boots, breeches, and a tightly buttoned blue jacket. This proved to be the body of Enver Pasha.[17]

Jemal Pasha's Afghan exploits had taken place three years before Enver's and were not directly related. Jemal soon completed the task that had been given him by the Red Army and left the Soviet Union to settle in Germany. He apparently felt no qualms about his role in the events that were exposed in Constantinople, for in an interview four months after the trials, he maintained that he was not responsible for the Armenian massacres.[18]

However, Jemal spent considerable time reconstructing the events through which he, Talaat, and Enver had become notorious, compiling his memoirs, which were published late in 1919. But for anyone expecting a truthful behind-the-scenes account of the Armenian atrocities from the one member of the triumvirate who claimed innocence of those events, the book proved vastly disappointing.

Jemal's account is vitiated at the outset by his claim that in all Turkey "there was not an Armenian who could speak Armenian . . .

and in the churches Mass was said in Turkish.'' By writing in these terms about the oldest national Christian Church and one of the oldest languages in the world—the two keystones of a 1,600-year-old Armenian culture—Jemal destroyed his credibility. He also reverted to the argument used by Turkey throughout the war (and again in its postwar comments on the atrocities), namely that the massacres were instigated by the Armenians and that more Turks died than Armenians. Nevertheless it must be granted that Jemal allows for the deportation by the Ittihadists ''of one and a half million Armenians from the East Anatolian provinces, and that 600,000 of them died, some murdered, some collapsing on the way from hunger and distress.''[19] That figure is at least double what current Turkish historians and apologists concede.

Jemal Pasha spent the next two years in transit, eventually finding himself in Tiflis in Soviet Georgia. For a politician of such notoriety this destination was surely unwise. Tiflis always had (and still has) an Armenian population of half a million. On July 22, 1922, Jemal was assassinated by two Armenians in Tiflis.[20]

When news of Talaat Pasha's escape from Turkey reached Europe, it seemed to arouse greater furor than that of Enver or Jemal. A measure of that anger may be seen in a letter from an Italian reader, printed on the editorial page of the *London Times* under the heading ''A Great Criminal.'' It reads in part:

> Recently hundreds of thousands of Armenians were sent to their doom by the same Talaat who openly declared that he would ''settle the Armenian Question by the extermination of the Armenians.'' The worst orgies of Abdul Hamid, the Red Sultan, pale before the crimes of this monster in human form. Is he to be allowed to escape?[21]

Talaat arrived in Berlin in November 1918, using the pseudonym Ali Salih Bey—the same he had used in his early Ittihadist days in Salonika—and rented a two-room apartment that soon became a meeting place for exiled Ittihadists. There they discussed developments in Turkey and also issued an information bulletin that was sent to many addressees.[22] But Talaat led a wary existence and went out in public infrequently at this time.

In January 1919, when the trial was announced in Constantinople, the Turkish ambassador in Berlin received an order to have Talaat arrested. At that time the bulk of the Turkish community and most of the embassy staff consisted of individuals of a revolutionary character who promptly drew up a list of Turkish war criminals and demanded that the German government arrest them and extradite them to Turkey. The order from Constantinople cited the murder of eight hundred thousand Armenians as the basis for the request. But the German government did not comply, and Talaat—realizing that his situation had become more hazardous—changed his residence and assumed an even lower profile.

In Berlin Talaat's main pleasure was playing bridge with his intimates in the afternoon, when the loss or gain of fifteen or twenty marks was the only subject of discussion. He rarely went to the theater, although his German—thanks to an aptitude for languages—was more than adequate. He did, however, keep up with international events, and during 1919 and 1920 he sent letters to loyal followers in Switzerland, Denmark, Sweden, Holland, and Italy, traveling to Italy himself in March 1920 and again in January 1921. Uncertain of the political attitude of the Italian government toward the Young Turks, he even shaved his thick mustache, hoping thus to pass unrecognized.

When the military tribunal systematically exposed the Ittihadists' crimes, Talaat told intimates that he intended to publish his memoirs in order to enlighten the public. He even composed an explanatory preface, which he sent to a number of European political figures, including David Lloyd George. The replies he received—with none from the British prime minister—discouraged him, and he temporarily abandoned the idea of publication, although he continued to work on the book.

Despite a desire for anonymity, Talaat never lost an opportunity to justify what his regime had done to the Armenians as anything but lawful and in the interests of the state. But in a portion of the manuscript (published posthumously by Talaat's wife), he confessed:

> I admit that we deported many Armenians from our eastern provinces . . . the deportation was not carried out lawfully everywhere. In some places unlawful acts were committed. . . . Similar security measures had been taken during the war by many countries, but in those countries the regrettable consequences were consigned to silence, whereas our operations became known in the entire world because everyone's eyes were upon us.[23]

A few weeks before he was killed, Talaat had made another revelation that could not have pleased his colleagues or his erstwhile German allies. In the German town of Hamm, he met with British

Tory MP Aubrey Herbert, a politician known for his pro-Turkish leanings, and told him that "he himself had always been against the attempted extermination of the Armenians. . . . He had twice protested against the policy but had been overruled by the Germans."[24]

On the morning of March 15, 1921, Talaat left his nine-room villa on Hardenbergstrasse, unaware that he was being watched by the survivor of one of the many massacres he had conceived and ordered. A few minutes later the morning air was shattered by the pistol shot that ended Talaat's life.

A new book by Johannes Lepsius about the Turkish annihilation of the Armenians had meanwhile been published in Europe. Entitled *Germany and Armenia 1914–1918*, this third and most comprehensive of Lepsius's works on this subject was a compilation of diplomatic communications and classified documents he had taken, with permission, from a more sympathetic German Foreign Ministry. The content of that book and the testimony of Lepsius himself were to have significant impact on the trial of the young Armenian who had fired that fatal shot.

7

The Trial Resumes

*J*ohannes Lepsius's professorial appearance belied the tireless activism that had characterized his life for a quarter of a century. His labors on behalf of the Armenians—the orphanages, lectures, articles, and books—had established him as Germany's foremost authority on the wartime events in Turkey. Thus, the respect for him was so great that even the prosecution agreed he should appear as the first of two expert defense witnesses despite his pro-Armenian sympathies. It was the defense's purpose to provide the court with an historical overview of Turkish-Armenian relations, thereby placing the 1915 tragedy and Tehlirian's crime in perspective, and there was no one better qualified to do this than Johannes Lepsius. With his starched wing collar, pince-nez, and short, pointed beard, Lepsius exuded authority and commanded the attention of the entire court.

Judge Lehmberg addressed two essential questions to him:

You know what the issue is. I ask you to limit yourself to the following: in the Armenian massacres of 1915, were there other atrocities similar in scope, and, do the depictions of the witnesses and the accounts by the accused of his personal experiences deserve credibility?

Lepsius fixed his clear blue eyes on the judge and began what was to be the trial's most focused testimony, delivered in a measured and deliberate manner that enhanced its authority. The German respect for scholars was evident in the rapt attention accorded him. Speaking without notes, Lepsius displayed total mastery of the subject to which he had devoted his entire mature life.

He began with a description of the old homeland of the Armenians in eastern and central Turkey and moved directly into the matter at hand, charging that the deportation of the total Armenian population of Anatolia—1,400,000 people—was carried out on the highest orders. The Armenians were moved to the northern and eastern ridge of the Mesopotamian desert, to such final stopping places as Deir Zor and Mosul.

"What significance did these deportations have?" Lepsius asked rhetorically. "Talaat signed a decree in which he said: 'The goal of the deportations is annihilation.' Consequently, of the entire number of Armenians deported south from the East Anatolian provinces, 10 percent survived, while en route, 90 percent were murdered, or, if women and children were not sold and dragged off by Turks and Kurds, died of hunger and exhaustion."

Lepsius continued his testimony:

The general deportation was determined by the Young Turk Committee, ordered through Talaat Pasha as minister of the interior— together with Enver Pasha as minister of war—and executed with the help of the Young Turk Committee.

Officially, it was stated that the deportations were preventive measures, but privately, authoritative persons said quite openly that their purpose was the annihilation of the Armenian people. The Turks said they were inspired by the example of the British in South Africa with the Boers, which gave them the idea of concentration camps.

When a substantial mass of some hundred thousand Armenians was compressed into a concentration camp on the edge of the desert, most were destroyed through systematic starvation and periodic massacres. Thus, when the concentration camps were filled through new deportations, columns of inmates would be led into the desert and slaughtered.

Dr. Lepsius paused, removed his pince-nez, rubbed his eyes, and wiped the glasses with a handkerchief.

What I tell you is evident in the documents from the files of the Royal Embassy in Constantinople and from the German Foreign Office, which I have already published. They are primarily reports from German consuls stationed in the inner parts of Turkey, and from the German embassy as well.

Today, you have heard two reports—from Tehlirian and from Mrs. Terzibashian—of their experiences in the deportations. Similar reports are available in German, American, and British publications. The facts are not to be doubted and the methods of execution correspond to those of the two witnesses.

Otherwise, the question would have to be asked: How was it possible to kill a million people in so short a time? That could only have been possible by resorting to the most brutal methods as was shown in the trial before the Military Tribunal in Constantinople of Talaat Pasha and his comrades. The first of the five points of the accusation concerned the Armenian massacres. The judgment of the Military Tribunal of July 1919 was to condemn to death Talaat, Enver, Jemal, and Dr. Nazim, as the main authors of the massacres.

Dr. Lepsius explained that the carrying out of the annihilation measures was entrusted to local officials, but that some refused and were deposed. He noted that terror was on occasion practiced by Turkish officials against their own population, which, he observed, "manifestly disapproved of the mass measures." The commander of the Third Army, which was in charge of the Anatolian provinces, issued an order announcing that any Turk who gave support or protection to the Armenians would be killed in front of his house and his house burned to the ground. Any official guilty of supporting Armenians would be tried before a military court.

Pointing out that the total Armenian population of Turkey numbered 1,850,000, Lepsius repeated the figure of 1,400,000 representing the Anatolian deportees. Of the remaining 450,000, he noted that some 200,000 were rescued by Russian troops, which had occupied eastern areas of Anatolia. The 250,000 Armenians who did not perish were to be found in the major cities, he said, and were spared the horrors suffered by their compatriots primarily through the intervention of highly placed Germans in Turkey.

You will hear from General Liman von Sanders himself how he prevented the deportation of Armenians from Smyrna. In Baghdad, Field Marshal [Baron Colmar] von der Goltz, the supreme commander of Turkish Forces, learned how Armenians had been deported from there to Mosul and told the governor to announce that he, von der Goltz, had forbidden the deportations. When new orders for deportation arrived, however, von der Goltz submitted his resignation. Only then did Enver Pasha, minister of war, give in, but not without noting in a letter that von der Goltz could not justify his authority by intervening in the internal affairs of the Turkish Empire. In Aleppo Consul Rössler was primarily responsible for the preservation of the Armenians.[1] In Constantinople it was the intervention of the German ambassadors which prevented the deportation of Armenians.

Once again Lepsius paused, this time to wipe his forehead. Resettling himself in his chair, he now sought to illuminate the origins of the ethnic conflict that had taken so many bloody turns in recent history and looked beyond the borders of the Ottoman Empire for an answer.

The Armenian question was a creation of European diplomacy, he said, and the Armenian people the victims of the political interests of Western nations. When Abdul Hamid II saw that the European powers seemed reluctant to enforce the reform plan they had imposed on him, he had responded with a whole series of massacres.

The massacre of Sassun in 1894, the motivation for the reform plan, cost thousands of Armenians their lives. The massacres of 1895–96, which followed on the heels of the reform plan, took two hundred thousand Armenian lives; the massacres of 1915–18 produced one million victims. This scale represented a graphic curve difficult to equal in the history of world massacres, Lepsius said.

The courtroom was totally silent. All eyes were on the frail figure pouring out names, dates, and statistics as though he had been born with the information. Even Judge Lehmberg seemed mesmerized by the theologian, so astonishingly conversant with the fate of this ancient, persecuted people.

Dr. Lepsius had no kind words for the Great Powers, which had called for Armenian reforms so often but had not "lifted a finger to rescue those they had pledged to protect or to call for the punishment of the murderers." The Armenians were pawns in the diplomatic chess games of England, Russia, and France, he claimed. Nonetheless Lepsius, the good German, bore his country no malice, despite the countless obstacles he had had to overcome in order to reach the German public with his message. His charity toward his own country may have been dictated by a combination of patriotism and humanitarianism. German documents would prove Germany's benevolence and understanding, he maintained, but for all that, his nation had been maligned as the one power that had stood behind the evil deeds of the sultan and of the Turkish government.

In 1913, I was in Constantinople. During the negotiations [for Armenian reform], the Young Turks were extremely agitated and embittered by the fact that the Armenian reform question was again preoccupying the powers. At the time, it was heard said by the Young Turks: "If you Armenians lift one finger to implement these reforms, the massacres of Abdul Hamid will be as child's play.

Dr. Lepsius now introduced an element of even-higher drama into his testimony by pointing out that the Young Turks and the Armenians had made the revolution against Abdul Hamid together, and during the elections, the leaders on both sides supported each other. But in the first months of the war, that friendliness disappeared.

Suddenly, in the night of April 24-25, 1915, to the astonishment of all Constantinople, the cream of Armenian intellectual life was arrested, taken to prison and then deported to Asia Minor. Of the total number of six hundred deported, only fifteen survived. One of the few Armenian intellectuals who remained free was Vartkes, the Armenian member of parliament and a personal friend of Talaat Pasha's. He went to Talaat to ask what was happening. Talaat said: "In the days of our weakness, you were at our throat and threw open the reform question. So now, we will take advantage of the situation in which we find ourselves to disperse your people in such a way that we will drive reform ideas out of your heads for fifty years!"
Vartkes responded: "Does that mean then that you intend to continue the work of Abdul Hamid?" Talaat replied "Yes."
It happened as it was promised. The trials of the military tribunal in Constantinople, as reported in the *Official Gazette*, brought to light the evidence that the deportation was decided by the Young Turk Committee and that Talaat Pasha—the soul of the committee and its strongest figure—ordered the extermination and did nothing to diminish the terror. The evidence is in German and Turkish documents.

Dr. Lepsius seemed to sag in his chair, exhausted from the strenuous effort, which had taken more than an hour. His scholarly overview of the bloody deeds of successive Turkish governments had been essential in judging the one act of vengeance that had put the Armenian youth on trial. While previous witnesses, mostly victims themselves of the massacres, had concentrated emotionally on their personal experiences, Lepsius lent to those events an objectivity and historical sweep that aided the court in understanding the causes and effects of the tragedy. The end of his volunteered testimony sent a ripple of animation through the public and the court.

As people shifted in their seats, Defense Attorney Werthauer, intending to broaden the jury's understanding of Turkish motivations, directed a question to the theologian: "You said that the diplomatic game between Russia and England contributed to the annihilation of the Armenians. Why so?"

"Because they implanted in the Turks the fear that the reforms would make Armenia autonomous whereby the stability of Asiatic Turkey would be endangered."

"Earlier we heard the reason that the Turks were Mohammedans and the Armenians Christians, and that the hatred went back hundreds of years."

"The fantastic idea to create a pan-Turkish, pan-Islamic empire in which there would be noplace for Christians is initially traceable to the Young Turk Committee and to Enver Pasha."

"In other words, just as one would say 'all-German,' or 'all-Russian,' or 'all-Turkish,' one would destroy everything that was not pure Turkish?"

"Yes," Lepsius answered.

Supplementing this line of questioning, aimed at eliciting ethno-religious causes for Turkish actions, another defense attorney intervened at this point in an attempt to simplify what in the final analysis may have been the bottom line of motivation for the Young Turks' policy towards the Armenians.

"Is it not so that the Armenians were the last oppressed Christian people on Turkish territory whom the Turks could count on dominating? All the Balkan and other peoples dominated by Turkey had risen and thrown off the Turkish yoke. In order to prevent the Armenians from also doing so, their annihilation was decided upon. Is that point of view correct?"

"Yes," Lepsius said, and he cited a report by Count Wolff-Metternich, German ambassador in Constantinople in 1918, to the effect that the Armenians were finished and the Young Turk "pack of hounds" was preparing impatiently for the moment when Greece would turn against Turkey, at which time the Greeks would be destroyed like the Armenians.[2]

Lepsius's testimony had now come to an end. The earlier witnesses who had spoken of the massacres, primarily Soghomon Tehlirian and

Christine Terzibashian, had been tragic victims of Turkish policies, and their testimony had been devastatingly personal. But Lepsius spoke from the perspective of history, philosophy, theology—objective disciplines Germans viewed with the utmost respect. Above all, he was a professor, and in the eyes of the court and the public, no calling commanded greater esteem.

Lepsius's impact on the courtroom was evident. The public engaged in excited whispering; the jurors, who had been taking notes, were hurriedly writing down his final words, as though no transcript would be provided. Prosecutor Gollnick, immersed in a stack of papers, was solemnly rubbing his head; and Judge Lehmberg appeared stunned.

Lepsius, "advocate of the Armenian people," stepped down. No witness could have been more different from the one who followed.

———

Retired General Otto Liman von Sanders was tall and strong for his sixty-six years, the most critical five of which he had spent in Turkey. Sent by Kaiser Wilhelm in 1913 as head of the German Military Mission, von Sanders had reorganized the Turkish Army, and in August 1914—three months before Turkey entered the war on the German side—had organized the country's conscription system. So deeply involved was he in Turkish military affairs that he was widely known as Liman Pasha. Perhaps his greatest hour came when he commanded the victorious forces at Gallipoli; his worst was undoubtedly his subsequent defeat by General Allenby and Colonel T. E. Lawrence (Lawrence of Arabia) in Palestine.

While the defense knew very well the kind of witness it had in Lepsius, von Sanders, the second expert witness, was in many ways of a different ilk. He had spent his entire life in the military serving the kaiser, and knew little of politics or history. As a patriot von Sanders could be expected to defend his country's role in Turkey, but would he hold the same views as Lepsius toward the Turkish government—Germany's wartime ally—views a professional soldier might consider treasonous? It must be remembered that Enver Pasha, the Turkish minister of war, had been von Sanders's superior. As a witness for the defense, von Sanders was being called because of his service in Turkey, which embraced the period of the deportations and massacres. During that time he was one of the prominent German commanders of all the Turkish troops, and therefore he could be expected to have some insight into the events discussed at the trial.

Having heard from Lepsius the historical and political factors that provided background for the massacres, the defense now looked to von Sanders to supplement that information by focusing on the execution at the actual operational level of the deportation and annihilation orders. In accordance with established German court procedure (wherein the presiding judge could initiate questioning or intervene at any point), Judge Lehmberg asked von Sanders to address the question of the organization of the guards assigned to the transports.

Von Sanders first said that he wished to add to what Dr. Lepsius had said from a military standpoint, and noted that the overall subject of the "Armenian massacres" should be divided into two parts. The first concerned the orders to deport the Armenians. Von Sanders stated flatly that the Young Turk government should be held responsible both for the orders given and their consequences. The second part related to military reasons; that is, to the conflicts arising from the Armenian attempts at self-defense and from Armenian defections to the Russian side.

"The government instituted the deportation and, what is more, on orders of the highest military and civilian authorities, both of whom viewed it as a military necessity to evacuate East Anatolia of Armenians," von Sanders said.

Aware that it was common knowledge that the Turkish Army was under the command of German officers, von Sanders made his first of several attempts to absolve the German Army of wrongdoing. He pointed out that all such recommendations from the field had come from Turks and that any charges against German officers were "false and inaccurate."

Thinking he had straightened out the record on that score, he now addressed Judge Lehmberg's question. Here he was quite frank in his condemnation of the Turkish police.

The carrying out of the deportation orders fell into the worst imaginable hands. Before the war, the Turkish gendarmerie was quite good. It numbered eighty-five thousand men and was an elite troop. But later, it was enrolled into the army, was split up, and installed as auxiliary military police, which did not consist of the best elements. Some were thieves, others unemployed. There was little discipline. They were not Turkish soldiers but a very bad military substitute created out of an immediate need. These things must be mentioned when speaking of the atrocities inflicted on the Armenians.

It cannot be overlooked that this escort personnel had been influenced by the concept of ''holy war,'' in which they saw before them Armenian Christians and believed that to act vigorously against them was a meritorious honor.

Further, Turkish provisions were so poor that not only Armenians died but many Turkish soldiers as well because of illness and a lack of care and poor organization in the Turkish Empire. After the Gallipoli campaign, in my army alone, thousands of soldiers died because of under-nourishment.

Von Sanders's testimony at this point appeared to be a virtual apology for the Turkish persecution of the Armenians. The court was seeking to ascertain details about the operational aspects of the deportations, but von Sanders's emphasis on the lack of discipline—the perennial complaint of professional, often German, commanders—appeared to be yet another oblique attempt to exonerate the forces under his control of blame. Additionally, though his mention of a lack of provisions and poor medical care seemed to be a rationale for the large number of Armenian dead, it was irrelevant because it offered no explanation for the barbarity with which the gendarmerie had executed their orders.

Von Sanders again reverted to his *idée fixe*—the honor of the German Army:

> I can say that no German officer ever took part in any measure against the Armenians. On the contrary, many of us intervened when we could. I never received an order from Talaat concerning the Armenians. I did receive orders signed by Enver, which sometimes were quite absurd. For example, an order once came from him to remove all Armenians and Jews from our staffs. Of course, it was not carried out because we needed the Armenians and Jews as interpreters. Such orders were nonsensical.

The German government had done everything possible, he said, but it had been difficult. He said he knew of strong protests raised by German Ambassador Wolff-Metternich protesting the measures taken against the Armenians. The general also cited instances of his own personal intervention. One graphic example, he pointed out, was also described in Dr. Lepsius's latest book on the massacres.

I went to Smyrna, where the Turkish Governor had dragged six hundred Armenians from their beds in the middle of the night, shoved them into wagons to deport them. I intervened and told the Governor of Smyrna that if even one Armenian was disturbed, I would have my soldiers fire on his gendarmes. The order was rescinded.

I should like to stress that at no time did I take measures supporting the Turkish side against the Armenians, nor was I asked to. On the contrary, everything was done in secret from us so that we could not even have any political insight into the inner political relations of the country.

The general seemed to be under stress as he pulled a silk handkerchief from his pocket, wiped his broad forehead, and inserted two fingers between his neck and collar.

How deeply Talaat was personally involved in the deportations, the chief decree on which is of May 20, 1915, I cannot say. But it was the Young Turk Committee which created it and the Ministerial Council which approved it.

The execution of the decree lay in the hands of the Governors, the local officials and above all the horrible gendarmerie. I feel duty bound to state that in the more than five years I have been in Turkey, I have never seen, witnessed or carried out any written order or measure from Talaat.

General von Sanders's testimony was a curious performance. In a sense it was of little use to either side. The role of the German army in the Armenian massacres had not been at issue, and von Sanders's protestations seemed directed less to the court than to those foreign critics who wondered, with good reason, how the savage persecution of Armenians by Turkish military and paramilitary forces could have taken place without German involvement, when the overall command of the Turkish armies was under von der Goltz, von Sanders, and an influential contingent of German military officers. More likely they had been under orders from Berlin not to interfere on the grounds that, as Enver and Talaat had insisted, the Armenian problem was an internal Turkish matter in which the Turks would brook no interference even from their most powerful ally.

Von Sanders laid the blame at the door of the Young Turks in Constantinople, but only for having issued the deportation decree. The brutal execution of that order he ascribed in part to local officials but mostly to the Turkish gendarmerie, whom he depicted as men of the lowest order. Von Sanders may have been speaking from ignorance but, in any event, he was certainly understating the case.

The vast evidence presented before the military tribunal in Constantinople two years earlier had revealed that Talaat had empowered Dr. Behaeddin Shakir to release criminals from the provincial jails and create the Teshkilat-i Mahsusa expressly for the purpose of dealing with the Armenians. Von Sanders may not have been familiar with the proceedings of the tribunal. But the extent of German involvement with the Turkish military made it implausible that he did not know what was happening. There is, after all, a certain difference between the "thieves and unemployed" of his description and the murderers and rapists identified by the Turkish court.

Von Sanders's inadequacy as a witness was further evident in his comments on the Turkish mistrust of Armenians, which focused on the military need for evacuating Anatolia and on the fact that some Armenians had defected to the Russians to fight against the Turks; in other words, by his account, Turkey had had to defend itself against Armenian treachery. These were two notions floated by the Turks that von Sanders had apparently accepted. In fact, the Armenian "defectors" were refugees fleeing Turkish persecution and finding refuge with their Armenian compatriots—more than one million—in the Russian-administered Transcaucasus, where for a century they had enjoyed relative well-being. As for the question of Turkish security, it struck someone as young and unread in history as Tehlirian, as well as many others in the courtroom that governments do not destroy an entire people because of "military necessity." Even Germany, threatened on all sides, had not behaved in this manner toward its ethnic minorities living in regions bordering on Russia.

Tehlirian stared at von Sanders and, contemplating his testimony, wondered by what stretch of the imagination hundreds of thousands of innocent and harmless women and children could have been considered a threat to Turkish military interests.

A further question hanging in the air had already been raised and resolved in the Constantinople proceedings: If the deportations and massacres had violated the Turkish Constitution, every official had the right to protest and refuse to execute them. But no such argument was voiced in Berlin.

Something else troubled Tehlirian as he turned von Sanders's testimony over in his mind. The general conceded that the deportations had been decreed by the Young Turk Committee in Constantinople, but he seemed to give greater weight to the improper execution of those decrees by unsavory elements in the gendarmerie. He seemed to be implying that what the Young Turks had really had in mind had been a benign fulfillment of their decrees, but that it had gotten out of hand. Thus, even as he assigned responsibility for the atrocities to the Young Turks, he minimized their guilt by laying greater blame on those "lower-class" elements they themselves had unleashed on the hapless Armenians.

As von Sanders left the stand, however, the defense knew that the testimony of the next witness would settle the question of Talaat's guilt and bring the trial to a climax.

Looking older than his forty-two years, Bishop Krikoris Balakian, who had come from Manchester, England, to testify, took the stand and was sworn in. Persecuted and killed in large numbers by the Young Turks, the clergymen who had survived, such as Bishop Balakian, had escaped and established parishes in foreign countries where they conducted services, founded Armenian schools, and kept alive the traditions of their ancient culture.

The Armenian bishop had entered the clergy twenty years earlier and had learned some German, as many educated Armenians had. But he said he had not spoken it for the last five years. He had been in Berlin in 1914 but left when the war started, returning to Constantinople. There, Balakian was among the first Armenian intellectuals to be seized and exiled on April 24, 1915. He was thus an early victim of the movement to annihilate the Armenian people. His graphic testimony supplemented that of Dr. Lepsius and served as an antidote to that of General von Sanders. He first described his own ordeal. For thirty-six hours his group traveled by train to the vicinity of Angora. About 190 were exiled by caravan to Ayash and the remainder by wagons to Djangere, about twenty-four hours beyond, reorganized into groups of twenty-five, fifteen, ten and five persons, taken back to Angora and killed. "Of the 190, only sixteen remained alive. I am one of them."

The courtroom was silent as those present weighed the import of this testimony. The murder of 85 percent of the Armenian intellectuals in this initial phase of a calculated genocidal plan bespoke a frighteningly efficient method, even as it foretold the numberless similar catastrophes yet to come. The bishop continued his terrible story in calm tones.

In Djangere there were some 250 Armenians who, together with the sixteen survivors from Constantinople, were exiled to the des-

ert at Deir Zor on orders from the Ministry of the Interior. But the
local Governor, Reshad Pasha, refused to carry out the order from
the Ministry and was immediately removed. His Deputy, who was
also the local Secretary of the Ittihadists, wanted to carry out the
order but we gave him about 800 Turkish pounds in gold and he
kept us there until February 1916.

We then heard that the Governor of Angora—who we heard was
responsible for the deaths of 82,000 Armenian men, women and
children—was sent to replace Reshad Pasha. He carried out Talaat
Pasha's order and we were deported to Deir Zor. At first, forty-
eight men were deported and when we were asked if we wanted the
women and children with us, I advised against it. Later we learned
that the women and children had been killed.

The deportees were forced to march in caravans through a succession of Turkish villages; the bloodiest stretch lay between Yozgat and
Boghaslian. The bishop realized by now that although the official
name of the action was "deportation," in reality it was "an organized policy of annihilation."

Because we had some money—about fifteen to sixteen hundred
gold pounds—we thought that in the general custom of the Orient
known as *bakhsheesh,* we could perhaps save our lives. That is to
say, we hoped at least to accomplish with money what we could
not through other means. We were not wrong. If I stand here alive
today, it is because of *bakhsheesh.*

The caravan was treated badly; deportees were not allowed to slake
their thirst even when close to a river, neither were they allowed to
buy food. Nonetheless everyone seemed gratified to be fortunate
enough to be alive. But then they encountered a monumental horror.

When we neared Yozgat, the bloodiest place of all, we saw near us
in a valley hundreds of heads with long hair—the heads of women
and children. Our caravan consisted of forty-eight men led by a
Captain of Military Police with a mounted escort of sixteen gendarmes. I asked the Captain if it were true that only Armenian men
were to be killed and not the women and children. "Well," he replied, "if we kill only the men and not the women and children,
then in fifty years there will be a couple of million Armenians. We
have to kill women and children so that there will be no internal or
external trouble."

The bishop pursued the question, asking why the women and children in the towns had not been killed. The captain was very forthcoming and explained that that was forbidden because in 1895–96 Sultan Abdul Hamid had ordered that everyone in the towns had to be killed. But when Europe and the entire civilized world found out, they did not tolerate it. Now, continued the captain, no one would be left alive as witnesses to come before some future court.

"The Captain said to me: "I can tell you all this because you are going into the desert and will die of hunger and will not be able to bring any of it to light." Originally, the captain said, he had led fourteen thousand men out of the town of Yozgat and surroundings into the valleys and killed them. The surviving family members were told that the men had arrived safely in Aleppo and had asked the government to permit the families to follow where they would find dwellings. The families were told that permission was given and all portable goods could be taken. Thereupon, the families packed everything—gold objects, silver, jewelry, rugs, whatever was portable.

The captain told me that the women now believed their husbands to be alive and [were] prepared to join them. There were about 840 carts altogether, half of them oxcarts, the rest drawn by horses. Of the 6,400 women and children who were deported to Aleppo, many went by foot.

I now asked the Captain why he allowed these women and children to go to Aleppo and he replied: "If we had killed these women and children in the towns, we would not have known where their riches were, whether buried in the ground or otherwise hidden. That is why we allowed precious items such as jewelry to be taken. But after we had proceeded for about four hours, we came into a valley. With us were some thirty Turkish women who began to go through the clothing of the Armenian women and girls and took away the money and jewelry. It took them four days."

When it was over, the captain told the Armenians a new order had come pardoning them and that they could return to their homes. The carts and coaches with their goods were sent on ahead as the caravans now reached a plain some four hours from Yozgat. The Captain sent his gendarmes into the nearby villages of the district to arouse the Turkish peasants to wage a *jihad*—a holy war. About twelve thousand peasants armed with wood-axes and other iron instruments fell on the Armenian women and children and hacked them to death. The only ones spared were the prettiest girls.

The court, which might by now have been inured to such harrowing testimony, was nevertheless stunned by these new revelations. The bishop, who seemed to be reliving the most torturous moments of his life, recovered his faculties and continued.

Women and children were killed without any regard whatsoever. I asked the Captain whether he had any pangs of conscience, whether he did not feel responsible to God, to humanity, to civilization. The Captain replied: "I am not responsible. I received the order from Constantinople. I am a Captain of the gendarmerie. They gave us the order to kill all the men because we have declared a Holy War. If a soldier kills someone in war he is not guilty. That is what I did, and after the slaughter I delivered a prayer and therefore was not guilty."

Defense Attorney von Gordon asked the bishop whether, when he was in Djangere, he had not gone with one of his old professors to see the governor, and whether the governor had showed him a telegram from Talaat Pasha containing a certain question.
"Yes," the bishop said.

The professor was Diran Kelekian of the University of Constantinople but also chief editor of the Turkish newspaper *Sabah*. He invited me to visit the Vice Governor Asaf Bey. I wondered whether it wouldn't be better if we hid ourselves, but the professor said, "Have no fear, Asaf is my student, he kisses my hand and displays great respect. We have often discussed these matters."
We visited Asaf Bey and he received us with great courtesy. We asked him what we could do to rescue ourselves and get to Constantinople. He replied to the professor, "Dear teacher, whatever you want to do, do fast, otherwise it will be too late." Naturally, we asked why it would be too late. We said we had no idea whether massacres had begun in Asia Minor. We didn't even know what was happening two hours away. Asaf Bey replied, "I cannot tell you more but you, Professor Kelekian, are my teacher, and you [turning to the bishop] are a clergyman who keeps a secret, I have great trust in your religious position. I shall show you a dispatch." Asaf then showed Professor Kelekian a telegram I read with him. I cannot confirm every word in it, but it read approximately like this: "Telegraph us directly how many of the Armenians are already dead and how many still alive. Signed, Minister of the Interior Talaat."

The bishop paused for a moment, then continued.

It is impossible for me to even think that an entire nation should be destroyed by slaughter. That has never happened before. Professor Kelekian asked Asaf Bey: "What does this mean? I do not understand it."

Asaf Bey replied, "You are a wise man, after all, you are a chief editor. . . . The telegram means: 'Why are you waiting? Carry out the massacre!' ''

Balakian became distraught, hesitated, then resumed.

Professor Kelekian began to cry. Then he said, "I have not raised my children to the point where they can fend for themselves. There remains nothing further for us to do than that you—meaning me—go with me to church and give me the Sacrament."

Asaf Bey advised us to work hard but quietly so that within two weeks we would be in Constantinople. In fifteen days, he told us, he would be leaving his post. And then he said, "I was in Osmani in 1909 when large-scale massacres took place in Adana. I was accused of having mistreated the Armenians and it was with great difficulty that I was saved. *I do not want to take part in another Armenian massacre because the time will come after the war when all high-level responsible persons will have to flee abroad. And then, we will be held responsible for these massacres and will perhaps be hung.*"

There was a long silence in the courtroom, which was finally broken by the unfamiliar voice of a juror, who asked, "Whose signature was on the telegram?"

"The signature on the telegram was 'Talaat.' I saw it with my own eyes," the bishop answered.

Defense Attorney von Gordon asked the bishop to tell the court how he had eventually been saved, and the bishop related his experiences in fleeing further Turkish persecution, finding refuge with German engineers who were building tunnels for the Baghdad Railway through the Amanus Mountains of central Turkey. The engineers told him to get rid of his beard and his clergyman's garb and wear European clothes. During the four months he spent there, he observed that some eight thousand Armenians were employed and protected by the Germans. But an order came that the Armenians had to be deported and killed, so the bishop fled again, this time to the Taurus Mountains, where other German engineers were also building a tunnel. His stay there was short, however. Turkish officials discovered he was an Armenian priest, so he fled to Adana. He stayed there for five months, again under German protection, dressed like a German soldier and taught to behave like one.

Balakian paused to voice his gratitude for the help and protection he had received from the German engineers and soldiers. Then he continued his narrative.

When the Allied armies had taken Damascus and marched on to Aleppo in late 1917, the Turks in Adana told the Armenians that they would not be allowed "to live and laugh and do harm to the Turks." Several thousand Armenians who had survived the earlier massacre in Adana were taken to a place between the mountains of Sis and Hajin and slaughtered.

Another German officer gave Balakian a uniform, and so clad, he came with German military personnel by train to Constantinople, where he hid until war's end. Then, collecting all available reports on the atrocities, he went to France in the hope of laying the evidence of Turkish crimes before the Paris Peace Conference.

Defense Attorney von Gordon now sought to tie up loose ends by connecting Bishop Balakian's testimony with that of Dr. Lepsius and General von Sanders.

"His Excellency Liman von Sanders has brought upon us a great conflict of conscience. He maintained that it was not Talaat Pasha who bore the responsibility for the atrocities but the subordinate organs which carried out the deportation orders. That contradicts the general conception which prevails among Armenians and the conviction of Dr. Lepsius.

"I should like now to ask the witness a question. Do not the Armenians hold the absolute conviction that Talaat was personally responsible for these massacres?"

"It is not only the general view, it is the truth," the bishop answered. "I am a synodal member of the Armenian Patriarchate in Constantinople and over a long period of time have had much opportunity to know Turkish affairs. I, naturally, also knew Talaat Pasha personally. His influence was total. He did everything with full awareness. When he wanted something for the Armenian Patriarchate, he would tell us, 'You need not go first to the other ministers, come directly to me. You need not write anything down, just tell me personally.' Talaat did it that way so he did not have to be accountable to anyone else."

"Do you know that among the Armenians these words of Talaat's have been circulated: 'I have done more on one day for the solution of the Armenian problem than Abdul Hamid did in thirty years!'?''

"Not only in thirty years. Talaat has done what has not happened in five hundred years! When I was in Djangere in September 1915, when all of Anatolia had been emptied of Armenians and massacred, there came from Erzerum to Djangere a Turkish major from the Russo-Turkish front on his way to Constantinople. With great pride he announced, 'What all our former Sultans have not done we have accomplished. We have wiped out a historic people in two months.' ''

For the first time in a long while, Judge Lehmberg intervened.

"Was this the overwhelming understanding with Armenians and Turks? And the fact is correct that through Talaat, in fifteen months the Armenians suffered more destruction than in many years?''

"Yes. But I never heard that from the mouth of Talaat himself."

In his lengthy testimony, Balakian had introduced two new aspects of the Anatolian tragedy: the fact of mass theft through the confiscation of personal property and the violent participation of Turkish peasants. There was also his inclusion of a horror even grislier than any described before.

After he had allowed the import of the bishop's words to sink in, Defense Attorney von Gordon addressed a question to General von Sanders.

"Your Excellency, you have said, not in positive form but nevertheless have expressed the idea, that the subordinates should be held responsible for the atrocities?''

"For the horrors, not for the deportations."

"Contrary to that view, I must do my duty and submit five original telegrams received from the vice governor of Aleppo. I should like to read two of these telegrams. Professor Lepsius has examined them all."

Judge Lehmberg pointed out to von Gordon that if he read the telegrams out loud, he would be anticipating the evidence.

"I must first tell you what there is in the telegrams," von Gordon said. "They will prove that Talaat personally gave the order in those five telegrams to attack all Armenians, including Armenian children. At first the order was given to hold back on the children only to the extent that they should not remember what happened to their parents. Later, in March 1916, the order became sharper, namely, that all children were to be removed from orphanages and destroyed because they would comprise dangerous future elements for the Turks.

"The witness Aram Andonian can testify as to the authenticity of these telegrams. He received them directly from the vice governor of Aleppo and delivered them to the British, who then made them available to the Armenian Delegation in Paris. I personally think it possible and even probable, and hope that the jurors believe that in the deepest recesses of his heart the accused—and not without good reason—is absolutely convinced that Talaat Pasha was the author of these terrible atrocities against the Armenians and therefore responsible for them. If that . . . is accepted, then I am prepared to forgo reading these telegrams."

Prosecutor Gollnick quickly intervened.

"I request that the proposal be declined. The presiding judge—quite generously—has already allowed discussion as to whether Talaat is guilty of the Armenian massacres. This question, however, is irrelevant because it cannot be doubted that the accused believed that in the person of Talaat, there stood before him the one who bears the guilt. Thus the motive is completely explained. I am also of the view that it is quite out of the question to clarify the issue of Talaat's guilt here in this court of justice. That must be a historical judgment, for which entirely other documents and evidence are required than those we have here."

Von Gordon withdrew his proposal to read the telegrams, but Tehlirian spoke up to insist that Aram Andonian's testimony be heard. Judge Lehmberg consulted with the jurors and addressed Tehlirian: "The jurors believe . . . that in the commission of the deed, you were convinced that Talaat Pasha was the one responsible for the massacres," thereby obviating the need to hear Andonian's testimony.

There remained one final piece of evidence to be heard: the expert testimony of the five doctors who had been patiently waiting to present their evaluation of Soghomon Tehlirian's state of mind at the time of the murder.

Central to the testimony of all five were the cardinal issues of Tehlirian's illness—how it affected his state of mind and whether it relieved him of responsibility. Such evidence would determine the applicability of Paragraph 51 of the criminal code, which—if Tehlirian was not in control of his senses—would absolve him of the crime.

Epilepsy and *free will* were the words that repeatedly echoed in the courtroom as the doctors offered their medical opinions. The task confronting each of them was to prove the presence or absence of free will. This question hinged on whether Tehlirian suffered from epilepsy, and if so, from what form.

The testimony of Dr. Robert Störmer, privy medical councillor to the court, was the longest of the five and was based on his examination of the accused, conducted at the state prosecutor's request. Störmer said flatly that Tehlirian was an epileptic.

He was never seriously ill until 1915, when he was an eyewitness to the massacres. He described to me the killing of his loved ones. He remembers that with a shuddering fear of the moment when he saw the ax of a Turk come down on his brother's head splitting it in two. The terrifying impression of this murderous deed, connected to the physical injuries to his head, arm, and knee, have robbed him of recollection.

For three days he was unconscious, and when he finally awoke, he was covered by corpses and the smell of corpses, which is embedded for all eternity in him and his soul. He told me that whenever he reads about this or when he recalls the massacre, the odor of corpses presses so on his olfactory organs that he has never been able to overcome it.

Störmer described in detail the effects of the attacks—sudden fatigue, loss of energy, fainting, then, on regaining consciousness, a great thirst and an urge to sleep. The first attack had come in 1916, the second at his parental home in Erzinga. Since then he had had four more. Always there was the odor of corpses. Störmer said these symptoms corroborated his diagnosis of epilepsy of a psychic nature—one of whose characteristics, he said, was tenacity.

As for the vision of Tehlirian's mother and her sharp, accusatory words, Störmer said this was not a hallucination but a dream image transposed into a waking state, as is often the case in epilepsy. Consequently, although the epilepsy had an unpredictable influence on the accused, it did not exclude the exercise of free will. On the contrary, Störmer said, the accused was very alert on the day of the crime and took some cognac only to give himself courage.

After observing Talaat emerge from the house, he seized his weapon and hurried to the street. He explained to me that he had

convinced himself that it was Talaat Pasha and that he had shot
him from behind because otherwise Talaat would have seen the
pistol and thwarted the assassination. He had carefully observed
Talaat's clothing and fired the shot between the hat and the coat.

While I see nothing that has to do with epilepsy on the morning
of March 15, the horrible experiences he had in Armenia had an
unmistakable influence on the deed. But this influence did not go
so far as to exclude his exercise of his free will.

After Judge Lehmberg instructed the interpreter to inform
Tehlirian that Dr. Störmer held him responsible for the deed, a juror
asked whether in the rush of events, when the terrible images of his
experiences came before his eyes, Tehlirian could not have sunk into
a morbid state. Störmer did not think so. Defense Attorney
Werthauer asked whether—if it could be proved that Tehlirian had
suffered an epileptic attack during the night—he could still be
held responsible. But Störmer was adamant. Even if such an attack
had taken place, there would still have been no absence of free will.

The issue had plainly caught the attention of the court, for now
another juror asked if it was possible that Tehlirian had no idea that
he had had an epileptic attack in the night. Störmer said it was
possible and that it was a common occurrence in insane asylums, but
it didn't shake his position.

One of the two associate judges, Dr. Lachs, now entered the
discussion, asking whether in the interim between attacks, responsibility was complete or reduced. Störmer said it was reduced. Lachs
then asked whether between attacks the epileptic was in a condition
of psychic compulsion. Very seldom, Störmer said, not swerving
from his previous position.

Defense Attorney Niemeyer had the last word, however, before
Störmer left the witness stand. He remarked: "The medical expert
cannot tell us the condition of the accused at the moment of the
deed."

Dr. Hugo Liepmann, a professor at the University of Berlin and a
psychiatrist, agreed with Störmer on the issue of free will. But he was
less absolute in identifying epilepsy. Liepmann was one of the doctors
who had examined Tehlirian prior to the trial, and he had done so
(as he now told the court) on three occasions.

He began by praising the accused, saying he possessed a rare
sincerity, was candid, adopted no pose, and was resigned to whatever

fate might befall him—he was no longer interested in life. Liepmann then addressed the question of his illness.

"In my view, *epilepsy* is not the magic word that is the key to the psychic life of the accused. Rather one must turn to the less-well-known area of psychopathology . . . and the aftereffects of a severe emotional shock in especially despondent people."

When a healthy person has a shattering experience, Liepmann explained, it rages within but eventually peters out. More sensitive natures, however, may be derailed by such experiences, which do not fade away and remain fixed in the soul. Always present, the experience gradually becomes overpowering, asserts itself repeatedly, and can propel the individual into unintended actions.

Liepmann described the impact of such a "psychic wound" on the seventeen-year-old youth who had traveled restlessly, unable to compose himself or organize his thoughts, and examined its nature, pointing out the absence of what according to him were the symptoms of genuine epileptic attacks—tongue biting, lip biting, urinary discharge, and a flailing about. He was convinced, he said, that the attacks were instead the expression of a severe psychic injury. Further, Tehlirian had told Liepmann he was aware that Christianity forbade him to kill; but after the spirit of his mother had appeared, he believed he was on the right path. He was acting under emotional pressure—not compulsion, Liepmann emphasized.

Ending his testimony, Liepmann said that while he found a certain limitation of free will, he could not find Tehlirian completely unaccountable: "Therefore, he does not come under Paragraph Fifty-one, but so close . . . that it would have required special moral inhibitions to resist the pressure."

Thus the first two experts held that at the moment of the crime, Tehlirian was in control and acted with free will. Dr. Cassirer, the psychiatrist whom Tehlirian had consulted after several attacks in Berlin, appeared next. His testimony was similar to Liepmann's.

When Tehlirian first came to him, Cassirer said, he had assumed that the attacks were symptomatic of epilepsy and accordingly prescribed medication of a sedative nature. It was not until the trial and the testimony he heard there, Cassirer confessed, that he had changed his mind. Now he was more in accord with the preceding opinion that the illness was in fact a psychic injury.

"I reach the same conclusion and for the same reasons as Privy Councillor Liepmann. This psychic instability has led to abnormal psychic apparitions, such as his mother seen in a dreamlike vision. He himself said that when he felt unwell he saw the image of his mother. This condition is purely psychopathic, and I consequently conclude that he is a severe psychopath.''

Cassirer then made the judgment that everyone was waiting to hear on the matter of responsibility.

''I am of the opinion that very fundamental morbid events played a role in the execution of the deed, but I do not maintain that he was in a state of total responsibility when he acted, as relates to Paragraph Fifty-one. But he stands very close to it, and for us psychiatrists, the lines are not so sharply and clearly drawn.''

Before the next witness, Defense Attorney Niemeyer, as he had with Dr. Störmer, asked Cassirer if Tehlirian's condition at the moment of the deed could really be known. Cassirer replied that it could only be assumed. Niemeyer again appeared satisfied.

Thus far, while they disagreed on the nature of Tehlirian's illness, all three experts held the view that when he committed the crime he was fully responsible and that there were no mitigating circumstances. Attention now turned to the two remaining medical authorities.

Professor Forster, a psychiatrist from Berlin's world-famous Charité Hospital, began with a verbal bow of respect to Drs. Cassirer and Liepmann, and then directly opposed their opinion that Tehlirian was a psychopath.

> When one hears what the accused has endured, then one has the
> . . . feeling that he obviously had to kill Talaat, whom he holds responsible as a murderer. Would a normal person do that? Other Armenians who lived through the same terror, perhaps even the same vengeful thoughts, did not commit this crime. So the deed is obviously no proof that the perpetrator is pathological.
>
> What we are dealing with is not genuine epilepsy but emotional epilepsy. Before the accused experienced the emotional event, he did not have these attacks. Now he describes them clearly: When he sees the images of the horrors, he sees the corpses and smells their odor. Then come the attacks, but not with a simple crying out and a convulsion, as in epilepsy, but a moaning and then falling down. He experiences the horrors so vividly that he loses consciousness. What he experienced in reality emerges so graphically before his eyes that the same emotions are released as in the reality.
>
> It is the same mechanism as when you run water through the mouth of a hungry person when he is thinking of a thick steak. The

imagination works similarly here, too, as if a steak is actually being eaten.

Forster said he was convinced that Tehlirian did not want to take revenge, but the compulsion of his morbid imagination and his mother's demand, returned time and again to shake him because the deed was contrary to his nature. And now Forster, too, came to the key issue of responsibility.

Do the conditions of Paragraph Fifty-one pertain? One cannot answer the question, Insane or not? with a simple yes or no. In contrast to the openly insane, here we are dealing with gradations. Every fanatic, every person who is driven by a strong idea, has something of the psychopath in him. Here, too, the question whether his morbid transformation was so powerful that it meets the conditions of Paragraph Fifty-one is very difficult to answer with a yes or no. How does one draw the line? I am generally inclined to draw a very fine one. In this case, however, I believe there are enough indications that Paragraph Fifty-one comes into play, and therefore I say that the exercise of free will was out of the question.

The courtroom was silent after this carefully drawn and measured judgment, which held that the defendant was not responsible for his actions. The fifth and final expert, a neurologist named Dr. Bruno Haake, was brief and direct. Sensing perhaps that the medical testimony may have been protracted and tedious, he spoke only six sentences, concluding: "I should like to go a bit further than my predecessor and give a completely affirmative answer to the question of whether free will is out of the question."

Thus, only two of the five had testified favorably for the defense, that Tehlirian was not responsible for his actions when he fired the fatal bullet.

All the evidence was now in, and only final arguments and summations by the defense and prosecution remained before Judge Lehmberg would charge the jury and ask it to deliberate and deliver its verdict.

Tehlirian lay in his cell that night and dwelt on the day's complex testimony. He understood that his life hung in the balance and that it rested particularly on the evidence of the medical experts—the psychiatrists and neurologists—who had examined him. Yet his thoughts did not center on their arguments. Rather, he concentrated on the vivid testimony of Johannes Lepsius. For it was Lepsius who had really spoken for him and had said everything that he, Tehlirian, had wanted to say at his first interrogation and later at his trial—the entire story of the fate of the Armenians.

As he lay on his cot, his thoughts alternating between images of Anahid and Lepsius's account of the events of the last twenty years, he lapsed into a dream:

He was walking in an endless desert, and everywhere in this immense space were sand dunes, like petrified waves. Looking down, he saw human footprints, which were sometimes visible and sometimes abruptly vanished. Suddenly he saw his mother, lying on the ground, in rags. He rushed to lift her.

"No, my son," she said, in a profoundly tired voice. "I am dead, it won't help, go home. But do you see what they have done to me? There isn't even a bit of earth on me. At night it is bitter cold and I freeze, especially my torso."

"Wait, mother, I will cover you."

"Yes, cover me, my child, cover me."

He covered her bare feet, her exposed torso, and her breast with sand, but when he tried to cover her head, she said: "No, my child, let my head stay free so that I can breathe. Now it is better. May you live a long life. Now go home."

Tehlirian opened his eyes in the dark cell and sensed that he had been eased of a great burden. Despite the judgment awaiting him the next day he fell asleep, suffused with a warm glow.

8

Justice in Berlin

*T*he next morning, an even greater crowd packed the courtroom, especially in the standing-room area, and it seemed to Tehlirian that more officials were also present. The newspaper accounts of the first day's proceedings had obviously excited the public's imagination.

Judge Lehmberg rapped his gavel at 9:15 A.M., noting that all necessary participants were present and that all relevant evidence had been heard. Then, in accordance with German court procedure, he read three questions, which he had drafted to clarify the issues for the jury:

1. Is the accused, Soghomon Tehlirian, guilty of deliberately having killed Talaat Pasha on March 15, 1921?

That question concerns homicide. Now comes the second question, concerning murder, which is to be answered only if the first question is answered in the affirmative.

2. Did the accused carry out the killing with premeditation?

Now comes the third question, to be answered only if the first, concerning homicide, is answered affirmatively but the second, concerning premeditation is denied.

3. Were there mitigating circumstances?*

*In fact, it was precisely the "mitigating circumstances" that proved to be the pivotal elements in this unusual case. The distinction between a premeditated act and one committed under emotional stress—raised later by von Gordon—had to be understood for the jury to reach its verdict.

If no further information is needed in the formulation of this question, I give the floor now to the prosecuting attorney.

Before Gollnick could begin his final arguments, von Gordon interrupted to say that Armin T. Wegner, who had been invited as a witness and who had taken photographs of the massacres was standing by. After some discussion, it was agreed that his testimony was no longer needed.*

Judge Lehmberg asked the prosecutor to address the question of guilt. It took the prosecutor some time to do so, for he apparently relished having an international audience before whom he could paint a picture with the broadest strokes. His opening paean to Talaat Pasha was not short on hyperbole, even as it reflected the government's attitude.

"It is the victim's personality that gives the deed its special meaning; out of the mass of the unknown and the unnamed, there reaches out the hand of a man who—himself the son of a people at a time of the most powerful international struggle—directed the fate of his fatherland and as a loyal ally of the German people has been transported to the heights of history."

Gollnick reviewed the events of March 15 and observed,

> The killing of a human being is punishable according to German
> law; it is punishable if it deals simply with the killing of a person.
> It also makes no difference whether the slain person is a German or
> a foreigner. According to Paragraph Three of the German Penal
> Code, the penal law of the German Reich embraces crimes com-
> mitted in all parts of the German Reich. The circumstance that the
> victim and the accused were both foreigners is, penally speaking,
> of no consequence. According to our laws, the accused merits
> punishment and certain circumstances do not render the deed un-
> punishable.
>
> First of all we must establish whether the slaying is a murder or
> manslaughter, because these two types of slaying are differentiated
> by the law, and you know that murder is the most severe crime

---

*Wegner was a prolific German publicist who had volunteered as a Red Cross medic in Turkey. In 1919 he wrote a long open letter to President Woodrow Wilson calling attention to the atrocities; in 1921 he wrote the introduction to the transcript of Tehlirian's trial; in 1933 he was arrested and tortured by the Gestapo for writing against the Nazis, then released through foreign intervention; in 1968, while in Soviet Armenia, a street was named after him in Yerevan; in 1972 he visited the United States, and six years later died at his home in Italy.

punishable by death, while manslaughter, that is, a killing committed under emotional stress, is viewed as being milder.

For anyone in the court who did not understand the meaning of murder, Gollnick spelled it out in the finest detail:

I can assume that it is known that murder is that form of slaying in which the deed is executed with premeditation, and that premeditation is a calm, clear, reasonable activity in which the perpetrator, in carrying out the deed, is still in the condition, and has the capacity, to clearly understand the significance of the deed, his motives, the means by which to carry it out, the consequences, the moral inhibitions, and counterreasons that could possibly argue against the deed, and to weigh all of these, and after all that, to reach his decision.

Gollnick argued that the motives for Tehlirian's crime were political—"political hate and political revenge." There could be no question, he stressed, that "horrors have happened, terrible deeds [been] committed against the Armenian people," and it was equally beyond doubt, he continued, that the accused and his family met with horror, that fate had delivered his family to death, and that he had seen it all happen.

Having accepted the two major points that the evidence thus far had irrefutably established, Gollnick now sought to prove that Talaat was not responsible for the atrocities and therefore Tehlirian had killed the wrong person: "The accused saw in Talaat Pasha the originator of the fate that he, his family, and many compatriots had met. Further, in Talaat he saw not only the minister of the interior but the personal and moral author of this crime. The establishment of these motives suffices completely for a criminal judgment. But, gentlemen, the question arises whether Talaat was truly the personal and moral author of these crimes."

But the prosecutor soon became so entangled in his efforts to prove that Talaat was an innocent bystander that Judge Lehmberg intervened with a reprimand, noting that Gollnick was entering territory not supported by testimony.

Gollnick again expressed the official views of the German government when he disputed the arguments of Johannes Lepsius, leaning instead toward the judgments of General Liman von Sanders, who had drawn a sharp distinction between decisions made in Constantinople and the execution of those decisions in the field. But Gollnick went further, invoking the Turkish argument of Armenian treachery, by claiming that Armenians had conspired with the Allies to stab the Turks in the back and achieve independence. On the grounds of such reports, he argued, Constantinople decided to issue the order for deportation. How that order was executed, Gollnick stressed, had to be considered separately from the order itself.

Here the prosecutor imputed a degree of barbarism to Asia Minor and suggested that the peoples who inhabited Turkey did not behave toward one another as did the civilized nations of Europe. He again referred to von Sanders's testimony about the Turkish gendarmes—"recruited rabble"—in whom "the worst instincts of human nature, robbery, and murder came to the fore."

Conceding that atrocities took place, he simply sought to absolve Talaat of any moral responsibility. He not only questioned the validity of the incriminating telegrams signed by Talaat but even disputed the findings and decisions of the Turkish military tribunal, concluding: "The evidence has not supported in the slightest the claim that Talaat Pasha was the moral author of these crimes."

In view of the severity of the crimes, he continued, and of the conviction that Talaat was responsible, Tehlirian's motive was clearly one of revenge, a motive that "should be humanely understood as long as human beings comprehend love and hate." Gollnick then sought to prove his central point of premeditation.

He reviewed Tehlirian's travels and his arrival in Berlin, "possessed of the fantastic idea of revenge, drawn as if by a magnet to the door of his victim's house." He cited Tehlirian's testimony that the decision to kill Talaat Pasha was made fourteen days before the deed; how he had changed his residence, moving directly opposite Talaat and observing his habits; how on March 15 he approached Talaat face-to-face to confirm his identity before shooting him from behind; how after the deed he called out that he and the victim were foreigners and that Germans need not be concerned.

> Gentlemen, all these circumstances lead one to say that the deed was carried out in a cold-blooded, circumspect, and premeditated manner. Then there is the temperament of the accused. Is he a hot-blooded person, easily excited? On the contrary, he is introverted, quiet, melancholy, not given to merriment or bursts of rage, a man who lets himself brood in thought. This too, in my view, supports his having acted with premeditation.

The prosecuting attorney now raised the issue of Paragraph 51, involving the matter of responsibility and the exercise of free will. He regretted that all five medical experts did not agree, but noted that the accused was an epileptic.

The epileptic loses his ability to reason in an attack but is otherwise a normal person. So, did the accused have an attack when committing the deed? Or shortly before? If not, then he must be viewed as a normal person. The court itself must decide.

Further, his behavior here shows him to have high intelligence. His replies are sharp and on target. We agree with the view of those who testified that Paragraph Fifty-one is not applicable. The existing penal code does not recognize mitigating circumstances, but we should not have only the interests of the perpetrator in mind but must think also of the victim.

We must consider here a man, torn from life at a time when his powers were at their peak, his death mourned by his widow and family, a man who stood in reputation as a great patriot and honorable man in the eyes of his national and religious compatriots.

Finally, gentlemen, also take into account the circumstances [that] favor the accused, namely the granting of a pardon.

Therefore, gentlemen of the jury, I ask that you find the accused guilty of murder.

Judge Lehmberg asked the interpreter to inform Tehlirian that the prosecuting attorney had asked the jury to find him guilty of murder with premeditation. It was not, however, to be Gollnick's last word in the trial.

The judge then asked the defense to present its final arguments. It was already midmorning, and Tehlirian's three attorneys had much ground to cover before the noon recess.

━━━━

Defense Attorney von Gordon lost no time in responding to Gollnick's summation and especially to his final point.

Gentlemen of the jury, the state attorney has indicated that even if you find the accused guilty of murder and condemn him to death, . . . the president of the Reich would certainly pardon him.

That is no way to influence you in this courtroom. If you find him guilty, he will be condemned to death, and we don't know what the president of the German Reich will decide. The issue here is not a pardon but the law.

Von Gordon's firm voice now took on an edge of sarcasm.

In the highly honored prosecuting attorney, I am pleased to greet a defender; to be sure, not a defender of Tehlirian but of Talaat Pasha. Unfortunately, however, he does so only on the basis of facts reported to him by various people. I cannot go along with that.

I have here a battery of telegrams. I have a witness who received these telegrams and confirms their authenticity. I wanted to read them but withdrew when it was evident that Tehlirian and all his people were convinced that Talaat was the author of the atrocities. You, too, have recognized that. At one point in this trial, Bishop Balakian said: "I went to the governor of Djangere and asked for help and he showed me a telegram in which Talaat asked: 'How many in the transport were already dead? And how many alive?' We understood what that meant." That is the only moment in which Talaat's authorship of the atrocities came up in testimony.

It suffices to know the simple fact that in a few months, an undisputed 1,400,000 of a total of 1,800,000 human beings were deported, and of those deported, 1,000,000 were killed. Could that have happened without systematic direction from on high? Was the Turkish Government so weak that it could do nothing to oppose that? You may believe that if you wish, but I do not!

Von Gordon moved on to the initial interrogation on March 16 and the transcript taken at the time. He called the jury's attention to Kevork Kalustian:

Here sits the interpreter who was called to police headquarters for the first statement; who enthusiastically saw in the accused "a great man." And Soghomon Tehlirian, who was in a feverish state after being roughed up, answered yes to everything. The interpreter told us Tehlirian would have answered yes to anything, he was so disoriented, and in consequence, the interpreter did not sign the Protocol because it was not completely genuine.

The defense attorney next reminded the jury of the events of June 10, 1915, when the deportation of the Tehlirian family began.

The first column was of the well-to-do, with horse and wagon. The second included Tehlirian and his family. Outside the gates of

Erzinga, Armenians from neighboring villages were forced into the columns. Tehlirian couldn't see the front or the rear, he was in the middle with his family—two sisters of fifteen and sixteen, another of twenty-six with a small child, two brothers of twenty-two and twenty-six, and his mother—the entire family was in an oxcart.

They were soon attacked—but by whom? By the gendarmes, the military police identified here by His Excellency Liman von Sanders, and also by a mob of Turks and Kurds. First the weapons were taken away, even umbrellas, then the money, gold, and the food. Then they gratified their lust with the women. The young girls—the sisters of fifteen and sixteen—were dragged into the bushes, and from a ditch the family heard the terrible screaming of the two girls and knew what was happening to them.

The two girls did not survive. When the accused regained consciousness, he saw the corpse of one sister. And of the brothers? The accused saw the most horrible sight—the head of his twenty-two-year-old brother split in two with an ax, a horrible sight he still sees when disturbed. Before his eyes he sees his mother collapse, apparently hit by a bullet; the others disappear never to be seen again.

He himself saw nothing more because he was struck on the back of his head by a blunt instrument. That wound has been confirmed by doctors today. He collapsed into unconsciousness and when he came to toward evening, lying among thousands of corpses, he discovered he had two other wounds—a bullet through the arm and a bayonet in the knee. Both scars are still there. In the semidark he tried to orient himself, find a family member. But he was the only survivor.

Gentlemen, this terrible massacre is so unbelievable that at first we wondered whether you, the Gentlemen of the Jury, would believe him.

Von Gordon paused, brought his hands together, looked at the jurors for a moment as though waiting for them to respond. Then, his voice strained, he continued:

A few days ago, a somewhat hysterical brochure appeared, representing the opposing side, entitled "The Secret of the Murder of Talaat Pasha." Of course, there is no secret; the matter has been cleared up. According to the brochure, "the young Armenian who was delivered as the murderer of Talaat Pasha"—the implication is that a certain great power was behind the affair—"is a tool of the barbaric rage that typifies his race, acting without deliberation and without consciousness of what he did. His pathetic story about the deportation of his parents by the Turks is naturally intended to arouse the sympathy of the judge.''

If the author of this brochure had been in this courtroom yesterday and heard the report of Mrs. Terzibashian, he would have had to retract such an observation. We wanted to introduce far-reaching evidence in this direction. Two German nurses who were at that precise time in Erzinga and sent reports to our Foreign Office, were present here. I decided to forgo their testimony because Mrs. Terzibashian was also transported in the long columns [that passed] through Erzinga. I need not repeat the gruesome events she reported. She saw the corpses of the earlier deportation columns and how the men and children were thrown into the river. That is clear proof of Tehlirian's portrayal. His statement is true to the core and not a ''pathetic fiction.''

Von Gordon reviewed the events of Tehlirian's return to his parental home and his emotions on recalling the relatively happy times of his childhood. But the images of the massacre passed before his eyes, and he had had his first attack. The smell of corpses filled his nose and mouth and indeed his very being, followed by the spasmodic collapse and unconsciousness.

Speaking slowly and stressing every phrase, von Gordon reiterated Tehlirian's discovery of survivors in Erzinga, and recited the telltale figures with special emphasis.

"Of 20,000 Armenians, only two families were left, who saved themselves by adopting Mohammedanism, and a few others widely dispersed—altogether twenty Armenians out of 20,000.'' Suddenly, his voice burst out in the courtroom: "Gentlemen, these are impressions never to be forgotten throughout one's life!''

Von Gordon described Tehlirian's travels after he left Erzinga, minutely, finally coming to his life in Berlin. He pointed out Tehlirian's reserve in discussing his earlier life, never wishing to describe what had happened in any detail, if at all. Once, he said, seeing a book by Johannes Lepsius in Apelian's hand, Tehlirian had torn it away, crying: "Let the old wounds be!''

These were not the actions or the words of someone who brooded incessantly about his own tragedy, von Gordon emphasized. On the contrary, they showed that he had tried to overcome them. Neither, after his chance encounter with Talaat Pasha, did he speak of it to anyone. The sight of Talaat did not arouse in him the decision to kill the Turk; the experience passed, there were no thoughts of revenge . . . until the night he dreamed that his mother disowned him because he had not avenged his family.

At that moment he was overcome by the feeling that he wished again to be the son of his mother when he joined her in heaven. For Orientals, such apparitions play a quite different role than for us, who look on them with philosophical and medical eyes. Remember the bible stories of your childhood, in which it was said: "And an angel appeared to him in a dream." Important, essential events were transposed to dreams. This happened to Tehlirian. The next morning he went to Hardenbergstrasse in order now quite consciously—and not as the prosecuting attorney said, somewhat picturesquely, "drawn there magnetically"—to quite consciously find a room from which he could observe Talaat. . . . He even sacrificed the rent for March, thus paying double, to get this new room. He said to himself: "I have decided to murder Talaat and therefore I must get closer." In this moment, he wanted to kill him.

The defense attorney, observing that the Armenians were Christians, said that Tehlirian had reminded himself of the commandment "Thou shalt not kill," and that he wavered often. Yet he did not pursue the deed. Instead he worked on his German and played music. Any plans against Talaat were not evident in those first ten days in the new room. Then came March 15.

That he had drunk some cognac "for courage" was not pertinent von Gordon said. He drank it with tea because of an unsettled stomach. The fact that he drank it at 9 A.M. made it untenable that he was seeking courage, since he could not have known that Talaat would appear on that day at around 10. Tehlirian saw Talaat come out on the balcony. He still had made no decision to kill him. Suddenly, a quarter of an hour later, Talaat left the house, and images of the massacre and of his mother passed before Tehlirian's eyes. That was when he seized his gun and rushed out.[1]

Von Gordon now addressed the issue of premeditation, weighing "cold premeditation" against the possibility, which he believed to be the case, that there was in the accused "a storm of passion, of feelings and images." He cited the German Supreme Court's concept that in the commission of a criminal act, it was the time of execution that was crucial and not the time of decision, and then gave the court's explanation of the distinction between a crime committed with premeditation and one committed with emotion.

> The perpetrator executes the deed with premeditation only if he acts with an adequately clear weighing of the consequences of the killing by which he achieves his purpose, a weighing of the motives that press him to action, as well as a weighing of the requisite activity that brings about the realization of the desired result. In emotion, the situation is that a person, in natural rage, has the idea of killing another [and] is dominated in his conduct to an exclusive degree by emotional excitement.

Von Gordon now turned to Judge Lehmberg's three questions and to the relation between "guilt" and the medical testimony presented by the five experts.

"With full hearts and with total conviction, we defense attorneys ask you to reject the question of guilt. The judge will tell you the first question begins with the words: *Is he guilty?* Not questioned are the exclusion of free will, the morbid disturbance of his mentality, and so forth, but in the word *guilty* is the answer to the question of whether you hold the accused responsible or not in the moment of the deed."

The defense attorney examined the testimony of each of the five experts. Dr. Störmer, he said, was an experienced physician but not a psychiatrist, who had based his negative judgment on the belief that physical epilepsy was present. That was not true. Dr. Störmer had asked: "Is this epilepsy of the kind that affects the psyche? That suspends free will?" His reply was that free will was greatly reduced, but not completely suspended.

Professor Liepmann, on the other hand, offered another explanation, von Gordon continued, namely that the symptoms were not due to an illness of the central nervous system but rather to a powerful psychic impression that caused a physical condition similar to epilepsy.

> But this cautious, older psychiatrist has come to the conclusion that a complete suspension of free will is not the case here. "I cannot draw such a conclusion," he says.
>
> Professor Cassirer agrees and says that he has no answer to the question of whether Paragraph Fifty-one is operative here, but adds that the condition of the accused at the moment of the deed

can only be assumed. The rest is beyond his scope and belongs properly to the judge and the jury.

Now comes the younger generation: Professor Forster from the Charité Hospital's Psychiatric Department, a quite prominent specialist in the field of psychiatry. He agrees with the views of Liepmann and Cassirer, but on the basis of his experience, he views all this with skepticism. He finds it hard to favor the application of Paragraph Fifty-one. Professor Forster says: "Here, a serious illness was at work. For the psychiatrist, these are difficult matters; whether we can confirm or deny the exclusion of free will is a difficult question." Nevertheless, Professor Forster said that the provision of Paragraph Fifty-one—the suspension of free will—applied.

Then came the neurologist, Dr. Haake, who said he would go further than three of the other experts—"This is an emotional act. The perpetrator committed the deed under the compulsion of his imagination. I regard him as unaccountable."

Thus you see the younger generation. Professor Dr. Forster is only forty-two. The younger generation goes a bit further, the older generation is somewhat more cautious. But both admit that it is a difficult matter.

With that, the entire responsibility has been shifted onto you. Properly! Gentlemen—medical experts are always only helpmeets to the judge. They help us to form our judgment. But the judge is the ultimate authority . . . and you are free to make your own decisions."

Von Gordon noted that the freedom of human will was a controversial question in philosophy and theology, but that (in a court) the slightest doubt as to whether free will was exercised at the moment the deed was committed must lead to acquittal:

Ask yourselves whether you can say with certainty that the accused —in that moment when he saw Talaat Pasha leave the house and was seized by the idea of killing him [and] took his pistol and ran after him—that he was in a position to crystallize his collective psychic powers into a uniform decision, or whether his dead mother, the terrible images, the memories of his mistreated people, and everything else that ran through his head were the things that forced the weapon into his hand? The doctors leave you in the lurch; they transfer the responsibility to you, and two of the doctors say no; one cannot confirm that he was responsible.

Defense Attorney von Gordon was now nearing the end of his summation, and he briefly focused on the victim, Talaat Pasha, to balance the prosecuting attorney's favorable words about the Turkish politician:

> I know that people will say it is sad and disagreeable that someone has been given hospitality on German soil and shot down. In our time, when conflict is to be found everywhere, when Armenians and Turks continue to fight and blood flows—the prosecuting attorney himself referred to that—one has the perception that, in any case, because of Talaat's government, a sea of blood has flowed—of at least one million Armenians—of children, women, the elderly, and of valiant men—to which on Hardenbergstrasse one drop was added.
>
> Talaat and his comrades strove to annihilate the Armenian people for the purpose of creating a pure, all-Turkish state, and used means that are unbearable to us Europeans. It is also wrong to say that one can understand such atrocities in Asia, where human life is less valued. But I will not, from a higher standpoint, make the man who now lies under the earth personally responsible. A terrible fate has been revealed to us, and to it also belongs this small part—the deed on Hardenbergstrasse. But it would be terrible if a German court added to this fate by an injustice against this man who has been so sorely tested. I hope that you, gentlemen of the jury, will take these thoughts to heart.

Although Adolf von Gordon had covered all the major points of the case, his colleague Friedrich Werthauer, citing colorful examples, augmented many of the same points with an intensity and passion that gripped everyone in the courtroom.

Werthauer began in a low key, but his soft voice rose in volume as he developed his arguments. He focused initially on the relevance of the German Penal Code, especially Paragraph 51 and the matter of free will.

> Gentlemen of the jury! The first question concerns the killing. Whether you answer yes or no is the subject of this trial. . . . The question provides a secure handle for a no, because it does not ask "Did the accused kill Talaat Pasha?" but "Is the accused *guilty* of having killed Talaat Pasha?" This difference will accompany you into the jury room. The eyes of the world are watching us, and your verdict will be considered a just verdict for thousands of years.

In this word *guilty* lies a series of factors that embraces the entire penal code. Paragraph Fifty-one deals with the perpetrator's mental state. But two paragraphs later there is a similar one, which deals with self-defense. Self-defense is understood to mean warding off attack. [This paragraph] states that even if such self-defense is not in question, when a person is gripped by fear and dismay and exercises self-defense, he remains not liable. I shall return to these paragraphs because they are the only ones essential to your decision.

Werthauer was setting up his argument like a chess player who first moves his pawns into position. As yet, however, his audience could not determine how self-defense entered the case, when it had been clearly admitted that Talaat had been unarmed and was shot from the rear. Addressing the relevance of Paragraph 51, Werthauer said that as a consequence of the testimony, there were three possibilities: Tehlirian was healthy; he was not healthy but his intellect was morbidly influenced; or the state of his mind was unknown. If there was any doubt, then Tehlirian had to be acquitted.

May I note a folk saying, something people have said for thousands of years: "I saw red!" That means that free consciousness is disturbed. When that happens, I do what I would not normally do. . . . You must take into account that the accused belongs to a southern people who are known to be more easily inflamed than the cooler northerners. Further, that country has a bloody tradition. It is known that Turks, no matter where they went, carried the banner of blood.

We have seen the Turks standing before the gates of Vienna in 1683; had they then come here, there would not have been much left in Germany either. There is a certain bloody tradition with the people from the south, not only with Turks but with Armenians also. The Armenians and Turks have always been enemies. When the accused shouted: "I'm a foreigner, he's a foreigner, this doesn't concern Germany!" he need only have added: "We live in a permanent state of war and revenge."

Werthauer now turned to the trial of the Young Turks. Prosecuting Attorney Gollnick fidgeted in his chair with displeasure but began to take notes assiduously.

"The death sentence on Talaat Pasha was delivered by a military court. I am no friend of war and military courts. I value general justice. . . . But I do not have the slightest doubt that the intelligent and cultivated judges who delivered the verdict after careful examination in Constantinople reached the correct judgment.''

Referring to Gollnick's earlier comments about the tribunal's validity, Werthauer continued:

It was said that the judgment was made under the pressure of English naval cannon. I have never heard that English judges were affected in this way in their judgments. One can speak for or against England as one wishes, but English justice has been a model for all times and all countries.

Had anyone examined the reasons for the verdict, he would have seen that the Armenian massacres had been confirmed and that the death penalty for the accused in that trial in Constantinople was appropriate. That accused has now actually been executed.

After the death penalty, Talaat had to flee and hide under a false name to escape execution. Every just and right-thinking Armenian said to himself: This man has been condemned to death, has committed the crimes, and deserves the punishment of death.

Obviously, Defense Attorney Werthauer was preparing a case for self-defense. He also disputed claims that Talaat had been a ''guest'' in Germany or that the German government would permit ''refugee criminals'' to hide there under false names. He continued:

Enver Pasha once again is together with the Bolsheviks in Russia, forging new plans for war and the further destruction of the Armenians. If Talaat, as he surely wanted to, had followed Enver, new atrocities against the Armenians could have been expected in eight to fourteen days. Anyone who—as the savior of his people— wanted to see these criminals cut down would have thought: This man is the enemy of the Armenian people; if he leaves Germany and joins Enver Pasha and the Bolsheviks, then our women and children will be massacred again!

That is why, even if [it does not do so] legally, the question of self-defense in a broad sense obtains here. [Tehlirian] had that fear when he saw Talaat again.

Werthauer now turned to the medical experts and their conflicting testimony. The experts could only give evidence on the basis of their scientific knowledge, he said; they should not trespass on the pre-

serve of the jurist. The question of the applicability of Paragraph 51
was not their concern, Werthauer insisted.

It is true that we do not know whether he had an attack the night
before or on that morning. Such attacks [can] come and go without
a person's knowledge. Even Dr. Störmer said he couldn't know
that. If attacks such as that happen, the psychic echo can last for
days. But Dr. Störmer didn't know.

The doctors say that when the accused awoke from his unconsciousness after the massacre to which his family fell victim in
1915, he perceived the odor of corpses, and that later, when images
of that moment came to him, he always perceived the same odor.
That is a sign that the soul of the accused has been affected, so that
when the images came, he was no longer master of his will.

If I am master of my will and I smell my inkwell, I do not smell
the odor of corpses. If, however, I know that someone had been
killed by my inkwell, and that when I smell my inkwell, I believe
myself to be smelling a corpse, then I am no longer master of
my will.

[Tehlirian] had not thought of Talaat when he came to Berlin,
even after he had been here for weeks, until he saw Talaat on the
street, people bowing to him, addressing him as pasha.* He
saw red.

Werthauer apologized for introducing politics into the courtroom
but explained that he was compelled to do so because the prosecuting
attorney had spoken in favor of Talaat.

It has been said here than an "ally" of Germany has been killed.
That is not correct. Talaat and his Committee of Young Turks were
allies of the then Prussian and German military government.
These Young Turks were never allies of the German people. They
overthrew the old Turkish government and through a sea of blood
held power for some ten years.

It is correct that the German government of that time formed an
alliance with them, but that government did the same with Lenin
and Trotsky, who were transported through Germany in order to
make a revolution in Russia.

---

*Inasmuch as this conflicts with the truth, and in view of the impeccable credentials
of the defense team, it is obvious that Tehlirian had not fully revealed his past to his
attorneys.

His voice rising, Werthauer made some comments on German policies that were highly discomfiting to General Liman von Sanders and like-minded people in the courtroom and beyond.*

> Talaat was in a cabinet of militarists, and a militarist is . . . the opposite of justice. The militarist is a man of violence, as opposed to the man of law who holds justice above all else. Militarists believe in justice only insofar as it is in harmony with "military necessity." They are not bound to any people, any border, any nation: they are to be found everywhere on the planet. They form one unified caste. We have sent some to Turkey to train the military there, which shouldn't really have been our business.
>
> Militarists want war and they want power, and these power seekers, not the Turkish people, are the ones who destroyed the Armenian people.

If the Young Turks knew that the "good gendarmes" were not available, but only the rabble, Werthauer argued, the deportation order should not have been given. While the gendarmes had to be held responsible for their deeds, more blame should be placed on those in Constantinople. The government had to bear the full guilt for the issuance and execution of the deportation orders.

Werthauer rested for a moment in the silence of the courtroom as he collected his thoughts for the final phase of his summation. Having covered the questions of guilt, the admissibility of Paragraph 51, medical doubts and conflicts, accountability, self-defense, traditional enmities, the military tribunal in Constantinople, premeditation, German government liability, militarism, and Young Turk culpability, he now focused on the Turkish argument of military necessity:

> Even if the Armenians had been allied with other nations, if some deluded leader had practiced treason and joined the Russians, the Young Turks knew that thousands of women and children knew nothing of such things. They also knew that the first provision of a deportation order is strict adherence to caring for women and children.
>
> In fact, it is a distinct pretense to maintain, as it has been outside this courtroom, that the deportations were instituted because

*Aware that a defeated Germany was being blamed for its militaristic policies and therefore justly punished, Werthauer was now appealing to the jury to reject that disastrous heritage, as personified by Germany's wartime ally Talaat.

the Armenians had allied themselves with the Russians, consequently for military necessity.

Werthauer digressed to describe the area of the Caucasus and Mount Ararat, where the Armenians had lived under constant attack and fear of invasion for two thousand years.

"One foreign race after the other has thundered over Armenia; just as the Turks laid waste to Hungary and came to the Rhine, people like Attila the Hun, whom even our children know of, have invaded Armenia in the most horrific way to annihilate people."

The outbreak of war gave the Ittihadists their excuse to "settle the Armenian question" once and for all, Werthauer continued. They flung themselves on the Armenian nation, not just for political but religious reasons as well. The court had heard how only two Armenian families had survived the Erzinga massacre by converting to Mohammedanism, confirming the religious hate and fanaticism of the Young Turks.

They wanted to slaughter Christians, they wanted Armenians only as Mohammedans because they believed that through the Koran they could better implement the pan-Turkish idea of power.

The pan-Turkish empire rests on the idea of military power, which contradicts the teachings of the Old and New Testaments—perhaps even a properly understood Koran—above all the idea, Love thy neighbor as thyself. The Young Turks destroyed this singular Christian nation in distant areas but not the Armenians in Constantinople, where they [the Ittihadists] took Christians and Jews into some [government] ministries.

To the distant areas the Young Turks sent telegrams, which lie before us, to the individual governors, with the order: The Armenian nation shall be relegated to oblivion. Thus we have before us the murder of a nation, the responsibility for which falls on the Young Turk Committee and especially on its most authoritative minister, Talaat.

To drive his points home—and no doubt hoping to render Tehlirian's motive and action less foreign—Werthauer drew a parallel with one of the most famous legends in European history.

Let us take the case of William Tell. Gessler the governor scorns the people, erects the symbol of slavery, forces Tell to shoot an apple sitting on the head of his son. This governor is of the same blood as the pan-Turks, of the men of violence. The idea that animates William Tell also stirs Tehlirian. What jury in the world would have condemned William Tell because he killed Gessler?

"I ask: Is there anything more humane than what we have heard here? The avenger of a million murdered souls, the avenger of an entire nation, confronts the one responsible for the murder of that nation, the architect of that huge misery. Do we need the image of his mother to have external medical notions of compulsiveness? His mother says to him: "You are no longer my son!" This thought pervades him as he seizes his gun and runs out. He is running to represent the spirit of justice as opposed to the spirit of violence.

Werthauer's impassioned peroration was spellbinding, and his voice rose higher in the courtroom.

"He is the representative of humanity against the representative of inhumanity, of sunny justice against dark injustice, of the oppressed against the symbolic representative of the oppressor . . . he represents one million murdered souls against one who, with others, bears the guilt for those deeds . . . he represents his mother, aged fifty-two—I mention that because it was said earlier that Talaat Pasha was in the full strength of his manhood—his sister, brothers, brother-in-law, and the two-and-a-half-year-old child of his sister.

The Armenian nation, a thousand years old, stands behind him to the smallest child. He carries before him in spirit the flag of justice, of humanity, of the honor of his sisters and his family. He confronted the man who allowed an entire nation to be physically destroyed. He became a spiritually weak and ill human being, and you, gentlemen of the jury, have to judge what took place in his mind when he committed the deed and whether he was master of his free will.

Gentlemen, I firmly believe that you are already of the opinion that it has not been proved that [Tehlirian] was master of his free will. Consider, gentlemen, that the eyes of mankind look on your verdict. . . . Say simply: "He is not guilty! Everything else is of no concern to us."

Thus, despite the many points of his summation, Werthauer's final plea was not legal but moral, his fundamental argument that the slaying of the Turkish politician was not an act of murder but indeed of retribution. The summation of Tehlirian's third attorney would attempt to erase the distinction altogether.

Noon was drawing near and Defense Attorney Niemeyer, aware that his colleagues' wide-ranging speeches had taken close to an hour apiece, made his the briefest summation of all.

Addressing the issues of premeditation and free will, Niemeyer employed two arguments to exclude both: Drs. Störmer and Cassirer both admitted not knowing the state of mind of the accused, the former even going so far as to say that no one could know that. Consequently it was not possible to determine the exercise of free will. As for premeditation, he argued, the accused lacked any plan. He could, for instance, have spent more time observing and pursuing Talaat; and certainly, there could have been a more favorable opportunity for the crime than to have committed it in broad daylight and on such a busy thoroughfare. But Niemeyer laid the greatest weight on the following consideration:

The paragraph on which you must decide your verdict, Number Two-eleven of the penal code, reads: "Whoever deliberately kills a human being shall, if he has carried out the killing with premeditation, be guilty of murder and be punished by death."

Assume you answer in the affirmative, assume that the head of Soghomon Tehlirian is to fall under the executioner's ax, and assume that someone raises the accusation of murder against the executioner. Remembering the language of the paragraph, gentlemen of the jury, must you punish the executioner with death?

Niemeyer turned the jury's attention to the tenets of German jurisprudence: "At the time of the deed, the Turks and Armenians were in a state of war. They were enemies in the sense of international law, and Article Four of the German constitution, whereby the recognized principles of international law form a component of German law, does not come into consideration."

What was relevant, however, was that in this instance, the accused's consciousness of illegality appears to have been determined on ethnic grounds. Niemeyer was implying that the Armenian concept of legality was based on a fusion of all elements of its culture and not, as in other countries, only on the law. He explained:

Consciousness of legality or illegality is determined in Oriental peoples quite differently from us. In judging the soul of Tehlirian and especially the consciousness of illegality, we must proceed from the fact that for the Orientals, to whom the Armenians belong although they have been Christians since the year three hundred, law, religion, and custom are completely one and the same.

Every Turkish sect, on the other hand, has a different law. The Persian Shiites have Shiite law because only the Koran is valid. Therefore the consciousness of law differs because they have different confessions.

The Armenians are quite a special religious people. In certain aspects their rites, their narrow dependence on religion in their daily customs, resemble Islam, with its washing and prayers. The Armenian lives in a totally religious atmosphere. A few ugly comments have given the Armenians a bad reputation: 'A Greek sells three Jews, an Armenian sells three Greeks,' and others like that. But the Persians, who know the Armenians best, have a proverb: "Take bread from the Kurds but sleep in the house of an Armenian." In other words the Persian, who is a Muslim, takes food from a Kurd and not from an Armenian. But he accepts hospitality not from his coreligionist but from an Armenian because the Armenians do not steal! The security of property, the conscious respect for property, is nowhere more certain than among the Armenians.

Niemeyer reminded the jury of Tehlirian's answer when Judge Lehmberg asked whether he admitted his guilt. When he said no, the judge had asked, "Why not?" Tehlirian replied, "Because my conscience is clear."

"For him," Niemeyer continued, "ethical and legal correctness are synonymous. He does not know, cannot imagine, that something ethically correct can be legally incorrect; he cannot imagine that something ethically good makes him guilty of death. I am totally convinced that he in no way acted against the true, correct law, the only law that mattered to him."

Niemeyer thus attempted to persuade the jury that Tehlirian had taken a violent action that was nonetheless entirely consistent with his own legal and ethical norms. He saw himself as the avenger of his people, and as the mere executor of a collective will he could have no consciousness of criminality. Indeed, his consciousness of individual identity itself was very weak. Niemeyer now went further, drawing for his concluding arguments on the history of the Armenian people—something neither of his colleagues had done—to dramatize their plight under Ottoman rule and, by extension, further validate Tehlirian's actions.

He began with a detailed review of Armenian history, when it was a large empire in the first century but was eventually absorbed by

Süleyman I in the sixteenth century. The Armenians, Niemeyer continued, always remained hopeful that despite their difficulties within the Ottoman Empire, reforms, self-administration, and security would be accorded them. When, in the nineteenth century, the many nations in the empire revolted against oppressive Ottoman rule and began its disintegration, the Armenians remained calm and patient. Not only could the Sublime Porte not complain about them, but the Armenians themselves never complained. But the Turks feared that the Armenians would become dangerous, and despite the absence of cause, the first persecutions and massacres began, "for no reason," Niemeyer emphasized. Only then did the Armenians organize themselves into political groups in the hope of achieving the reforms they had expected.

This knowledgeable review of Turkish-Armenian relations was climaxed by a personal note, which Niemeyer interjected into the conclusion of his summation.

In 1899 I was in Constantinople twice and heard from eyewitnesses myself of the massacres in August 1896. They made a fearful impression on me. And when on March 16 of this year I read what had happened on Hardenbergstrasse, three images came before my eyes that I am unable to forget. I personally witnessed none of the three, but it is just as though I had.

On August 26, 1896, when the Armenians had organized a revolutionary incident,[3] and it was exposed by informers of the Turkish police, the Turkish government—that is, Sultan Abdul Hamid— did nothing to prevent it, instead even welcomed it. A mob was armed with clubs and ordered to kill every Armenian encountered on the street, from noon August 26 on, and I have heard German women and children relate how they saw the murders happen: a typical incident was when the men—wielding clubs, bared to the waist, and in baggy pants, accompanied by Turkish policemen— approached an Armenian; the victim would kneel, raise his hands in prayer, bow his head, and be killed with one blow. Ninety percent of those killed in this way had this head wound.

The second image concerns how Talaat Pasha entered the government in 1908. He came with his comrades to the office of the then Grand Vizier, who casually lit a cigarette and asked what Talaat was doing there. At that moment, a pistol shot rang out and the man Talaat Pasha wanted to do away with lay dead, shot in the throat.

And now comes the third scene—of March 15, 1921—which we all know. This trial is unlike any other. It forces us to understand the broader ramifications, to understand other peoples, other circumstances, and to apply justice to them. . . . I do not believe that Soghomon Tehlirian will be found guilty of murder. But he would rather die, he would prefer to lay his youthful martyr's head on the block; his mother will appear to him, and he will die a blessed death. One could almost wish that for him.

An acquittal will not bring his mother, brothers, and sisters back to life. The acquittal will also not bring him back his health. He will never be like the rest of us. But you cannot find that Tehlirian was responsible. He acted as he had to, did what he could not leave undone. Whether you want to explain this compulsion as a demonic, or ethical, or noble, or morbid psychosomatic or emotional epileptic-arisen condition—certainly, all these elements must be considered. But you must also consider the overall aspect of the case and ask: What will be the consequence of our verdict, not in a political or other sense, but in the cause of higher justice, in the sense of that goodness for which we live, which makes life worth while?

Niemeyer's summation placed Tehlirian's deed in a historical context for the first time in the trial. By underscoring various points—Armenian problems within the Ottoman Empire, patience and hope for reforms, Turkish persecution for no cause, and finally organization and political consciousness—supported by some personal reminiscences, Niemeyer sought to impress on the jury that the crime they were judging had a moral justification, by reason of which the defendant should be acquitted but for which he was prepared to die.

Four summations had now been delivered and the logical step would have been for the presiding judge to charge the jury. But state prosecutor Gollnick now arose to make what to many appeared an odd statement. He accused the defense attorneys of not having informed the jury that the presiding judge was compelled to deliver judgment according to the law. Besides this, his presumed rebuttal of the three defense attorneys lacked in substance and was more a parade of debating points. He took issue with Werthauer's division of the world, as he put it, into militarists and men of law; but he saved his most acrimonious remarks for Werthauer's comments about Talaat Pasha—"a loyal ally of the German people."

The Turks, he said, had fought shoulder to shoulder with the Germans and were allies of the German people. It was not honorable to disavow the past no matter what the political views of the individual. "Therefore," he concluded, "I must raise the sharpest protest against the defense attorney's description of these two advocates of Turkish policies, Talaat and Enver, in such an insulting way as refugee criminals."

All three defense attorneys were permitted a final reply. Von Gordon was enraged: "Gentlemen, we have been reproached by the prosecuting attorney that we did not say even once that the judge is compelled to judge according to the law. Yes, gentlemen, I would be ashamed of myself to say that to you—it is so obvious."

The courtroom broke into laughter, easing the tension of the morning. Von Gordon moved on to Gollnick's assertion that the Turkish people had fought side by side with the Germans: "But the Turkish people are not guilty of the massacres, they condemn them, as every normal, feeling person would. This systematic annihilation of the Armenians originated not in an emotional outburst of the people but as a fully considered, administrative political measure by leading circles, a measure carried out by rabble, by Turkish military police."

Werthauer next responded to Gollnick's umbrage at descriptions of the Young Turks as refugee criminals with a powerful rebuke of his own:

> Talaat Pasha, together with Enver Pasha, Jemal, and Nazim, has been condemned in a public military tribunal that consisted of the most respected judges, after detailed exhaustive testimony, and was found guilty of the profane crime of massacre of the Armenians and of the persecution of innocents. This judgment is valid, and it is incorrect and contrary to German law if, because I label as a criminal someone who has already been found guilty and condemned for a most heinous crime, I am to be considered guilty of an insult. Whether these refugee criminals who stayed here under false names had the support of any militarists is unknown to me.

He acknowledged that the Turks had fought together with the Germans but pointed out that neither people had anything to do with their countries' entering the war, which in any case was not at issue in the trial: "People like Enver Pasha, Talaat Pasha and the others are at issue here not because of the war but because they undertook the deportations, because they caused these crimes against the Armenian people, the most cruel crimes in the history of mankind."

Tehlirian himself was "a man of justice who saw red and no longer knew what he did." He was not guilty, Werthauer said, because his will was not healthy and therefore not free. Further, when he ran down into the street after Talaat, "he did not go down alone because with him were millions of murdered Armenians."

Though it seemed almost unnecessary for the third defense attorney to add anything, no one was prepared for his final comments which, at the very end of the two-day trial, forthrightly introduced for the first time the issue of German complicity in the tragic events—an issue that even Johannes Lepsius had not raised. Niemeyer pointed out that the defense had avoided transforming this into a political trial, as the presiding judge had requested. But the comments of the prosecuting attorney incited and now compelled him to speak:

> During the war, military and other organs of both Germany and Turkey kept silent and even hid the Armenian atrocities in a way bordering on inadmissibility. Yes, some tried to stop the atrocities, but the Turkish population said—"It is impossible that this is happening without the will of the Germans." We Germans have been made co-responsible in the Orient and in the whole world for the Armenian atrocities. There is extensive literature in America, France, and the Orient that says the Germans have been the real Talaats in Turkey.
>
> If it happens that Soghomon Tehlirian is acquitted, then this idea will no longer be supported in the world. The world will then greet acquittal as an act of true higher justice!

Niemeyer's words echoed in the courtroom and laid before the jury the opportunity to absolve the German nation of its pervading sense of guilt for the crimes of its wartime ally.

With the summations now concluded, Judge Lehmberg asked the defendant if there was anything he wished to say. Tehlirian said he had nothing to add.

Judge Lehmberg fixed his eyes on the twelve Berliners seated to his left and, promising that he would be brief, began his charge to the jury.

> Our penal code's point of departure is that a normal person is in full control of his will. Paragraph Fifty-one of the penal code states that there is no punishable act if the perpetrator acted in a

state of insensibility or of morbid disturbance of his mental state, wherein the exercise of free will is excluded. Free will is present when a person is in a position to control his actions, his drives, his impulses, through his intelligence, through his intellectual personality.

The law requires that the condition you shall determine must be such that it not only impaired and obstructed free will but also excluded it. You must also ask yourselves whether the epilepsy established in the accused, together with the other occurrences which expert medical testimony provided, created such condition in him relative to his personality and experiences that he could not fully avail himself of his senses, feelings and mind when he committed the crime on March 15, 1921.

If you assume that a substantial part of his sensibility or certain sides of his intellectual personality were so injured that the accused was no longer in the position to freely activate his will, then you must, on the basis of Paragraph Fifty-one, deny criminal responsibility and acquit the accused. That is the first test you have to face because the question begins with the words *Is the accused guilty.* . . .

Judge Lehmberg let the first part of his charge sink in before he continued on to his second question, which dealt with premeditation: "You must ask yourselves whether the accused wanted to kill Talaat, and whether he knew that he had killed a human being. If so, and you do not deem Paragraph Fifty-one operative, then you must decide in the affirmative on the question of guilt."

Premeditation, he stressed, would lay the basis for a verdict of murder. If that were the case, he said: "You must be convinced that in the moment when he fired the shot, the accused acted with premeditation. But if you accept the existence of a state of inner turmoil, you must unquestionably deny the issue of premeditated homicide."

The judge dismissed the issue of consciousness of illegality as not germane to the case, underlining that the central questions were Did Tehlirian know that he killed and Did he want to kill? The death penalty was valid only in the case of murder, he explained. But in the case of manslaughter under mitigating circumstances, the minimum sentence was six months' imprisonment.

"I request now that you assume your responsibility on the questions posed to you in the same way as you elected the foreman, who will be in charge of your deliberations and voting."

A guilty verdict required, he said, a two-thirds' majority, or eight votes, clarifying once again that if the jury found in the affirmative, it would signify that Paragraph 51 was excluded and criminal responsibility existed. The same two-thirds' majority held true on the question of premeditation. On the other hand, if the jury found mitigating circumstances in evidence, then only a simple majority of seven votes was necessary.

Judge Lehmberg signed the three questions as was customary in a German court of law and handed them over to the jury. All twelve jurors rose and withdrew to the jury room. The courtroom suddenly came alive with the hum of conversation and sounds of movement as the spectators rose, uncertain as to how long a decision would take.

Soghomon Tehlirian slumped in his chair, drained of all emotion. The last two days had revived for him the horrors he had sought to dismiss from his memory, and the thought went through his head that any punishment would be light compared to what he had suffered in the trial. He sat immersed in thought and in memories of happier times.

To everyone's astonishment, after only one hour the court was informed that the jury was ready. The spectators hastily and noisily returned to their seats, and Judge Lehmberg rapped for order. The foreman, Otto Reinicke, arose and holding a sheet of paper close to his eyes, read with a quivering voice: "On my honor and conscience, I witness the verdict of the jurors: 'Is the accused Soghomon Tehlirian guilty of having deliberately killed a man, Talaat Pasha, on March 15, 1921, in Charlottenburg?' No."

The courtroom erupted with cheers and applause in a spontaneous demonstration that drowned out Judge Lehmberg's announcement that the accused had been acquitted.

Tehlirian stood up, unable for the moment to grasp his good fortune until his three attorneys congratulated him and made him understand that he was once again a free man.

Now he was surrounded by his Armenian compatriots and his two interpreters, Vahan Zachariantz and Kevork Kalustian, and their shouted words of happiness filled him with joy. Total strangers, Berliners and other Germans, slapped him on the shoulder or shook his hand, and the thought occurred to him that the German people wished to redress the wrong that had been done him.

Judge Lehmberg and his two associates had already departed the courtroom, which continued to resound with vigorous applause and shouts, when one of the police guards indicated to Tehlirian that he had to return briefly to the prison for the formality of signing papers.

When Tehlirian emerged from the prison again, a crowd had gathered, and when he appeared on the street the cheering was renewed as another demonstration began. Two policemen stood by a car into which he was pushed by his Armenian colleagues. He fell into the rear and as the doors closed he looked out the window and saw three women—Frau Stellbaum, Frau Dittman, and Fräulein Beilinson—all smiling and waving their handkerchiefs.

Ahead were some ten cars moving slowly through the streets toward a destination where the joyous Armenian community had already gathered to celebrate what they regarded as not only a judicial but a moral victory.

His mission now over and his actions vindicated, Tehlirian sat in silence in the moving car, his thoughts once again on the image of the lovely and devoted woman with whom he longed to spend the rest of his life. Would Anahid be waiting?

The jury's unexpected verdict burst like a bombshell on public opinion abroad. In view of a century of close German-Turkish relations—the rapport between the sultan and the kaiser, the alliance during the war, and the irrefutable fact that Talaat Pasha and his cohorts were living and conspiring in Berlin with the knowledge and protection of the German government—the acquittal of the Armenian student by a German jury seemed incredible.

Why did the jury's decision turn out as it did? What motivated the jurors to free this slender, diffident youth who, to all appearances, seemed thoroughly incapable of any act of violence?

Soghomon Tehlirian was acquitted on a technicality that today would be called "temporary insanity." Clearly the jury accepted the argument advanced by all three defense lawyers and by two of the medical experts that because of a mental state brought on by a variously described epilepsy, Tehlirian was not in full control of his senses. Obviously the jury had embraced the premise of Paragraph 51, which recognized the absence of free will and had therefore decided for acquittal.

Judge Lehmberg had submitted his three questions, dealing first with guilt, second with intent, and third with premeditation. The second two would be inoperative if Paragraph 51 came into play.

It is not known how the voting went, but it was obviously not much in dispute. A verdict of acquittal required eight votes, and since the deliberations took only one hour, there was little time for argument and repeated voting. One may speculate about the basis on which one or more of those eight may have voted. But the plain fact had been brought out in pretrial interrogation and in court testimony that Tehlirian freely admitted to the murder.

Most revealing and indeed most thought-provoking were Tehlirian's own statements: "I do not regard myself as guilty because my conscience is at peace," he said, and, "I have killed a man but I am not a murderer." These Dostoyevskian pronouncements, taken together with other testimony—Tehlirian's traumatic shock on awakening in a sea of corpses, his growing awareness of a huge personal tragedy, the shattering accounts of Mrs. Terzibashian and Bishop Balakian, the calm and comprehensive testimony of Dr. Johannes Lepsius, and the Turkish military tribunal's condemnation of the Ittihadists—all these could not help but produce in a jury of ordinary people an empathic emotional response to the fate of Tehlirian and the entire Armenian population in Turkey.

Paragraph 51, the relevant section of the German Penal Code, with its language pertaining to the exercise of free will, had a psychomedical aura. It offered the jury a plausible resolution to the dilemma of having to judge a man for whom it had great sympathy but who, at the same time, did not deny the fact that he had slain another human being.

It did not take public opinion long to come to the conclusion that the basis for the Berlin verdict—a medical technicality—had been merely a convenient outlet for the jury in this politically charged case and that the real meaning of the acquittal involved the broader realm of international relations and, indeed, of German history. The most telling demonstration of this understanding came in an article printed by the *New York Times* in its monthly political magazine, *Current History*. Written only weeks after the trial, the article— entitled "Why Talaat's Assassin Was Acquitted"—presents in the original Turkish and in English translation ten telegrams—nine signed by Talaat, one by the Young Turk Committee—calling for the deportation and annihilation of Armenian men, women, and children. These telegrams placed responsibility for the massacres squarely on Talaat Pasha and the Young Turks—which is to say, on the central government in Istanbul.

The draconian measures described in these telegrams were a shock to American readers, and some of the phrases left no room for doubt about the intent of the Young Turks: "the noble project of wiping out of existence," "uproot and annihilate," "submit women and children to the same orders as males," and finally a telegram sent to the prefect of Aleppo, which concluded, "An end must be put to their existence, however tragic the measures taken may be, and no regard must be paid to either age or sex or to conscientious scruples," and was signed "Talaat, Minister of the Interior."[4]

The *Times* wrote: "This evidence directly linking the murdered Talaat with the inhuman deeds that were covered by the general term 'deportation' was irrefutable and overwhelming. The documents established once and for all the fact that the purpose of the Turkish authorities was not deportation but annihilation."[5]

Soghomon Tehlirian's acquittal thus recognized, first and foremost, the huge injustice against Tehlirian himself; it acknowledged the crimes against the Armenian nation by the Young Turk regime headed by Talaat Pasha and his coconspirators; and, by denying Tehlirian's guilt, it denied Germany's guilt and absolved Germany of complicity in those crimes. But in voting for acquittal, the Berlin jury actually turned the case on its head by acknowledging that Soghomon Tehlirian, the defendant, was in fact the victim, while Talaat Pasha, the murdered man, had been the real criminal.

———

The assassination of Talaat Pasha on the ides of March and the acquittal of Soghomon Tehlirian ten weeks later sent waves of exhilaration throughout Armenian communities everywhere. For the first time in their tortured history, Armenians experienced the satisfaction of retaliation, of emerging from their grief to strike a blow against their oppressor. To be sure, the taking of one life did not balance the loss of a million, but the symbolism of Tehlirian's deed was sufficient to act as a balm—temporarily at least—for the pain of their huge national tragedy and to gratify their craving for vengeance and justice.

Hundreds of thousands of Armenians who had survived the massacres had fled Turkey and found refuge and new lives in the Western world. But the memory of the horrendous events of 1915 would never leave them. This act of revenge lifted from their souls a sense of guilt at having fled, and they looked upon the young man who had done what had to be done as the instrument of their will.

A deeply religious people, the Armenians did not close their eyes to the fact that Tehlirian's was an act of terrorism. But they weighed this individual act against Talaat Pasha's many acts of state terrorism, and condoned it as a moral assassination.

Armenians everywhere underwent a national catharsis, a purging of emotions pent up not just for a few years but for centuries. In community activities, social gatherings, religious ceremonies, and wherever jubilant Armenians congregated, the phrase was repeated over and over: "We kiss the hand that killed the tyrant."

In the wake of the assassination and the trial, the flood of commentary in the Armenian press echoed the sentiments of its readers in phrases that spoke of the "gratification of revenge" and the "victory of justice." Three days after the assassination, *Hairenik*, the ARF organ in Boston, published an editorial entitled "Nemesis" (the first public mention of the network), with a warning that "sooner or later justice will triumph and . . . no one should consider himself beyond *Nemesis*'s reach."[6] Political rivalries were overlooked as Tehlirian became a hero to all. Although he was a member of the ARF, its bitter political foes pulled no punches in praising his courage and will for having slain the former Turkish grand vizier who, some papers said, operated against the true interests of the Turkish state and people.

This last phrase was a statement of remarkable generosity, given the instances in which marauding Turkish villagers descended on the hapless caravans. At a time when it would have been all too easy to raise such a specter, this phrase apparently dismissed the concept of what today would be known as "collective guilt." And in fact, despite the intensity of emotion unleashed by the events in Berlin, the Armenian press showed a certain restraint and perspicacity even in discussing the German people. A dispatch from Berlin separated the views of the German people from those of Kaiser Wilhelm, "who always smiled at and applauded the crimes of the Sublime Porte." It continued: "We cannot believe that the German people do not feel in the depths of their soul a certain satisfaction in seeing the corpse of the great barbarian lying in a Berlin street."[7]

It was Soghomon Tehlirian, however, who was the focus of every word, spoken and written, blessing his hands and wishing him a long life. "He redeemed our national honor," said one Marxist editorialist.[8] Another observed, "But even more overjoyed than we are the martyrs of Deir Zor, so many of whom lie unburied on the hot desert sand."[9]

If the Armenian press in all its political hues reveled in the news from Berlin, Turkish editors were reluctant to explore the ramifications of the case, aware that to do so would only expose the wartime atrocities and Tehlirian's motivations. One Turk, however, who apparently had no hesitation in voicing his convictions concerning the assassinated Ittihadist was a prominent *littérateur* named Jenab Shehabeddin. He wrote that the only way Talaat Pasha could have earned his pity would have been if "instead of shamefully and guiltily escaping, Talaat had shown the courage to remain where fate had raised him to such heights, and had walked Robespierre-like to the guillotine. Then perhaps, I might have felt some pity."[10]

Perhaps. Had Talaat been executed by his own people rather than by a survivor of his colossal crime, justice would have been served equally well, but the vast hunger for revenge of a devastated nation would have remained ungratified.

Conclusion

*T*he echoes of Soghomon Tehlirian's deed in Berlin were to resound in the months ahead in the streets of Rome, again in Berlin, and in other cities where former Turkish officials had found refuge. For while Tehlirian was the first of Nemesis's emissaries of revenge, others were already on the hunt for the remaining perpetrators of the ruin of an entire nation.

The second was Arshavir Shiragian, and just as Tehlirian wrote his recollections of those suspenseful days after thirty-five years, so did Shiragian fifty-five years later. But even after so much time, neither made any mention of Nemesis.

In Rome, Shiragian's target was Said Halim Pasha, the Turk who had been grand vizier before Talaat and who had contemptuously dismissed Armenian pleas for mercy when the April 24 deportations had begun. Said Halim, Jemal Azmi, and Dr. Shakir, together with their servants, had been transported by the British to Malta, where, after a brief stay, they were released. Jemal and Shakir then fled to Berlin while Halim found refuge in Rome. Shiragian killed Said Halim on December 5, 1921, on a major Roman thoroughfare, leaping into the horsedrawn carriage in which the former Turkish premier was riding with his bodyguard and firing at point-blank range.

Although Shiragian escaped the Italian police, who were preoccupied with demonstrations by Mussolini's fascists, word spread rapidly throughout the expatriate community, that it was Shiragian

who had killed Said Halim. Hidden from official eyes, he was nonetheless decorated by the Greek Consul in Rome (whose own countrymen had good reason to welcome Shiragian's deed), and then
informed by Armenian accomplices that a new mission awaited him.

In the company of another Nemesis recruit, Aram Yerganian,
Shiragian found his way back to Constantinople, often protected in
his travels by Greek diplomats, whose pro-Armenian sympathies
stemmed from a shared experience of suffering under Turkish rule.
Shiragian pleaded with his superiors there for the assignment he most
ardently desired—to go to Baku in Azerbaijan to kill Enver Pasha.
Instead he was directed by Nemesis to Berlin where, with several
accomplices—one of them the same Hrap who had assisted
Tehlirian—he was to assassinate both Dr. Behaeddin Shakir and
Jemal Azmi.

After three months of surveillance and planning, this was accomplished around midnight on April 17, 1922, only a few yards from
Uhlandstrasse 47, where the two Turks and some friends, among
them Talaat's widow, had dined. Since this happened barely a year
after the assassination, only a few streets away, of Talaat Pasha,
memories of Tehlirian's trial were still fresh.

In reporting the murders, the Berlin press seemed united on three
points. First, it was said that Germans themselves bore some guilt
since a Berlin jury had exonerated Tehlirian one year earlier for the
same crime; second, the papers alleged that the assassinations were
being carried out under the direction of a secret Armenian organization based in the United States; third, they complained that while
thousands of Berliners were homeless as a result of the terrible
postwar depression, Turkish émigrés, especially former high-ranking
officials, were living in luxury in exclusive areas of Berlin. This third
point was hammered home by the liberal *Berliner Tageblatt*, which
made no secret of its resentment at the fact that among the five
thousand Turks then living in Berlin, some prominent families who
had deposited money in Swiss banks during the war could find such
splendid accommodations when desperate Germans were searching
for the most modest of apartments.

The nationalist *Deutsche Allgemeine Zeitung*, on the other hand,
consistent with its progovernment and pro-Turkish coverage of
Tehlirian's trial, expressed outrage at what it called Germany's "loss
of political capital in the Moslem world," and said that Berlin had
become "an arena for foreign assassins." It also severely criticized
the prosecuting attorney of the Tehlirian trial for having used "weak

words to condemn a political murder" and also for his choice of witnesses "who were of greater service to the murderer than to the unfortunate victim."[1]

Despite the elimination of four former highly placed Turkish officials, the work of Nemesis continued, others responsible for the massacres still being very much at large. Indeed, Shahan Natali, one of the most avid seekers of revenge and the guiding force in Europe of the Nemesis network, was reputed always to have at hand a long list of Turkish targets; he, like Tehlirian, had lost almost his entire family in the massacres. Although Tehlirian never mentioned Natali in connection with his mission, Shiragian was constantly guided and abetted by him.

Of the more prominent Turks, Jemal Pasha—the last of the Young Turk triumvirate—was the next to be killed. Jemal was gunned down on July 22, 1922, in the Georgian city of Tiflis by two Armenians who also escaped. The fate of Enver Pasha has already been noted, leaving only Dr. Nazim to be accounted for. However, it was not an Armenian who ended his life but his fellow Turks, who hanged him for treason in Ankara in 1926, when he was discovered in a plot to assassinate Mustafa Kemal, the president of Turkey.

The Armenians recruited by Nemesis thus killed five, possibly six, prominent Young Turks, including Talaat, Jemal, and Enver. With these executions, plus those of a number of lesser-known Ittihadists, the wave of vengeful terrorism came to an end. Meanwhile, Armenians, fleeing both the Turks and the communists, dispersed to the far corners of the world, never forgetting what had happened to them but realizing that the world was not interested in their fate. In fact, the world's attention was centered on the Great Depression, the emergence of Stalin, then of Hitler, and eventually World War II, followed by revelations of the Holocaust.

Their own holocaust having been obscured by time and these major events, the Armenians who had settled abroad—primarily in the United States, Western Europe, and the Middle East—now sought to become loyal citizens of their adopted countries while preserving the traditions of their ancient culture.

Even as they pursued these aims, however, their sufferings as a people under Turkish rule never left their consciousness. Yet, in the spirit of their ancient Christianity, Armenians sought not revenge but recognition and justice for the crimes of 1915. The education of their young was wholly imbued with this tragedy of recent history, along with the great milestones of the past. Three dates stand out in this national record: the adoption of Christianity as the state religion in

A.D. 301; the creation of the Armenian alphabet in 406, whose first fruit was the translation of the Bible; and the defense of Christianity against the fire-worshipping Persians in 415 at Avarair, in the shadow of Mount Ararat.

But the devastation the nation had suffered remained always as an *idée fixe*, no matter what direction the educational process led. The message of the Armenian church, the bastion of the nation, continued to be: Let us forgive but not forget.

With the creation of the United Nations in 1945, the Armenians found a new international forum in which smaller nations had the same vote as the major powers. Human rights suddenly became a matter of universal concern. For the Armenians, although they were not represented in the United Nations, this was a major development since it once again focused attention on the great injustice they had suffered.

But justice was still not to be had, and once again it was Turkey that stood in their way. Even though since 1923 a Turkish republic, which had renounced and exiled the sultan, modern Turkey was reluctant to repudiate the policies and actions of the Ottoman regime. In 1973 the United Nations Subcommission on Prevention of Discrimination and Protection of Minorities drafted a report that included a reference to "the massacre of the Armenians, which has been described as the first case of genocide in the twentieth century." The Turkish delegation protested and brought such pressure to bear on the Human Rights Commission that the paragraph in question was withdrawn.

While Talaat's assassination in Berlin was an admitted act of vengeance, "blood revenge" was not in the Armenian tradition, as some elements of the German press suggested at the time. Had this been the case, Armenian retribution against Turkish injustices would have begun more than a century before, and Ottoman rulers would never have viewed the Armenians as "the most loyal nation" in the empire. The idea of retribution for official persecutions was conceived when Armenian political consciousness was born. This process began in the middle of the nineteenth century but only acquired concrete form with the establishment of Armenian political organizations around the turn of the century.

Until the end of World War I, with the exception of one isolated attempt on Sultan Abdul Hamid's life, there had not been any systematic, concerted acts of terrorism. But when the major Turkish criminals escaped the reach of the postwar military tribunal, the Nemesis network was established, and the campaign of revenge instituted.

Armenian political terrorism dormant since then, can be said to have resumed in 1973 when an elderly Armenian in Los Angeles who had lost his entire family killed two Turkish diplomats. This initial act in the revival of Armenian terrorism, followed by two more in the United States, was soon repeated in Europe, the Middle East, and as far away as Australia. By 1975 two Armenian organizations, based in Lebanon, had been activated and were waging a campaign of violence against Turkish installations and diplomatic missions beyond the borders of Turkey, which lasted for ten years, involved twenty countries and close to two hundred incidents. While some of the attacks seriously damaged property without loss of life, others proved fatal for twenty-two Turkish diplomats and as many members of their families.

On October 22, 1975, for instance, the Justice Commandos of the Armenian Genocide—for two jailed members of which in Los Angeles the ARF accepted donations—assassinated the Turkish Ambassador in Vienna, and two months later the Turkish Ambassador in Paris. At other times attempts on the lives of Turkish diplomats were made while they rode in their official cars, the assassins using 9 mm automatic weapons. This group appeared to focus exclusively on historic Turkish-Armenian issues.

The Armenian Secret Army for the Liberation of Armenia (ASALA), whose training was provided by the Palestine Liberation Organization (PLO), although at first also concentrating on Turkish targets, soon expanded its operations, as for instance on November 13, 1979, in Paris, when it bombed the offices of Turkish, KLM, and Lufthansa Airlines. Swiss offices were the target of fifteen Secret Army attacks. But Turkish targets remained their prevalent objectives, including a widely publicized incident on September 24, 1981, in Paris, when four ASALA members seized the Turkish consulate and held twenty hostages, eventually killing one and wounding three. In the last of the more sensational episodes, in April 1985 members of ASALA occupied the Turkish Embassy in Ottawa, but the ambassador, leaping out of a two-story window, escaped. ASALA accounted for the deaths of nine Turkish diplomats. In all, both terrorist groups claimed responsibility at one time or another for attacks on Turkish diplomatic posts in Vienna, Beirut, Paris, Madrid, The Hague, Athens, and the Vatican, as well as bombings of Turkish cultural attractions and business establishments.

The purpose of this campaign, of course, was to revive interest in the Armenian question. Instead, coming as it did on the heels of a far-more-spectacular PLO terrorist program, it only aroused universal revulsion. It did, however, goad the Turkish government into action with a countercampaign of revisionist history that vacillated between a total denial that Turkey had even inflicted harm on the Armenians and an admission that while perhaps three hundred thousand Armenians may have died as a natural consequence of war, twice as many Turks had been killed by Armenians, who, it was claimed, had initiated the massacres. This revisionist campaign was waged with remarkable persistence and tenacity by Turkish ambassadors and their staffs, especially in Washington, D.C., by scholars affiliated with Turkish institutes and by public relations lobbyists.

Turkey's sensitivity to accusations of guilt for the Armenian tragedy was nothing new. In the late 1930s, Metro-Goldwyn-Mayer had sought to make a motion picture of Franz Werfel's epic novel *The Forty Days of Musa Dagh*. The Turkish government filed a series of protests with the State Department, and the resulting pressure from State persuaded MGM to kill the project.

But by the 1970s, five decades after the massacres—not to mention the Nuremberg trials, the exposure of the Holocaust, and open discussions in the United Nations, the European Assembly, and the Helsinki Conference, as well as the mounting documentary evidence of the Anatolian disaster—it seemed both reasonable and right that after all this, Turkey would relent and admit not its own crimes but the wrongs of a previous government in the final years of the Ottoman Empire.

Neither reason nor morality has prevailed. Ironically, the Turkish campaign of denial and revisionism has moved the Turkish-Armenian debate from a whisper in the wings to center stage. The Turkish persecution of Armenians has in the 1980s become the subject of American presidential attention and of lengthy congressional exploration. While this has not been a cause for joy in Ankara, for the Armenians it has been a welcome departure from decades of international, and particularly, American indifference.

Since the apocalyptic events of 1915—which, through the policies of Mustafa Kemal, continued in abated form until 1923—there have been a number of mass exterminations of ethnic populations, but none has equaled the total devastation Hitler and his SS visited upon the Jews. Because of the liberating Allied armies, which beheld at firsthand the unmistakable evidence, as well as the efficiency and speed of modern communications, most of the top criminals of the Third Reich were caught and charged with crimes against humanity.

A quarter of a century before, other criminals—also in the guise of governmental officials—had been charged with such crimes. But they escaped and found refuge in the very country in which the Nuremberg Trials would later take place. Although similar international inquiries were not conducted by the victorious Allies after the Armenian tragedy, two trials did take place, one in Constantinople, the other in Berlin.

While the ultimate effect of the Berlin trial of 1921 cannot be known, one of its profoundest fruits was conceived at the very moment of Tehlirian's acquittal. Seated in the audience was a twenty-three-year-old German-Jewish law student, Robert M. W. Kempner. In an article published in 1978 in the Frankfurt periodical *Emuna*, Kempner said that Tehlirian's trial had such an impact on him that he vowed to create in his lifetime a forum of justice for crimes against humanity. After World War II Kempner—who had fled Nazi persecution and found refuge in the United States—returned to Germany as one of the American prosecutors at the Nuremberg Trials.

The Turkish tribunal, on the other hand, fell far short of its intentions, largely because the major defendants had already escaped. But one may well speculate on the results and revelations of an international court of inquiry, had there been one within five years of the tragedy. In addition to the Ittihadist leadership, other participants, survivors, and eyewitnesses, as well as mountains of Turkish and German documents, all in fresh evidence, the court also would have heard the testimony of the American consuls who remained in Turkey until 1917, when the United States severed relations with Turkey—all of them trained, objective, and neutral observers. Above all, the international court would have heard from Consul Jesse B. Jackson, who made the single most compelling statement supporting the view that the massacres were authored in Constantinople when he wrote: "The deportation of Armenians from their homes by the Turkish Government has continued with a persistence and perfection of plan impossible to conceive in those who directly carry it out."[2]

As documentary evidence now shows, the Turkish persecutions were tolerated by the German government, which stood by and committed what has been called a "crime of silence." Two questions linger even today in the minds of all Armenians: Why did Turkey do it? And why did Germany do nothing?

The second question is perhaps easier to answer than the first. Germany had two motives, one tactical, the other strategic. In World War I the Central Powers included Germany, Austria-Hungary, Bulgaria, and Turkey—which in 1914 meant the Ottoman Empire, embracing large parts of the Near East. Germany, in desperate need of allies, colluded with Enver Pasha to attack Russia and thus bring Turkey into the war. Consequently, Turkish forces served the German cause on many fronts in the Near East. But Germany also had long-term strategic plans for the territories that comprised the Ottoman Empire, plans that included economic exploitation of Anatolia, expansive if underdeveloped areas populated largely by Armenians. The Berlin-to-Baghdad Railway, which German engineers were then constructing, was the pathway to Near Eastern oil, an absolute prerequisite for German industrial expansion.

To have intervened with the Ittihadists on behalf of the Armenians would have undermined Germany's short- and long-range plans. If other evidence were lacking, those in attendance at Talaat Pasha's funeral made it clear; they included representatives of the German government and various ministries, especially the Foreign Office, the German military, and three major German banks.

Turkey's motivations are more varied and complex. The massacres of 1915 excised a major Turkish resource and impoverished the country by eliminating manpower from the military; doctors, nurses, and technical staff from the hospitals; tillers of the soil and harvesters of the crops from the land; and experienced local officials, industrious merchants, leaders of the intellectual community, and, above all, the most prolific taxpaying element in the country.

Yet, when Ambassador Morgenthau pointed these consequences out to the grand vizier, he dismissed them as unimportant. Talaat may have been cruel but he was certainly not stupid. Thus it defies logic that he would willingly have sacrificed Turkey's national interests by eradicating the most vital and productive minority within its borders. Hence, the answer must lie elsewhere. In fact, it is embodied in a number of motivating factors in the Ittihadist mind-set, factors powerful enough to override the exigencies of both the war and the economy.

The Young Turks' dream of a pan-Turanic greater Turkey extending from the Dardanelles to the far reaches of eastern Asia required a homogenous population purified of alien elements. While there were plenty of Jews, Greeks, Assyrians, and Kurds to corrupt that purity, there were also the more numerous Armenians, who, unlike the other Turkish minorities, played such a prominent role in the life of the country as to arouse in many Turks a sense of their own mediocrity and an accompanying resentment. With Turkey's entry into the war, many Armenians, including prominent political leaders, began to flee the persecutions that had already begun and to seek refuge in Russia, with many joining the invading Russian forces. This immediately led to accusations of Armenian collusion with the enemy, which, combined with the festering hatred of Armenians as infidel Christians—and as a potent and threatening ethnic minority within Turkey's borders—propelled the Ittihadists into a policy of national savagery.

Only a decade later, these same concepts of racial and religious purity, a fear of subversion, and a drive for expansion to the east emerged again as official policies of the National Socialists in Germany. The similarity is even clearer if one substitutes Armenian for Jew, Christianity for Judaism, Turan for Aryan. Small wonder that Hitler drew some of the inspiration for his maniacal policies from the Armenian tragedy. He could not have been unaware of Tehlirian's widely reported trial in 1921. Furthermore, in 1923 his top adviser was the same Max Erwin von Scheubner-Richter who had witnessed the massacres as vice consul in Erzerum. (He was killed later that year in Hitler's Beer Hall *putsch*.)

An international court of inquiry would have exposed the Young Turks' policies, their methods, and their guilt. There would today be no conflict of fact; justice and history would have been well served; and (not least important) some fifty Turkish diplomatic families would not have fallen victim to Armenian fanaticism.

———

The question remains of how Soghomon Tehlirian should be regarded today—as a murderer, a terrorist, or as a mere pawn in a larger scheme. His trial sought to clarify different aspects of murder: premeditation; manslaughter—that is, murder committed under mitigating circumstances such as emotional stress; and the presence or absence of free will, thereby linking it to the question of responsibility. His attorneys explored all these issues and drew a picture so compellingly positive that the jury set him free.

But his attorneys were arguing his defense on the basis of what he had told them, and it is a fact that he withheld important information—raising the intriguing possibility of an alternative trial outcome. The point was made repeatedly, especially in the summations, that Tehlirian's deed was committed as a justifiable and moral act of revenge for the murder of his family. Political motivations were set aside or suppressed as his attorneys emphasized the personal nature of his crime. But the missing element in Tehlirian's testimony, both at his police interrogation and in the trial, was the all-important planning and supervision by the ARF and its Nemesis network. Had all this emerged in the trial, there can be little doubt it would have brought into sharp focus the events prior to the crime, shed a truer light on its motivation, and perhaps led to a different conclusion.

That Tehlirian—emotionally obsessed, mentally unbalanced, and suffering from a form of epilepsy brought on by his excruciating experience—was manipulated cannot be questioned. Convinced of his sincerity and singleminded purpose to kill Talaat, the ARF saw in him an instrument for accomplishing its own objective, which also echoed the will of a battered nation. Therefore, it recruited, assigned, and abetted him. The ARF had fully expected that Tehlirian would escape—as all the later assassins did—and while it did not counsel a specific plan, it provided him with money. That he was caught was entirely due to his own failure to devise a plan and elude the irate mob that captured him. His ineptitude, however, brought about a double victory for the ARF—one it had neither expected nor planned.

The first was the full exposure in a court of law of the Turkish crimes against the Armenian people, furnished in gruesome detail by Tehlirian, by other survivors of the massacres, and by the distinguished humanitarian Johannes Lepsius. While the Constantinople tribunal two years before had received minimum publicity, its proceedings buried in the Ottoman archives, the Berlin trial was covered by international journalists who reported extensively on the testimony of eyewitnesses—a propaganda coup the ARF could never have achieved with its own resources.

The second victory was the acquittal. Despite the defendant's admission that he had murdered Talaat, and despite the testimony of three out of five medical experts that he had acted with free will—that is, responsibly—Tehlirian was found not guilty. That verdict encouraged and spurred Nemesis to pursue its other targets in the knowledge that, with the world now aware of Turkish atrocities, no court of law would convict Armenian assassins if they were caught.

In fact, one year later Nemesis arranged the gunning down of two more prominent Turks in the very same city.

Of the three possibilities, then—murderer, terrorist, pawn—it is clear that the first and the third were valid. Tehlirian did admit to having murdered Talaat, and although neither his attorneys nor the court knew it, he had already committed an earlier murder—that of Talaat's Armenian collaborator in Constantinople. As for being a pawn, of which he was probably unaware, it is equally clear that the ARF manipulated him into service, exploiting his naïvete for its own purposes.

Was Tehlirian, then, a terrorist? In contemporary terms, a terrorist is an agent of destruction, oblivious of the value of human life, and motivated by a political cause, to which he or she hopes to draw attention. This does not fit the image of Tehlirian. The most prominent terrorists in the late twentieth century have been agents of the PLO and Irish Republican Army (IRA) or of groups such as the Baader-Meinhof gang, the Basque nationalists, Italian Red Army Factions, and even Armenian separatist groups. All these were driven by a specific nationalist cause or an ideology into hijacking planes, spraying airports with gunfire, blowing up busloads of school-children, bombing sidewalk cafes or department stores—in other words, killing innocent people indiscriminately.

Soghomon Tehlirian, on the other hand, had but one unswerving goal—to wreak revenge on a man guilty of killing his family. Once that was done, the torment in his soul subsided and Tehlirian never killed again. The ARF's motive in having Talaat killed was political. Tehlirian's motive was vengeance. He was not a soldier in an ideological cause, nor fighting for territorial integrity, nor was he the agent of a political faction. Although a loyal member of the ARF, under whose auspices he carried out the assassination, he was a member in name only, executing the deed for his own sake rather than for any political program.

One of literature's most memorable terrorists, the assassin in André Malraux's *Man's Fate*, on the other hand, is a political animal, consciously acting in a great political cause. He encounters moments of weakness, experiencing revulsion at the thought of killing a sleeping human being who is incapable of fighting back. But at the critical moment he strikes because of the compulsion of his mission, which dictates that he must kill. Even so, after the deed he is filled with dread in the presence of death. This sensitivity sets him apart from the modern terrorists, for although he comprehends the need for his mission, he is a thinking and feeling individual and not the slave of mindless fanaticism.

It also sets him apart from Tehlirian, whose vision is too blurred for him to be operating in a greater cause. There is only one cause for him—dispatching the former grand vizier, at which he feels no revulsion as he points his revolver and fires, and experiences no dread as he looks down at the bleeding corpse. So intent is he on absorbing the reality of the moment that he loses precious time for escape. Unlike today's terrorists, he remains himself, in full control of his being, oblivious of causes and destiny. One can almost hear him say, "I have committed a terrorist act but I am not a terrorist."

The courts today would not be so lenient and so quick to acquit Tehlirian. They would wrestle at much greater length than the Berlin jury did with the larger issues of this emotional, politically charged case, and while recognizing its ambiguities and the motivation for Tehlirian's crime, would find it perhaps morally right but certainly legally wrong, and settle for manslaughter.

For Armenians, 1988 proved to be the year in which a major Soviet myth was shattered—the myth of security from Turkish oppression. For seven decades, despite its contiguity with Turkey, the Soviet Socialist Republic of Armenia appeared to provide a safe haven for its Armenian inhabitants from their traditional enemy on the western border. But throughout that time, Armenians had been troubled by the lingering fear that to the east, there existed a like enemy in the Soviet Socialist Republic of Azerbaijan, inhabited primarily by a Turkish-speaking people. During World War I, Azerbaijan, which like Armenia was part of the Russian Empire, had been slated for annexation in the Ittihadist vision of a pan-Turanic empire, a fact of which Soviet Armenians were desperately aware, even if the rest of the world was not.

Nestled within the Azerbaijan Republic was a tiny enclave, only ten miles from the Armenian border, known as Karabagh. In 1921 Josef Stalin had capriciously ceded Karabagh to Azerbaijan, despite its overwhelmingly Armenian population.

With the advent of *glasnost*, an Armenian delegation presented the Politburo with a petition requesting the unification of Karabagh with Soviet Armenia. The request was denied and within weeks events of such violence took place in the Soviet republics of Armenia and Azerbaijan that Red Army troops were called in to quell the insurrections—a phenomenon unthinkable only a few years earlier. The worst paroxysm occurred in the Azerbaijani industrial center of Sumgait, where gangs of Azeris went on a rampage, pillaging, raping, and killing longtime Armenian residents.

For seven decades, Soviet Armenians had lived with the uneasiness of a tenuous existence between Turkey to the west and Azerbaijan to the east. While a relaxation of Soviet authority was always welcome, it also carried the concurrent danger of tangible threats from across Armenia's borders. That situation came to pass with the reform-minded leadership in the Kremlin, and for all its positive and welcome features, *glasnost* unleashed centuries-old antagonisms. Armenians were once again faced with the nightmare of 1915. This time, however, it came not from without but from within the very borders of the so-called fraternal Soviet Union.

As the year went on, the bloodshed continued, only to be interrupted in December when a huge catastrophe struck this smallest Soviet republic. An earthquake registering 6.9 on the Richter scale, the strongest quake in the Caucasus in eighty years, killed and uprooted the lives of more than half a million Armenians. Its impact was so monumental that President Gorbachev cut short his first visit to the United States—for a summit with President Reagan—and flew to Armenia for a personal inspection of the devastation. The world (and the United States) ignored ideology and, reacting with huge generosity, poured out humanitarian aid in the amount of $200 million, contributed by the governments of fifty-three countries, including Turkey, while private groups from an equal number of countries gave liberally with money and material. But the question of Karabagh and the violence it generated would continue to haunt Armenians and the Kremlin leadership.

In the United States Senate, meanwhile, where there was strong sentiment for the small beleagured nation, the struggle for passage of a resolution acknowledging its suffering under the Ottoman Government failed passage again, in deference to America's ally, Turkey.

Dr. Johannes Lepsius returned from Holland to Germany in 1919 to discover that the same authorities who had earlier vilified him now viewed him with respect. When his seminal book *Deutschland und Armenien 1914–1918* (Germany and Armenia 1914–1918) was published, copies were also sent to the Paris Peace Conference, even if the Armenian cause was not being advanced by the victorious Allies.

Through the intervention of friends in the Foreign Office and under the sponsorship of the German government, he was assigned the monumental task of producing a forty-volume study, *The Major Policies of the European Cabinets—from 1871 to 1914*, a work that even today provides valuable source material on European and Armenian history. His interest in Armenian affairs never waned, and his office in the Foreign Ministry became a focal point for countless Armenians who sought him out for advice and assistance.

His latest major public appearance was as a pivotal witness in the Tehlirian trial. A few years thereafter, he became seriously ill and went to Merano in the South Tyrol for a cure. He died on February 3, 1926, and was buried there two days later, his grave marked by a *khatchkar*, an Armenian stone cross, dedicated by Catholicos Vazgen I, supreme patriarch of all Armenians.

Talaat Pasha died in 1921, but he was not to find a final resting place for twenty-two years. In 1943, during World War II, his remains were transported from Berlin to Istanbul where, in the presence of German Ambassador Franz von Papen, they were interred in a mausoleum on a hill overlooking the city. When the war ended, the Turkish government rehabilitated Talaat Pasha, naming a school in Istanbul and a boulevard in Ankara after him.

Soghomon Tehlirian married Anahid, who bore him two sons. They emigrated to the United States and settled in California. In the four decades he spent there, he was revered and acclaimed wherever he went. His earlier illness never recurred, but he developed diabetes and died of a stroke in San Francisco in 1960 at the age of sixty-three. Anahid died in 1979.

In Fresno's Ararat Cemetery, a statue of Tehlirian stands at his gravesite, on which are inscribed these words:

This monument has been erected by the Armenian people in memory of Soghomon Tehlirian, the national hero who, on March 15, 1921, brought justice upon Talaat Pasha, a principal perpetrator of the Armenian genocide of 1915 which claimed the lives of 1,500,000 Armenian martyrs.

A Personal Postscript

A chill wind was blowing from the East River as we mounted the dimly lit steps of the church in Manhattan. It was a Sunday evening and as often happened on weekends, my parents were taking me to a function at the Twenty-seventh Street Church, as it was known to all Armenians. But unlike the many other occasions when there was an air of frivolity, this night my father and mother seemed solemn and strangely silent.

The large basement under the church served as a hall for a variety of functions, from wedding receptions and holidays to many kinds of festivities designed to collect money for Armenian causes. All I had been told about this night was that it was a banquet in someone's honor, which for a little boy meant sitting silently, listening to long speeches in Armenian and being bored.

Entering the hall, I beheld long wooden tables at whose head, already seated, were our priest, several familiar members of the Armenian community, and a slender youngish man shyly looking this way and that. I cannot recall much else until dinner was over, when the inevitable speeches were made, and the young man was introduced. Suddenly I was jolted out of my lethargy by the sounds that filled the hall.

Over the deafening applause, men began to shout, among them my father, who was now standing and clapping his hands vigorously. He made me stand on the chair and ordered me to applaud. Finally, the tumult subsided and everyone sat down, as the young man spoke. I cannot remember anything he said, even though I understood Armenian very well. But many of the words were beyond my child's vocabulary.

Again, the hall reverberated with shouts, cheers, and hammering on tables. Then, women of all ages, ahead of the men, lined up to meet him, and as the shy youth faced them, each seized his right hand, kissed it fervently, and then bowed in homage, some women even kneeling and weeping openly.

Hypnotized by this astonishing scene, I stood on my chair until I felt my father lift me up and carry me to the end of the line. Creeping nearer and nearer, we finally stood before the guest of honor. My father spoke a few words, then took my hand and extended it to the youth, who after shaking it, kissed my forehead. A few moments later we left.

Driving home, the mood in the car seemed even more somber than before. I looked up at my father, who was staring straight ahead, his thoughts clearly back in the hall. Although I felt a tension in the air, it was hard to resist asking the obvious question: "Father, who was that man?"

He continued looking through the windshield silently for a few seconds, then said softly, "His name will not mean anything to you now, but someday it will."

"But father, why were those women kissing his hand?"

I realized years later that, as I waited for his reply, he must have been reliving the most dreadful moments of his life—his father killed before his eyes in the first massacre and his mother and sister victims of the second.

He turned, looking down at me in the front seat, and said in a trembling voice which I can still hear: "Because with that hand he avenged our people. Never forget him!"

The memory of that night almost seven decades ago is still vivid today, and this book is my response to my father's admonition to never forget Soghomon Tehlirian. In a sense that kiss on a child's forehead was like the passing of a torch intended to illuminate the Armenian people's arduous journey toward freedom, from the time of Christ to the newly proclaimed republic. The struggle is not over, but in our time it has made the greatest progress, and has achieved widespread recognition and encouragement because of the dedication of men like Soghomon Tehlirian. That is the legacy he has left us—of which he too was an integral part—and that fired my imagination in the writing of this book.

In the process, I have benefited from the wisdom of many hearts and minds whose generosity deserves recognition far greater than mere mention:

At the Library of Congress, I am deeply indebted to Dr. Yorguy Hakim of the Near Eastern Law Division and to Margrit Krewson of the German Department. To this I would add a personal tribute to the superb archives of that great institution. In this respect, gratitude must be expressed also to the National Archives of the United States and the State Department Library. Additionally, I am grateful to the many former colleagues in the U.S. Foreign Service who have encouraged me to pursue this work.

A large measure of gratitude is due my German informants: Dr. Hermann Goltz, Curator of the Lepsius Archives in Halle, whose invitation to attend the Lepsius Symposium in 1986 opened many avenues of information, Dr. Koehnke, curator of the State Archives in Merseburg, and Dr. Tessa Hofmann, a dedicated scholar and writer in Berlin.

In Hungary, Dr. Istvan Gal of the Szechényi Library, fervent defender of the rights of small nations, and many other Hungarian intellectuals were remarkably well-informed about the Armenian tragedy; two of these were the poet Gábor Devecséri and the composer Zoltán Kodály.

There are also a number of individuals from Turkey, Greece, Cyprus, Bulgaria, Romania, and the Soviet Union who, reflecting the hazards of our times, should probably remain anonymous. I can, however, safely acknowledge Anne Avakian, Erika Czulkowski, Ann Lochner, Diana Markarian, and Ogda O'Gulian.

I should also be grateful, even if perversely, to the attitude of many Turkish ambassadors and embassy officials with whom, in the course of a diplomatic career, I tried to carry on civilized discussions. Most recently, as a member of the U.S. delegation to several human rights conferences after the Helsinki accords, I was again struck by the adamantine rigidity with which senior officials on Turkish delegations and from the Foreign Ministry responded to congenial attempts at discourse. All their negative, often vituperative reactions galvanized my determination to set down the facts that are known to historians, diplomats, and most of all, to the ever-dwindling survivors of a great tragedy.

The four main sources of material for this book are the official German transcript of the trial of Soghomon Tehlirian, published in Berlin in 1921; the German press accounts of the assassination and the trial; John Giragosian's *The Young Turks Before the Tribunal*, published in Yerevan in 1982; and Soghomon Tehlirian's *Memoirs*, published in Cairo in 1956, which provided his private thoughts and emotions. Also informative was Arshavir Shiragian's *The Legacy*, published in Boston in 1976. The many other books, periodicals, and newspapers from which information was drawn have been cited in the end-of-book notes. The author assumes full responsibility for all translations from German and Armenian.

This book was never intended to be a detailed account of the massacres. In the telling of Soghomon Tehlirian's story, however, it was necessary to review some of the principal events surrounding the massacres in order to provide context and relevance to the murder of Talaat and the subsequent trial of Tehlirian in Berlin. Historians and Armenologists who have devoted a major part of their lives to this subject may be consulted for more detailed information. First and foremost is Johannes Lepsius's *Deutschland und Armenien 1914–1918*, also available in English and French.

In our time no one has explored the Armenian tragedy more thoroughly than Dr. Richard G. Hovannisian of UCLA, in books, articles, and lectures. Close behind are Dr. Gerard Libaridian, director of the Zoryan Institute for Contemporary Armenian Research and Documentation in Cambridge, Massachusetts, and Dr. Dennis Papazian of the Armenian Research Center at the University of Michigan. Equally informative, especially in historical detail, is Christopher J. Walker's *Armenia—The Survival of a Nation*, as are the publications of Dr. Vahakn N. Dadrian of SUNY and Dr. Kevork B. Bardakjian of Harvard.

Finally, a word of gratitude to my editor, Adam Bellow, whose critical eye, sense of perspective, and overall guidance have served this author beyond measure.

Notes

INTRODUCTION

1. Edouard Calic, ed., *Secret Conversations with Hitler* (New York: John Day, 1971), p. 81.
2. Louis P. Lochner, *What About Germany?* (New York: Dodd Mead, 1942), p. 2.
3. Henry Morgenthau, *Ambassador Morgenthau's Story* (New York: Doubleday, 1919), pp. 321–322.
4. Andrew Corsun, *Armenian Terrorism: A Profile* (Washington, D.C.: U.S. Department of State, Office of Security Feature, August 1982).
5. *Congressional Record.* Senate, February 27, 1990. S. Rept. 1731.
6. *Washington Post*, April 21, 1990, p. 10.

1. MURDER IN BERLIN

1. *Der Prozess Talaat Pascha* (Stenographischer Bericht) (Berlin: Deutsche Verlagsgesellschaft für Politik und Geschichte, 1921), p. 21.
2. *Vossische Zeitung*, March 16, 1921.
3. *Tägliche Rundschau*, March 16, 1921.
4. Ibid.
5. *Der Prozess Talaat Pascha*, p. 29.
6. Ibid., p. 30.
7. Ibid., p. 19.
8. *Deutsche Tageszeitung*, March 16, 1921.
9. *Deutsche Allgemeine Zeitung*, March 16, 1921.
10. *Tägliche Rundschau*, March 16, 1921.
11. "The End of Talaat," *Berliner Tageblatt*, Editorial, March 16, 1921.
12. *Germania*, March 16, 1921.
13. *New York Times*, March 18, 1921.

2. THE WEB OF HISTORY

1. Robert Melson, "Provocation or Nationalism" in *The Armenian Genocide in Perspective*, Richard G. Hovannisian, ed. (New Brunswick, N.J.: Transaction Books, 1987), p. 72.

5. BEHIND THE CURTAIN OF WAR

1. *Der Reichsbote*, September 11, 1896.
2. *Rheinisch-Westfälische Zeitung*, September 24, 1896.
3. *Der Reichsbote*, September 11, 1896.
4. Hovannisian, *The Armenian Genocide in Perspective*, p. 72.
5. *Abdul Hamid II—Seine Familie und sein Hofstaat* (Budapest: Sigmund Deutsch, 1901). In his other book on Abdul Hamid's policies, published five years later in Leipzig, Stern totally ignored the atrocities—a bias that had earlier aroused Lepsius's suspicions as to the objectivity of German newspaper accounts—considering the 1894 earthquake a more notable event than the sultan's decimation of his Armenian subjects.
6. J. P. D. Kinross, *The Ottoman Centuries* (New York: William Morrow, 1977), p. 579.
7. Cable by Richard von Kühlmann to the German chancellor, February 16, 1917, in Johannes Lepsius, *Deutschland und Armenien 1914-1918* (Potsdam: Tempelverlag, 1919), pp. 320-321.
8. Ernest E. Ramsauer, *The Young Turks* (Princeton, N.J.: Princeton University Press, 1957), pp. 16-17.
9. This incident is described in Christopher J. Walker, *Armenia—The Survival of a Nation* (New York: St. Martin's Press, 1980), pp. 164-166.
10. Kinross, *The Ottoman Centuries*, p. 562.
11. David M. Lang, *The Armenians—A People in Exile* (London: George Allen & Unwin, 1982), p. 14.
12. Henry Morgenthau, *Ambassador Morgenthau's Story* (New York: Doubleday, 1919), pp. 13, 15.
13. R. H. Dekmejian, as quoted in Hovannisian, *The Armenian Genocide in Perspective*, notes that the Berlin-to-Baghdad Railway, built with Armenian labor, was later used to transport Armenians to distant locations where they joined other deportees on foot in death marches into the Syrian desert.
14. Dickran H. Boyajian, *Armenia—The Case for a Forgotten Genocide* (Westwood, N.J.: Educational Book Crafters, 1972), pp. 4-6.
15. National Archives, Washington, D.C., on microfilm, Reel 44, File 867.4016/127. Other reports by Davis can be found in *The Slaughterhouse Province: An American Diplomat's Report on the Armenian Genocide of 1914-1917*, Susan K. Blair, ed. (New York: A. Caratzas, 1989).
16. National Archives, Reel 43, File 867.4016/105.
17. Ibid., Reel 44, File 867.4016/126.
18. Ibid., Reel 43, File 867.4016/Cable 289.
19. Ibid., Reel 44, File 867.4016/126.
20. Ibid., Reel 44, File 867.4016/155.
21. Ibid., Reel 44, File 867.4016/219.

22. Ibid., Reel 43, File 867.4016/74.

23. Morgenthau, *Ambassador Morgenthau's Story*, p. 326.

24. Letter from Dodd to Morgenthau, transmitted to U.S. Department of State on September 16, 1915. In National Archives, Reel 44, File 867.4016/189.

25. Letter (in German) from Johanson to Morgenthau, transmitted to Department of State on November 9, 1915. In National Archives, Reel 44, File 867.4016/226.

26. Morgenthau, *Ambassador Morgenthau's Story*, pp. 333–334.

27. Ibid., p. 339.

28. Ibid., p. 338.

29. Lepsius, *Deutschland und Armenien*, p. 79. Wangenheim nevertheless concluded his cable with a request to Berlin "to inform Dr. Lepsius that because of the political and military conditions in Turkey, those measures are unfortunately unavoidable"—certainly an indication of Lepsius's moral authority in the face of the German government's hostility toward him.

30. Gerard Chaliand and Yves Ternon, *The Armenians—From Genocide to Resistance* (London: Zed Books, 1983), pp. 63–66.

31. Ibid., p. 62.

32. Ibid., pp. 67–68.

33. Lepsius's meeting with Enver is re-created in chapter 5 of Franz Werfel's novel *The Forty Days of Musa Dagh* (New York: Modern Library, 1934).

34. It was learned only after the war that the copies sent to Reichstag members were confiscated. This and other information on Lepsius has been drawn primarily from two sources by Dr. Hermann Goltz, director of the Lepsius Archives in Halle, Germany: the first is "Zwischen Deutschland und Armenien," which appeared in *Theologische Literaturzeitung*, no. 108, December 1983, and the second a lecture he delivered at the Lepsius Symposium in Halle in February 1986.

35. Lepsius, *Deutschland und Armenien*, p. 126.

36. Walker, *Armenia—The Survival of a Nation*, p. 235.

37. "The Armenian question no longer exists," Lepsius, *Deutschland und Armenien*, p. 147.

38. Morgenthau, *Ambassador Morgenthau's Story*, p. 342.

39. This is actually the title of his book, which is subtitled "Events in Armenia in 1915," published by G. P. Putnam's Sons (New York, 1916). Gibbons was one of a number of Americans, largely missionaries and doctors, who wrote about their experiences in Turkey in books with titles such as *Horrors of Armenia—The Story of an Eyewitness* and *Letters from the Scenes of the Recent Massacres in Armenia*.

40. Lang, *The Armenians—A People in Exile*, pp. 28–29.

41. Lepsius, *Deutschland und Armenien*, p. 193.

42. Leon Ostrorg, *The Turkish Problem* (London: Chatto & Windus, 1919), p. 163.

43. In *The Blue Book* (London: 1916), *British Foreign Ministry*, published later as *The Treatment of Armenians in the Ottoman Empire*.

44. French historian Yves Ternon notes: "In August 1916 they were sent to Mosul and either swallowed up by the desert . . . or herded into caves where they were soaked with petrol and burned. Even today in the deserts near Deir Zor, children from nearby villages still go to these caves to pick through the bones in the hope

of finding a gold tooth or a wedding ring.'' From *A Crime of Silence* (London: Zed Books, 1985), p. 119.

45. Lepsius, *Deutschland und Armenien*, p. 80.
46. Although the Young Turks had collapsed, the Ottoman government, headed by the sultan, was still the ruling body in Turkey until the establishment in 1923 of the Turkish Republic by Mustafa Kemal, who moved the capital from Constantinople to Ankara.

6. JUDGMENT AND EXILE

1. Peter Lanne, *Armenia—The First Genocide of the Twentieth Century* (Munich: Institute for Armenian Studies, 1977), p. 135.
2. *Renaissance*, no. 80, January 19, 1919.
3. John Giragosian, *Yeridturkere Tadastani Archev (The Young Turks Before the Tribunal)* (Yerevan: State Press, 1982), p. 170.
4. According to *The Times of London* of February 8, 1919, other charges included profiteering, spoliation of Greeks, and ill-treatment of Allied—primarily British—prisoners of war.
5. Giragosian, *The Young Turks Before the Tribunal*, p. 183.
6. Ibid., p. 212.
7. Ibid., pp. 186–192.
8. Ibid., p. 191.
9. Op. cit.
10. *Tyurkje Stamboul*, December 23, 1918.
11. *Alemdar*, January 8, 1919.
12. *Takvim-i Vekayi* (Turkish Government Official Gazette), no. 3616, May 22, 1919.
13. *The Times of London*, May 3, 1919.
14. *New York Times*, July 13, 1919, p. 1.
15. Reuters dispatch, April 10, 1919.
16. Louise Bryant, *Mirrors of Moscow* (New York: Thomas Seltzer, 1923), pp. 152–159.
17. Louis Fischer, in *University of Virginia Review*, vol. 6, 1930. The Armenian hunger for justice has created a legend, believed by many, that the Red Army soldier who slew Enver was an Armenian.
18. *Frankfurter Allgemeine Zeitung*, November 27, 1919. Some historians do not dispute Jemal's claim, arguing that although he did not condemn the atrocities at the time, he did give orders in Syria, which was under his command, to prevent further massacres and even organized relief measures.
19. Jemal Pasha, *Memories of a Turkish Statesman—1913–1919* (London: Hutchinson, 1919), pp. 241, 280–281.
20. Richard G. Hovannisian, *The Republic of Armenia* (Berkeley: University of California Press, 1971), p. 420.
21. *The Times of London*, January 19, 1919.
22. This activity, plus the fact that Talaat was in Berlin on a special passport issued to him by Chancellor Friedrich Ebert, exposes as totally groundless the later German press claim that the government was unaware of his refuge.
23. *Current History*, November 1921, pp. 294–295.
24. Walker, *Armenia—The Survival of a Nation*, p. 233.

7. The Trial Resumes

1. Consul Walter Rössler, an eyewitness to many atrocities in the Aleppo area, had intervened often to save Armenian lives. He had been called as a defense witness, but the foreign ministry refused to allow him to appear—one of the German government's many ploys to reduce testimony to an absolute minimum. In private correspondence with the author, Dr. Tessa Hofmann writes that Tehlirian's attorneys wanted a five-day trial to permit more testimony concerning the political background of the massacres, but the German ministries of justice and foreign affairs wanted a quick and inconspicuous trial. The prosecution consequently endeavored to focus on Tehlirian's psychological problems, as later testimony will show, to avoid transforming the court into a political tribunal.

2. These were predictive words, for in 1922 the nationalist forces of Mustafa Kemal, former colleague and fellow officer of Enver Pasha, killed one hundred thousand Greeks and Armenians in Smyrna. See Marjorie Housepian, *The Smyrna Affair* (New York: Harcourt Brace Jovanovich, 1971).

8. Justice in Berlin

1. While von Gordon's sequence of events is correct, his statement that Tehlirian still had not made a decision to kill Talaat is clearly incorrect and must be construed as legalistic embroidery.

2. It cannot be known precisely how long each of the attorneys spoke, except that it took almost the entire three hours of the morning, but the quantitative imbalance of their summations may be perceived in the number of pages they occupy in the official transcript; Prosecutor Gollnick, seven; and Defense Attorneys von Gordon, Werthauer, and Niemeyer, thirty-five. This 1:5 ratio in the summations lends further credence to the argument that the German government wanted to have as expeditious a trial as possible, while the defense hoped for a prolonged and detailed exposition of its case.

3. The forcible occupation of the Ottoman Bank by members of the ARF.

4. *Current History*, July 1921, pp. 552–553.

5. Ibid., p 552.

6. Soghomon Tehlirian, *Verhishoomner (Memoirs)* (Cairo: Houssaper, 1956), pp. 450, 451 (quote from *Hairenik*, ARF organ).

7. Ibid., p. 455 (independent).

8. Ibid., p. 459 (quote from *Bahag*, Hunchak organ).

9. Ibid., p. 458 (quote from *Azk*, Ramgavar organ).

10. Ibid., pp. 471–472 (quote from *Peyam Sabahi*).

Conclusion

1. *Deutsche Allgemeine Zeitung*, April 18, 1921.

2. National Archives, Washington, D.C., Reel 44, File Number 867.4016/219.

Index